RESEARCH IN LAW AND ECONOMICS

Volume 5 • 1983

I.   ANTITRUST

II. REGULATION AND REPRESENTATION

Editorial correspondence pertaining to manuscripts should be sent to:

Professor Richard O. Zerbe, Jr., *Series Editor*
Graduate School of Public Affairs
DP-30
University of Washington
Seattle, Washington 98195
(206) 543-4920

Three copies should be sent. Manuscripts must be put into Journal's style before final acceptance.

RESEARCH IN LAW AND ECONOMICS

I. ANTITRUST
II. REGULATION AND REPRESENTATION

Editor: RICHARD O. ZERBE, JR.
*Graduate School of Public Affairs
and Department of Economics
University of Washington*

VOLUME 5 • 1983

 JAI PRESS INC.

Greenwich, Connecticut   *London, England*

The publisher recognizes and appreciates
the support given by the University of Washington

BOARD OF REFEREES

CONTENTS

LIST OF PARTICIPANTS   ix

I.   ANTITRUST

THE EFFECT OF MONOPOLIES AND CARTELS ON
MARKET PRICES
Daniel K. Benjamin   1

THE CHICAGO BOARD OF TRADE CASE, 1918
Richard O. Zerbe, Jr.   17

PRICE-FIXING AND THE ADDYSTON PIPE CASE
George Bittlingmayer   57

BERKEY PHOTO, INC. V. EASTMAN KODAK CO.: A
SEARCH FOR AN EXPLANATION OF KODAK'S
DOMINANCE OF THE AMATEUR PHOTOGRAPHIC
EQUIPMENT INDUSTRY
James W. Meehan, Jr.   131

A GUIDE TO THE HERFINDAHL INDEX FOR
ANTITRUST ATTORNEYS
Paul A. Pautler   167

II.   REGULATION AND REPRESENTATION

THE PROSPECT THEORY OF THE PATENT SYSTEM
AND UNPRODUCTIVE COMPETITION
Roger L. Beck   193

VOTER SEARCH FOR EFFICIENT REPRESENTATION
Roger L. Faith and Robert D. Tollison   211

LIABILITY RULES, PROPERTY RIGHTS, AND TAXES
Robert J. Staaf   225

AUTOMOBILE SAFETY REGULATION: A REVIEW OF
THE EVIDENCE
  Richard J. Arnould and Henry Grabowski   233

TABLE OF CASES   269

INDEX   273

The papers in the previous volume of *Research in Law and Economics,* Volume 4, *Evolutionary Models in Economics and Law,* were the product of a conference sponsored by the Liberty Fund, Inc. We wish to acknowledge their support.

The next volume of *Research in Law and Economics,* is devoted to topics of antitrust and regulation, with these authors and articles: Alan A. Fisher and Richard Sciacca, "An Economic Analysis of Vertical Merger Enforcement Policy"

Jeffrey A. Eisenach, Richard S. Higgins, and William F. Shughart II, "Warranties, Tie-ins, and Efficient Insurance Contracts: A Theory and Three Case Studies"

Richard J. Agnello and Lawrence P. Donnelley, "Regulation and the Structure of Property Rights: The Case of the U.S. Oyster Industry" Robert A. Rogowsky. "The Justice Department's Merger Guidelines: A Study in the Application of the Rule"

Dwight Dively, "Applications of Regulatory Theory to the Trucking Industry"

LIST OF CONTRIBUTORS

Richard J. Arnould   College of Commerce and Business
          Administration
          University of Illinois, Champaign

Roger L. Beck   Department of Marketing and Economic
          Analysis
          University of Alberta, Edmonton

Daniel K. Benjamin   U.S. Department of Labor
          Washington, D.C.

George Bittlingmayer   Graduate School of Business Administration
          University of Michigan

Roger L. Faith   Department of Economics
          Arizona State University, Tempe

Henry Grabowski   Department of Economics
          Duke University

James W. Meehan, Jr.   Department of Economics
          Colby College

Paul A. Pautler   Federal Trade Commission
          Washington, D.C.

Robert J. Staaf   Law and Economics Center
          University of Miami

Robert D. Tollison   Clemson University

Richard O. Zerbe, Jr.   Graduate School of Public Affairs
          University of Washington

PART I

ANTITRUST

THE EFFECT OF MONOPOLIES AND CARTELS ON MARKET PRICES

Daniel K. Benjamin

By utilizing the dominant firm model, equations are developed that show the extent to which the dominant firm will raise price above marginal costs as a function of market demand elasticity, the supply elasticities of the dominant and fringe firm(s), and the market share of the dominant firm. The methodology here allows one to determine the magnitude of the price-enhancing effects of cartels and dominant firms under alternative circumstances. These results are useful in indicating the circumstances in which price effects will be trivial, and the circumstances in which they will be large. For example, the effect of reductions in market demand elasticities in raising price is dramatically enhanced by larger market shares for the dominant firm. A high fringe supply elasticity will not prevent very significant price increases over marginal costs if the market share is sufficiently large. Finally, Judge Learned Hand's maxim that a market share of 90 percent constitutes a monopoly while 60 percent probably does not and 33 percent certainly does not turns out to be about right if one is speaking of the measurable effects of such market shares on output prices.

Research in Law and Economics, Volume 5, pages 1–15.
Copyright © 1983 by JAI Press Inc.
ISBN: 0-89232-419-8

Discussions of the effect of cartels or large, dominant firms (monopolies) on market prices typically focus on a short, fairly standard list of items: the elasticity of market demand, the market share of the cartel or dominant firm and the ability of fringe suppliers to expand output in response to price changes [see, for example, Bork (1) or Posner (6)]. After dutifully noting the way these aspects of market structure inhibit (or enhance) the ability of a cartel or monopolist to raise price above the competitive level, these discussions halt with no mention of the magnitude of the inhibitive effects. For example, does doubling the market elasticity of demand halve the effect of a cartel on price? Does doubling the market share of a large firm double its effect on market price? How does the importance of fringe suppliers vary with the market share of the cartel or dominant firm?

I focus on the effect of monopolies and cartels on market prices due to its importance in the enforcement of the antitrust laws. The courts have long recognized the probative value of market prices in determining the existence of antitrust violations. The origins of this recognition lie deeply rooted in English and American common law and quickly found expression in case law under the Sherman Act [see Letwin (5), chap. 2]. In the Addyston Pipe case Judge Taft of the Circuit Court and Justice Peckham of the U.S. Supreme Court argued that the pattern of price differentials between "free" and "pay" territories could be explained only by a combination in restraint of trade among the defendants.[1] Judicial doctrine on this matter is particularly clear in the Cement Manufacturers Protective Association decision:

> Agreements or understanding among competitors for the maintenance of uniform prices are, of course, unlawful and may be enjoined [and] . . . *an artificial price level not related to supply and demand of a given commodity may be evidence from which such agreement or understanding or some concerted action of sellers operating to restrain commerce may be inferred.* [Cement Manufacturers Association v. U.S., 268 U.S. 588, 604–606, 45 S.Ct. 586, 592, 69 L.Ed. 1104, 1111 (1925); emphasis added]

Sometimes the "artificial price level" produced by restraint of trade may be clearly discernible. Often, however, it will be necessary to account for cost changes over time or for cross-sectional cost differences. It may also be necessary to rely on samples rather than populations and the data may be subject to measurement error. The methodology I develop enables one to determine the magnitude of the price-enhancing effects of cartels and dominant firms under alternative circumstances. I show, for example, that under a variety of conditions even perfectly enforced cartels will have negligible effects on market prices. In the presence of sampling and measurement error such effects could be empirically undetectable; under such circumstances a failure to find a "break" in prices need not be inconsistent with the existence of a restraint of trade. Conversely, I show that under other conditions the price-enhancing effects of cartels and dominant firms will be quite large; in such circumstances the failure to observe an impact on market prices would be significant economic evidence against the existence of an antitrust violation.

In private antitrust suits the magnitude of the "artificial price level" takes on added importance, for it helps determine the magnitude of the damage award in the event of a guilty verdict. Damage computations in private antitrust suits typically center on estimates of the difference between the restraint-induced "artificial price" and the "competitive" price that would have prevailed absent the restraint [see, for example, Easterbrook (2), pp. 319–320]. My results provide a method of assessing both the plausibility and the internal consistency of estimates of this differential and, thus in principle, a means of avoiding excessively high or low awards.

I propose to analyze the price-enhancing effects of monopolies and cartels with the aid of a simple but general model. The qualitative results I obtain are familiar but the magnitudes involved are striking. For example, cartels with even substantial market shares will have trivial effects on the market price. Conversely, for cartels or dominant firms with very large market shares, the elasticity of supply of fringe firms turns out to be of negligible importance in constraining price increases. Finally, Judge Learned Hand's hoary maxim that a market share of 90 percent constitutes a monopoly while 60 percent probably does not and 33 percent certainly does not turns out to be about right if one is speaking of the measurable effects of such market shares on output prices.[2]

I. THE DOMINANT FIRM MODEL

The model I shall use to develop these contentions is the venerable "dominant firm" model, depicted in Figure 1.[3] The model supposes a market demand for some good, $Q_D = F(P)$, where P is the price of the good. The fringe firms act as price takers, supplying an amount given by $Q_s = G(P)$. The marginal cost curve of the dominant firm (or horizontal sum of the marginal cost curves of the conspirators in the case of a cartel) is shown by C. Absent price-searching behavior, the market supply curve would be S (the horizontal sum of Q_s and C) and the market price P_c. If the dominant firm or cartel acts as a price searcher, it will perceive a demand curve equal to the horizontal difference between the market demand curve and the fringe supply: $Q_d = F(P) - G(P)$. Given the associated marginal revenue schedule, MR, the profit-maximizing price is P_d. I seek to de-

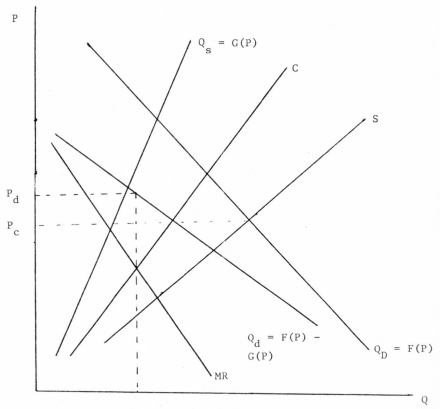

Figure 1.   The Dominant Firm Model

termine the extent to which P_d diverges from P_c. Noting that

$$\frac{dQ_d}{dP} = F'(P) - G'(P),$$

multiply both sides by P/Q_d to obtain the elasticity of demand facing the dominant firm:

$$\epsilon \equiv \frac{dQ_d}{dP} \cdot \frac{P}{Q_d} = F'(P)\frac{P}{Q_d} - G'(P)\frac{P}{Q_d} \, .$$

To put this in a more useful form, multiply the first term on the right-hand side by Q_D/Q_D and the second term by Q_s/Q_s, yielding

$$\epsilon = F'(P)\frac{P}{Q_D} \cdot \frac{Q_D}{Q_d} - G'(P)\frac{P}{Q_s} \cdot \frac{Q_s}{Q_d} \, .$$

Note that

$$\eta \equiv F'(P)\,\frac{P}{Q_D}$$

is the elasticity of the market demand, while

$$\omega \equiv G'(P)\,\frac{P}{Q_s}$$

is the elasticity of the fringe supply curve. Denoting the dominant firm's market share by θ, then $Q_D/Q_d = \dfrac{1}{\theta}$. Also it is true by definition that

$$Q_s + Q_d = Q_D.$$

Multiplying this expression by $1/Q_d$ and rearranging terms yields the result that

$$\frac{Q_s}{Q_d} = \frac{Q_D}{Q_d} - 1 = \frac{1}{\theta} - 1 = \frac{1 - \theta}{\theta}.$$

Thus, the elasticity of demand facing the dominant firm may be written[4]

$$\epsilon = \frac{\eta}{\theta} - \omega\left(\frac{1 - \theta}{\theta}\right), \tag{1}$$

which is merely an explicit way of saying that it varies directly with the elasticity of market demand (η) and the elasticity of the fringe firms' supply (ω) and inversely with the dominant firm's (or cartel's) market share (θ).

Knowledge of the elasticity of demand facing the dominant firm is not sufficient to determine its pricing policy, as reflected by the familiar condition describing the profit-maximizing price,

$$P\left(1 + \frac{1}{\epsilon}\right) = C,$$

where C is marginal cost. This expression can be rearranged to yield

$$\frac{P}{C} = \frac{\epsilon}{\epsilon + 1}$$

or

$$\frac{P}{C} - 1 = \left(\frac{\epsilon}{\epsilon + 1}\right) - 1.$$

I shall label the term $P/C - 1$ the "premium" (above marginal cost) charged by the dominant firm or cartel. The existence of this premium reflects the fact that any output restriction (i) pushes up the price and (ii) lowers the level of marginal costs. Depending on the responsiveness of marginal costs to the rate of output, a given premium (for example, 25 percent) can be comprised chiefly of a higher price or lower marginal costs or some mixture of the two.

As a matter of notational convenience in what follows I shall use a "hat" over a variable to designate the proportionate change in that variable. Thus, for any variable V, $\hat{V}$ represents the percentage change in V.[5] For values of P and C in the neighborhood of the competitive equilibrium (where $P/C = 1$), it is approximately true that[6]

$$\hat{P} - \hat{C} \approx P/C - 1, \tag{2}$$

which simply states that the combined effect of the increase in price and the decrease in the level of marginal costs equals the premium of price over marginal costs. Note that $\hat{P}$ represents the (proportionate) amount by which the cartel or dominant firm raises price above the competitive level.

Defining $\alpha = \hat{C}/\hat{Q}_d$ to be the elasticity of the dominant firm's marginal costs with respect to its output, we can substitute for $\hat{C}$ so that Eq. (2) can be expressed as

$$\hat{P} - \alpha\hat{Q}_d \approx \frac{P}{C} - 1.$$

Given that the elasticity of demand facing the dominant firm can be expressed quite generally as $\epsilon = \hat{Q}_d/\hat{P}$, we can substitute for $\hat{Q}_d$, yielding

$$\hat{P} - \alpha\epsilon\hat{P} \approx \frac{P}{C} - 1.$$

Rearranging terms and recalling that

$$\frac{P}{C} - 1 \approx \left(\frac{\epsilon}{\epsilon + 1}\right) - 1$$

produces the result that

$$\hat{P} \approx \left(\frac{1}{1 - \alpha\epsilon}\right)\left(\frac{\epsilon}{\epsilon + 1} - 1\right)$$

so that[7]

$$\hat{P} \approx -\frac{1}{(1 - \alpha\epsilon)(1 + \epsilon)}. \tag{3}$$

Equation (3) shows that the extent to which a dominant firm will raise price above the competitive level depends on the responsiveness of its marginal costs and on the determinants of the elasticity of demand it faces—the elasticity of market demand, the elasticity of the fringe firms' supply, and its market share.

II. IMPLICATIONS OF THE ANALYSIS

To illustrate the implications of Eq. (3) I shall select some "plausible" values of the parameters and then examine the effects of varying the values of the parameters. Initially, I assume that the market elasticity of demand is −1, chiefly because so many empirical estimates seem to cluster around this value. I also assume that both α and ω equal 1—in this case on theoretical grounds. For example, with a quadratic cost function, the elasticity of marginal costs with respect to output is bounded from above by unity while the (short-run) elasticity of supply is bounded from below by unity.[8] Similarly, it is possible to show that with a Cobb-Douglas production function the short-run elasticity of marginal costs with respect to output is $(1/a) − 1$ and the short-run elasticity of supply is $a/(1 − a)$, where a is the variable factor's share.[9] If that factor's share is one-half, unitary elasticities result.

Given these assumptions, the table and Figure 2 illustrate the effect of market share on output price.[10] Note first that the effect of market share on price is roughly exponential. An increase in the dominant firm's share from 10 percent to 25 percent increases the market price by only 1 percent while a change in share from 75 percent to 90 percent results in a doubling of price. Also significant is the fact that firms with fairly substantial market shares will have trivial effects on price. For example, a firm with a third of the market will raise price only 4 percent above the competitive level.

Figure 3 shows the dramatic effect of market demand elasticity on the ability of a dominant firm or cartel to raise price appreciably above competitive levels. (For clarity I have chosen the classes singled out by Judge Hand—33 percent, 60 percent, and 90 percent). As the market elasticity of demand rises above unity, the cartel with 33 percent of the market becomes virtually undetectable and even the cartel with 60 percent of the market quickly becomes a force not to be reckoned with. For example, with a market demand elasticity of −2, such a cartel would be able to raise price less than 7 percent above the competitive level. The proportionate effect on pricing is most striking for the cartel or dominant firm with 90 percent of the market. An increase in the market elasticity of demand to −1.5 cuts its effect on price in half and when $\eta = −2$ its effect on price is only one-seventh as large as when market demand is unit elastic.

Figure 4, in which I revert to the assumption that market demand is

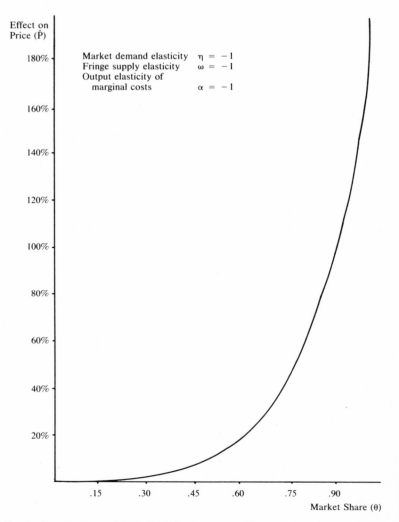

Figure 2. Effect of Market Share on Ability of Dominant Firm or
Cartel To Raise Prices above Competitive Level

unit elastic, shows the effect on price of allowing the elasticity of the
fringe supply to vary. For the cartel or dominant firm with a market share
of 33 percent, the fringe firms prove to be as inhibitory as the market
elasticity of demand. Increasing the elasticity of demand from -1 to -2
cuts the cartel's price to within 1.6 percent of the competitive level; doubling the fringe supply elasticity from 1 to 2 drives the cartel price to

Table 1. Effect of Market Share on Output Price

Function	Market Share, θ (in percent)							
	5	10	25	33	50	60	75	90
Dominant firm demand elasticity, ε	−39.0	−19.0	−7.0	−5.0	−3.0	−2.3	−1.7	−1.2
Price, P̂	.07	0.29	1.3	4.0	12.5	32.0	57.0	215.0

Note: When market demand elasticity (η) = −1, fringe supply elasticity (ω) = 1, and output elasticity of marginal cost (α) = 1.

9

within 1.3 percent of the competitive level. The effectiveness of the fringe against the medium-size cartel is diminished but not insubstantial: increasing the fringe supply elasticity to 2 cuts the cartel's effect on price by two-thirds and, with a fringe supply elasticity of 5, the cartel price is within 4 percent of the competitive level. The fringe firms are considerably less efficacious in restraining the comprehensive cartel (or Judge Hand's

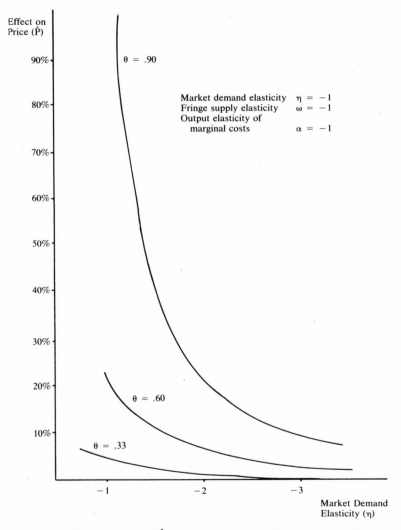

Figure 3.   Effect on Price ($\hat{P}$) of Allowing Market Demand Elasticity to Vary

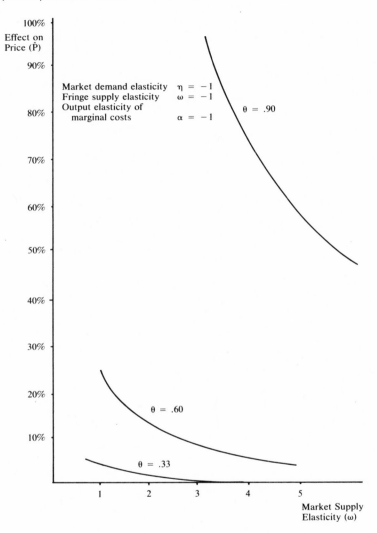

Figure 4. Effect on Price (P̂) of Allowing Fringe Supply Elasticity to Vary

"monopoly"). With a fringe supply elasticity of 2 the monopoly price is more than double the competitive price. Even with a fringe supply elasticity of 5 the monopoly price exceeds the competitive level by nearly 60 percent. In short, it would appear that the object of Judge Hand's concern can earn substantial rents in the face of a vigorous fringe of competitors— if that fringe is sufficiently small.

Figure 5, drawn under the assumption that market demand and fringe supply are both unit elastic, shows the effects of variations in the elasticity of marginal costs with respect to output. It reveals a familiar pattern. Under a broad range of conditions the ability of the small cartel to raise price above the competitive level is negligible. For the medium-sized car-

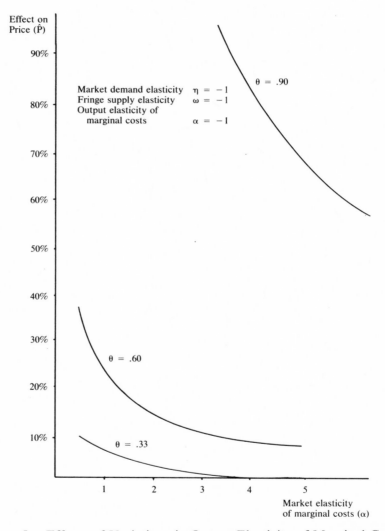

Figure 5.   Effects of Variations in Output Elasticity of Marginal Costs with Respect to Output

tel the effects range from trivial, where marginal costs are very sensitive to output, to substantial, where the converse holds. Finally, even in circumstances least conducive to a price increase, the large cartel still has a large effect on price.

III. CONCLUSIONS

Taken together, these results suggest several generalizations. First, the most important enemy of the large dominant firm or comprehensive cartel is the market elasticity of demand. Nevertheless, the price-enhancing effects of such an organization on the market price remain substantial over a wide variety of conditions. Of equal interest is the importance of the fringe suppliers in disciplining the large dominant firm; once its market share approaches 80 percent or 90 percent it can rightfully look upon its rivals with impunity. One way of viewing these results is that a substantial, clearly discernible effect on price should be the sine qua non of any comprehensive price-fixing conspiracy. Failure to find such an effect in the presence of an alleged comprehensive conspiracy implies that the conspiracy was a spectacular failure—or that the allegation is defective.

The ability of the medium-sized dominant firm or cartel to achieve detectable price increases is much more sensitive to market conditions. Its effect on price ranges from substantial to trivial, and its efforts at aggrandizement are largely thwarted once the market elasticity of demand is much above unity. Moreover, unlike the very large firm or cartel, it typically will be subject to effective discipline by its rivals.

The firm or cartel with market share in the 30 to 40 percent range will be unable to produce detectable price increases under virtually any circumstances. This suggests that a failure to find clear evidence of price enhancement in the presence of a small alleged conspiracy is at best weak evidence against the existence of the conspiracy. Further, antitrust damage claims alleging price enhancement of more than a few percentage points should be viewed with suspicion when raised against a small cartel.

Finally, if one's concern is with the effect of monopolies or cartels on the prices paid by consumers, Judge Hand's guidelines seem roughly right.

ACKNOWLEDGMENTS

Roger Latham, Keith Leffler, Patrick Minford, Richard Zerbe, and an anonymous referee provided helpful comments on an earlier draft of this article, as did members of the Faculty Workshop at the University of Liverpool.

NOTES

1. *United States v. Addyston Pipe and Steel Company*, 85 Fed. 271 (1898), 175 U.S. 211 (1899).

2. *U.S. v. Aluminum Co. of America et al.*, 148 F.2d 416,424 (1945).

3. According to Scherer (7), the origin of this model dates back to Forchheimer (3).

4. This formula has a venerable history in the literature. See, for example, Stigler (8) and Landes and Posner (6).

5. So $\hat{V} \equiv \Delta V/V = \Delta \log V$.

6. To see this, recall the well-known approximation

$$\log x \approx x - 1,$$

which derives from the fact that $x - 1$ is the first term in the Taylor Series expansion of $\log x$. Let $x = P/C$ be the ratio of the dominant firm's price to its marginal cost so that

$$\log(P/C) = \log P - \log C \approx P/C - 1.$$

Let P_c and C_c be the levels of price and marginal cost at the competitive solution where $P_c = C_c$ and $P_c/C_c = 1$. Then $\log(P_c/C_c) = 0$ and it remains true that

$$\log(P/C) - \log(P_c/C_c) \approx P/C - 1$$

or

$$(\log P - \log P_c) - (\log C - \log C_c) \approx P/C - 1.$$

Thus considering deviations of P and C from their levels in the competitive solution,

$$\log P - \log C \approx P/C - 1$$

which is the approximation asserted by Eq. (2) in the text.

7. Note that $\epsilon < 0$ and that profit maximization dictates that the dominant firm choose an output rate such that $|\epsilon| > 1$. Hence $\hat{P} > 0$.

8. For the quadratic cost function, total costs are

$$\alpha + \beta Q + \gamma Q^2$$

and marginal costs are

$$C = \beta + 2\gamma Q.$$

The elasticity of marginal cost with respect to output is simply

$$\frac{dC}{dQ}\frac{Q}{C} = 2\gamma \left\{ \frac{Q}{\beta + 2\gamma Q} \right\} = \frac{2\gamma Q}{\beta + 2\gamma Q} < 1$$

which approaches unity as output approaches infinity. The elasticity of supply is simply the inverse of this.

9. With variable factor L and fixed factor K the Cobb-Douglas production function is

$$Q = ALaK^{1-a}$$

and short-run marginal cost, C, is simply

$$C = (\partial L/\partial Q)w,$$

where w is the price of the variable factor. Thus

$$C = \frac{w}{AaK^{1-a}L^{a-1}} = \left[\frac{w}{AaK^{1-a}} \right] L^{1-a}$$

and the elasticity of marginal cost with respect to output is

$$\frac{\partial C}{\partial Q} \cdot \frac{Q}{C} = \frac{w}{AaK^{1-a}} \left[(1 - a)L^{-a}(\partial L/\partial Q) \right] \frac{ALaK^{1-a}}{(\partial L/\partial Q)w} \ .$$

Cancellation of the common factors in the numerator and denominator yields

$$\frac{\partial C}{\partial Q} \cdot \frac{Q}{C} = \frac{1 - a}{a} = \frac{1}{a} - 1.$$

Again the elasticity of supply is simply the inverse, $\dfrac{a}{1 - a}$.

10.   Although all of the results that follow are based on the "constant elasticity" model I am using, the results do not appear to be an artifact of this particular model. For example, assuming linear demand, supply and cost functions produce qualitative similar results—although the derivation of those results is considerably more cumbersome.

REFERENCES

1.   Bork, Robert. (1978) *The Antitrust Paradox,* New York, Basic Books.
2.   Easterbrook, Frank H. (1981) "Predatory Strategies and Counterstrategies," *University of Chicago Law Review,* Vol. 48: 263.
3.   Forchheimer, Karl. (1908) "Theoretisches zum Unvollständigen Monopoli," *Schmollers Jahrbuch,* pp. 1–12.
4.   Landes, William M., and Posner, Richard A. (1981) "Market Power in Antitrust Cases," *Harvard Law Review,* Vol. 94: 937.
5.   Letwin, William. (1965) *Law and Economic Policy in America,* New York, Random House.
6.   Posner, Richard A. (1976) *Antitrust Law: An Economic Perspective,* Chicago, University of Chicago Press.
7.   Scherer, F. M. (1980) *Industrial Market Structure and Economic Performance,* Boston, Houghton Mifflin.
8.   Stigler, George J. (1940) "Notes on the Theory of Duopoly," *Journal of Political Economy,* Vol. 48: 521.

THE CHICAGO BOARD OF TRADE CASE, 1918

Richard O. Zerbe, Jr.

The Chicago Board of Trade case of 1918 resulted in a classic rule-of-reason opinion. It involved a Rule (the Call Rule) fixing cash grain prices in the "to arrive" market after the close of the Board. Justice Brandeis found the Rule had no particular effect on grain prices but had a variety of other, intended, beneficial effects. Evidence not essentially presented in the record of the case shows the purpose of the Rule was, rather, to police the fixing of commission prices. The intended effects of the fixed commission and grain prices were complex. One intended effect was to enhance the efficient workings of the market. The rules increased the number of bids and brought more trade into the open market. Another effect was to enhance the position of one set of Board members vis-à-vis another set of members who had developed an especially favorable relationship with the railroads. The relationships with the railroads arose primarily from efforts by the railroads to cheat on ICC freight regulations. Finally, the price-fixing rules were intended in part, and this became the dominant motive as time obviated the other motives, to cartelize commission prices. The major grain markets all had market power and fixed commission rates. One could speculate that, if the Chicago Board of Trade had been differently presented, the subse-

Research in Law and Economics, Volume 5, pages 17–55.
Copyright © 1983 by JAI Press Inc.
All rights of reproduction in any form reserved.
ISBN: 0-89232-419-8

quent history of commission-fixing exemption from antitrust law on regulated exchanges might have been different.

I. INTRODUCTION

A famous antitrust case, *Chicago Board of Trade v. United States,* is often cited, fundamentally important, and prominently featured in trade regulation casebooks.[1] It is a bulwark of the "rule of reason," yet troubling, since the Supreme Court upholds a price-fixing rule whose purpose and effect are obscure. Brandeis noted in *Chicago Board of Trade*:

> The true test of legality is whether the restraint imposed is such as merely regulates and perhaps thereby promotes competition or whether it is such as may suppress or even destroy competition. To determine that question the court must ordinarily consider the facts peculiar to the business to which the restraint is applied; . . . The history of the restraint . . . the reason for adopting the particular remedy, the purpose or end sought to be attained, are all relevant facts.[2]

This is famous language. But, does *Chicago Board of Trade* meet the requirements of its own test? What is the history of the restraint, and what were its effects and the motives behind it?

My purpose in this paper is to explain the actions of the Board of Trade that led to the case and to examine the effects of the Board's actions and the Court's decision. The motives and effects of the litigious action of the Board, which Brandeis viewed as central to the antitrust judgment, are conflicting and compounded by a desire for the gains of market efficiency, harm to rivals, and attempts to monopolize.

At issue was the legality of the price-fixing part of a rule adopted in 1906 by the Chicago Board of Trade, and known originally as the Call Rule.[3] The part of the Rule to which the government objected essentially pegged the price of grain "to arrive" for that part of the day in which the Board of Trade was closed. For the period of the Call Rule (1906–1913) a "call" auction was held at 1:15 p.m., the close of regular trading on the Board of Trade. This auction established the price for the remainder of the day until the Board opened again the next morning. After 1913 the Rule was modified and known as the "To Arrive Rule." With modification the Rule existed until August 1955. In spite of the fact that the Rule fixed prices, the Call Rule was upheld by the Supreme Court in a decision by Brandeis.[4]

The Call Rule, as I will show, was primarily a product of conflict between two classes of grain dealers, both members of the Chicago Board of Trade: commission merchants and terminal elevator dealers, firms owning grain elevators in Chicago. This conflict arose out of the entry into grain merchandising by terminal elevators. This entry in turn was in part the result of changing technology, an unintended consequence of *Munn v. Illinois,* and especially an unintended consequence of the operation of the Interstate Commerce Commission.[5]

The effects of the Call Rule were several and complex, as we shall see. In part the Rule was an efficiency-enhancing rule aimed at increasing information and reducing risks. These effects increased the efficiency of the Chicago market, but also improved the relative position of commission merchants. The consequences of the Rule noted by Brandeis are explained by a delineation of these aspects of the Rule. The Rule also acted as a tax on Board members who were cash grain dealers, thus enhancing the demand for grain broker services of Board members, which were a substitute for dealer services.

But the Call Rule also involved the extension of fixed rates of commission into the direct buying of grain and the price-fixing of grain which was a device by which the fixed commissions could be policed. Again, part of the motivation was to improve the relative position of the commission merchants and part to exploit the power of the Chicago market. This latter motive was the dominant one after 1913. The dual nature of the Rule may explain why the economics of the case has so long been a puzzle.

Given the commission-fixing aspects of the Rule, might there have been a more powerful and interesting case which the government could have brought? Parts V and VI of this paper consider the existing law regarding fixed commissions and explore the possible consequences had *Chicago Board of Trade* been brought originally as a commission-fixing case.

II. BACKGROUND: THE COUNTRY MARKET

Major grains in the area, and in the period under discussion, were wheat, corn, rye, barley, oats, and beginning in the mid-1930s, soybeans. The great bulk of the farmers' grains, probably over 96 percent, was sold to the country elevator. Perhaps 1 percent was sold to other country markets. The vast bulk of grain shipped from country elevators, between 80 and 90 percent, was shipped to terminal markets.[6]

Terminal Markets

Terminal markets were large markets such as Chicago, which were the final destination of substantial quantities of grain. Nevertheless, much of the grain was resold or brokered for other destinations, mostly in the East.

The Call Rule is concerned with "to arrive" grain. This is grain that is bought in the country for future delivery (10 to 90 days) at a specified market.

Terminal markets had both brokers and dealers; commission men were primarily brokers. Terminal elevator owners were primarily dealers. Both classes were members of the Board of Trade. Before the late 1870s commission men handled virtually all of the business. By the time of the Call Rule, that is, before 1906, the greatest share of grain was being handled by terminal elevator dealers.

Elsewhere [Zerbe (22)] I have explained how attempts to regulate terminal warehouses and the regulation of the railroad by the Interstate Commerce Commission gave an impetus to direct buying by terminal elevators. An indirect result of the railroad regulation was that, at the time of the Call Rule, terminal elevators were receiving freight rebates. Not surprisingly then the portion of the business going to terminal elevators at the expense of commission men had been growing.

As part of their direct buying activities, terminal elevators began to establish country elevators, eventually to become significant factors in country buying competition,[7] and to exploit economies of scale in organizing cartel activities.[8]

Through the grain dealers' associations, the line elevator organizations became dominant factors in the political forces of several states, clashing with the farmers' groups in an economic and political battle. The growth of farm cooperative elevators proved to be their countermeasure in this rivalry.[9]

Thus, there was considerable antipathy between commission merchants and terminal elevators, and between farmers and terminal elevators. This first rivalry is relevant to the passage of the Call Rule.

III. THE CALL RULE

A. Passage of the Call Rule

To a large extent, the Call Rule arose from the conflict between commission merchants and the terminal elevator dealers.[10] For commission men as a class the question was one of survival. The commission merchants or receivers—men who previously had handled the process of bringing grain from the country and shipping it through the primary markets to consumption points—were being eliminated from business.[11] Warehouses owned at least three-fourths of all grain received in public warehouses in Chicago.[12]

Commission men were being driven out of business because first, terminal elevators had lower transport costs, as explained earlier; and second, elevator merchandisers were making their own market outside the regular hours of the Board of Trade.[13]

The elevators could "make a market," apparently, from cash grain business on the Chicago exchange. The movement of business from regular exchange hours to "off hours" was sufficiently large that J. P. Griffin, a commission merchant and member of the Board, testified: ". . . it was a question if the market would not go into decay, because the business . . . was being taken away from the open market. . . . The volume of business . . . in the open market . . . had dwindled down to small proportions" [*Record* at 143].

It is unclear why the elevator buyers were interested in their own closed market. The hypothesis most consistent with the evidence points to an attempt to eliminate the commission merchants who impeded the operation and policing of a buyers' cartel of terminal elevator grain dealers operating with respect to country purchases.

Commission merchants were in competition with warehouse dealers and had different marginal costs due to the differential freight. Since the optimum cartel price differs between the two classes, cartel agreement in this situation was more difficult to obtain. Probably more important, commission merchants made the operation of an elevator buyers' cartel difficult to police. Any agreement on country bid prices could be undercut by commission men. Terminal elevators attempted to control price-cutting by bidding only for grain in the territory of the railroad line with which the elevator was associated.[14]

Terminal elevators also bought from commission merchants. Commission men were under no "natural" inclination to restrict country bidding to a particular railroad. Thus, terminal elevator owners in buying from commission men were effectively undercutting their own cartel. As long as commission men were part of the market, policing of the terminal elevator cartel would be difficult.

The after-hours "secret" market raised information costs for commission men. "To find out what grain to arrive was worth prior to the enactment of the rule it was necessary to use your friendship to a great extent and to work in devious ways. . . . Very often with strenuous effort you could not find out what the bids were until the next morning" [testimony of William Eckhardt from *Record* at 112]. It is in this sense, as a device lowering the time costs of determining the after-hours price, that the fixed price part of the Call Rule acted as the business closing rule which Brandeis stressed in his decision.[15]

If elevator men had the power to make a market, why did they not form their own market separate from the Board of Trade; and since in a sense they were attempting to do this anyway, why not go all the way? Elevator owners opting out of Board of Trade membership would deprive themselves of member rate commission charges on futures business. This, though not the only reason for membership, should in itself have been sufficient. The natural monopoly aspect of the futures business would have made successful entry difficult or impossible.

As a result of the elevator men's activities, Mr. Griffin, who took part in the formation of the Call Rule, testified that: "The complaint that was finally made was that the market was becoming virtually a closed market; . . . The smaller merchants . . . rebelled; they claimed they were being driven out of business, and that they were denied equality of opportunity to engage in that business" [*Record* at 43]. The antipathy arising from this situation, great to begin with, had been accumulating. By 1905 "the relationship between [the two classes of dealers] . . . bordered on civil war . . ." [*id.*] and, in the same year, led to the formation of a "committee to investigate monopoly and dwindling trade." From this committee came the Call Rule.

B. The Call Rule and Market Efficiency

The Call Rule and related rules that were adopted simultaneously affected the grain trade in several ways. Market efficiency was increased by these antimonopoly measures in three ways. First, the utility of the regular market was increased by measures designed to move a large proportion of trading to arrive within regular market hours. Second, the informational advantages enjoyed by the terminal elevators during after-hours trade was eliminated. Third, an ancillary rule weakened or eliminated the elevator cartel by allowing bids accepted in the country for Chicago to be filled over the lines of any of the railroads arriving in Chicago. Testimony is that shippers found this advantageous [*Record* at 138].

Utility of Regular Market

Trading during regular hours was encouraged by the Board by (1) enforcing the closing rule for futures trading, (2) fixing the after-hours "to arrive" price, and (3) establishing fixed commissions for after-hours buying. Further, the closing rule for futures trading [Rule 4, Sec. 8 (1900); *Record* at 144] had not been enforced "for some years" [*id.* at 108]. The disadvantage of trading outside regular hours made it more difficult to hedge grain after hours. Much of the bidding in the "to arrive" market, especially in Chicago, was for "contract grade"—grain deliverable on futures contracts and thus capable of being efficiently hedged, lessening risk.[16] The Call auction was not in contract grades but in commercial grades, more satisfactory for cash buying but riskier because these could not be so efficiently hedged. However, the greater certainty of the call price reduced the need to hedge.

The fixed price provision of the Call Rule also moved more of the trading to within market hours, clearly the Rule's intent: "In the Call Rule we aimed—and it was the intention and object of the farmers [*sic*] of the Rule, that so far as practical, to force the trading in grain to arrive into the open market during the hours of regular trading . . ." [J. P. Griffin, *Record* at 144]. When the equilibrium price was above the fixed call price, there would be less grain supplied to the after-hours market and more grain would move to the regular market. When the equilibrium price was below the call price, the amount of grain demanded in the off-hours market controlled by the call price would be less and, again, grain would move to the regular market.

Abundant testimony supports the assertion that the Call Rule "did what its framers intended . . . [and] forced the business into the open market" [*id*]. George R. Nichols, who was instrumental in the passage of the Rule, testifies that after its passage "we installed six additional sample tables, which [was] 24 additional spaces" [*id*. at 110; see also at 108].

Unfortunately, no quantitative evidence showing the importance of the fixed price provision in strengthening trade during regular hours is available, either directly or through bids by time of day or of changes in bids with the Call Rule. The percentage decrease in off-hours trade is $E \cdot T$ where E is the elasticity of off-hours demand or supply, depending on whether the fixed price was above or below equilibrium, and T is the price distortion $\frac{\Delta P}{P}$ imposed by the Call Rule. No data exist for E and no way of calculating E is possible from available data. Trade during regular hours would be a very good substitute for off-hours trade and thus E would be quite high. An idea of the likely price distortion produced by the Call Rule can be obtained by examining the differences between market closing prices and opening prices the next day. These are not available for cash grain but are for futures contracts which serve as a reasonable proxy.

Differences between closing prices and opening prices the following day were examined for the six years preceding the Call Rule. For each year daily prices were examined for June, July, and August for wheat, corn, and oats.[17] The mean price differences for these grains over the six years were, respectively, 46 cents, 41 cents and 46 cents. The price difference as a percentage of the mean price for grain gives respective averages for the six years of 56 percent, 1 percent and 1.3 percent. The price difference exceeded one cent per bushel on 12 percent of the days examined for wheat, on 13 percent of the days examined for corn, and on 11 percent of the days examined for oats. Thus the meager quantitative evidence is consistent with the testimony to the effect that the Call Rule moved a significant portion of the off-hours trade into regular hours.

The Call Rule introduced fixed commission rates for direct buying *only during off hours* between 1906 and 1913. The price distortion in commission services introduced by the Call Rule was much greater than for grain prices. Nevertheless, fixed commissions were probably less effective than the fixed grain prices in moving grain into regular market hours because the demand elasticity was so much less for commission services than the comparable elasticity for grain. Nonmember commission rates were one cent per bushel for wheat and rye, and one-half cent per bushel for corn and oats. Member rates were one-half cent and one-fourth cent per bushel. It is reasonable to assume that purely competitive nommember rates would not be below the member rates, and would have been above them since there would be less financial risk dealing with fellow members.[18] Hence, the differential between nonmember and member rates of one-half cent for wheat and rye and one-fourth cent for corn and oats represents an estimated maximum extent of the "excess" rates which a Board of Trade member might have avoided charging, and shippers might have avoided paying by trading during regular hours. Thus, the percentage price distortion may have approached 100 percent. It can be shown that the elasticity of demand for commission services would be less than 1 percent of either the demand or supply elasticity of grain.[19] Even with a price distortion for commission services of 100 percent, the E·T for these services would be less than for grain itself. Thus the fixed commission for after-hours direct buying would probably have had a smaller impact than the fixed prices for after-hours grain in moving grain to within regular market hours.

The commission rate applied to direct buying in the after-hours market was too high for a monopoly rate. Assuming the member commission charge is at marginal costs, the 1906 nonmember commission rate for direct buying implies a price elasticity between .5 and 1 at the competitive price. This is certainly smaller than the actual elasticity for after-hours services for direct buying alone, since within-hours trading must have been a very good substitute. Moreover, the same rate was used after 1913 when fixed commissions for direct buying were extended to all transactions. Thus the after-hours commission charge was considerably higher than the monopoly rate. This supports the view that a purpose of the commission rate was to increase business during regular hours relative to off-hours business and that the commission men were at this time politically powerful compared to warehouse operators. By "taxing" off-hours direct buying, the demand for pure commission services was increased.

Informational Advantage

Information is a primary product of such a market as Chicago represents. Consider, for example, that the Board fought an expensive campaign to maintain property rights in its quotations about this time; in 1901 two telegraph companies were paying $2,500 per month for the Board's quotations [*Christie, supra* note 1].

Well-known results of bidding models, such as Teisberg's (14), show that large profits accrue to those with superior information. When market information reaches all bidders, profits drop, consistent with the attempts by warehouses to maintain their relative informational advantage by impeding the flow of information. The advantages to commission men, providing a more symmetrical distribution of information, are apparent.

Consider the effect of superior market information on the number of bidders. Assume that bidding is competitive and that each bidder is stochastically the same. Assume bidders seek to maximize gains from becoming informed net of the costs of information. Suppose further, following Teisberg and Gaskins (15), that each potential bidder is either informed or not and that marginal and average costs of information, C, are constant. Once informed, the bidder has no advantage in purchasing more information. Only informed potential bidders bid. (An assumption equivalent in its effects but more realistic would be that information costs increase sharply after some point.) Let

M = the number of bidders with C_2 information costs
N = the number of bidders with C_1 information costs
n = the total number of bidders
$\dfrac{E(n)}{n}$ = the expected gains per bidder as a fraction of asset value, V;
C_1 = constant average and marginal costs of becoming informed for most market members;
C_2 = constant average and marginal costs of becoming informed for members in advantageous position $C_2 < C_1$.

The market is segmented into two groups, a small "cartel" group with limited membership and C_2 information costs, the other with C_1 information costs. The number of low-cost bidders is fixed. The number of "highest" informed bidders will increase so long as the expected gains exceed the costs of becoming informed. Thus, in equilibrium:

$$\frac{VE(n)}{M + N} = C_1. \tag{1}$$

Since $C_2 < C_1$, members of the informationally superior group will have expected economic profits of $M[C_1 - C_2]$ where M is the number of bidders with the advantage. Suppose now that costs for all bidders are lowered to C_2. Then

$$VE(n) = (M + N)C_2 \tag{2}$$

A decrease in information costs from C_1 to C_2 will increase the number of bidders and decrease $\dfrac{E(n)}{N}$.

A similar result is obtained when the industry as a whole is considered the decision maker and when E and C are functions of the quantity of information.[20] Thus where the costs of information are primarily a function of exchange rules and market viability, a decrease in information costs due to a change in market rules may result in a substantial increase in the number of bidders and hence also in the number of bids. The new bidders have experienced a decrease in information costs and the share of business going to this group relative to the previously advantaged group will increase.

The Board of Trade can affect information costs and thus the number of bidders. It must also solve the related problem of how many members to allow. Additional members lower information costs for others, but also lower expected gross gains. The equilibrium number of members is reached when the marginal decrease in per capita costs just equals the decrease in per capita expected gross benefits.

In terms of the model here:

$$\frac{Vd\dfrac{(E(n))}{N + M}}{dN} = \frac{dc}{dN} . \tag{3}$$

For an asset with a given value, V, the seller may be expected to receive the value of the asset minus the expenditures to become informed, minus the commission charge. The seller then receives:

$$V - nC - A = (1 - E(n))V - A \tag{4}$$

where A is the commission charge. A lower C would increase the price received by the sellers, and this conclusion is not altered if a fixed commission is charged on each sale.

Weakening of the Elevator Cartel

The foregoing model and the hypothesis concerning the purpose of the terminal elevators merchants in shifting to off-market activity are consistent with the effects of the Call Rule. The most spectacular effects were (1) the increase in the number of bidders for grain to arrive; (2) the increase in the number of bids going to the country; (3) a reduction of risks for country sellers, and the increase in the number of sellers in Chicago able to offer grain in the East. The testimony concerning these effects is voluminous, clear, and consistent [*Record* at 98, 108, 114, 117, 121, 130, 133, 136, and 140].

Testimony concerning the increased number of bidders is very impressive. Nichols testified that: "It increased the number of buyers and sellers in the market to a degree that you would have to use the word 'multiply' " [*id*. at 108]. William Eckhardt, a commission merchant, testified that "there were also additions to the number of concerns who did . . . business . . ." [*id*. at 114]. Merritt, a commission merchant, testified: "The number of people exposing samples on the tables was very much increased, offhand I should say from fifty to seventy-five percent" [*id*. at 140].

The increased number of bids going to the country reduced risks to country dealers in buying farmers' grain. As Hubbard, a country grain dealer in Illinois, testified: "The effect of this [the fixed after-hours price] was to give us an assured market and we did not pay to take the risk of going over to the opening market next morning" [*id*. at 123]. The reduced risk allowed country dealers to work on a closer margin, as Hubbard, whose testimony is typical, noted: ". . . I feel that that element of risk was removed and we possibly were enabled to handle out grain upon a little closer margin" [*id*. at 124].

Clearly, the removal of the information barriers played the key role in increasing efficiency, with several notable results. (1) The increased trading during market hours improved the informational value of the trading process during regular market hours and gave a wider distribution to information. (2) The fixed after-hours price reduced or eliminated the informational advantages of terminal elevators and decreased the cost of determining the after-hours price in an important way. (3) These measures, along with the introduction of the option of allowing the seller to use any railroad, reduced or eliminated the informational advantage and monopoly bidding by terminal warehouse dealers.

We have Eckhardt's testimony that: "There was a complete reversal of the percentage of business handled by independent concerns as against the interests who received and handled business prior to the enactment of the Call" [*id*. at 114]. We have testimony, bearing out Teisberg's model, that "prior to the adoption of the rule, . . . those who did handle the commodity handled it at a larger margin of profit" [*id*. at 135 and see also 137]; and from Brennan, a commission merchant, who testified that "when this call was in effect, you could sell anything bought from the farmer, . . . and in that way he [the commission merchant] bid with a closer margin, because his margin of profit was assured" [*id*. at 131].

Further testimony indicates that the total volume of business done both during and after regular exchange hours increased [*id.* at 133 and 136]. In spite of the increase in the proportion of business done during regular exchange hours, it is by no means clear that even the absolute volume of trade in off-hours decreased. A decrease in information costs would, in terms of the model here, increase the bid price to sellers and the volume bought. An increase in the total volume of trade is consistent with the model: the cooperative elevators, which were a threat to both line elevator cartels and the independent elevators, were apparently beneficiaries of the reduction in the market power of warehouses.

"I remember very distinctly before the inauguration of the Call, that there were instances where it was thought advisable by certain of the large buyers of grain in this market and elsewhere, not to antagonize those who were unfavorable to the cooperative movement" [*id.* at 133; see also at 118–119, 130].

Thus the Call Rule and associated rules were in part concerned, at least initially, with information and market efficiency.[21] The story, however, does not stop there. By 1913 the purpose of the Call Rule seems to have been rather different.

IV. THE CALL RULE AND FIXED RATES OF COMMISSION

Minimum commission and brokers' rates for futures trading had been part of the Board's rules since the 1880s. Before 1900 commission rates were not enforced [Lurie (10), pp. 224–230]. In that year teeth were inserted into the enforcement processing, and in 1901 a member, Dickinson, was successfully expelled although he carried his case to the Illinois Supreme Court in a 1904 decision.[22] Immediately following this decision minimum rates were introduced for cash grain handled on consignment.

The Call Rule (Section D) applied these same rates to *direct buying after* regular market hours; it provided that "final bids on the 'call' less the regular commission charge for receiving and accounting may be forwarded by dealers.[23] The fixed price provision of the Call Rule was necessary to the enforcement of this extension of fixed commissions. Prices bid to country dealers by members of the Board were determined by subtracting from the price in the Chicago market freight charges and fixed commission charges. That is, the bid price to the country was:

$$P_B = P_c - F - C$$

where P_B is the bid price to the country dealer; P_c is the Chicago price, F is the freight rate, and C is the fixed commission charge. Records of bids to country dealers could be and were examined to determine if the required commission rates were charged. This would, however, only be meaningful if there was a definite or official Chicago price. Suppose, for illustration, that the "true" market price in Chicago is 100 cents per bushel, that the freight rate is 10 cents per bushel, and the required fixed commission is one cent per bushel. The bid price to the country then should be [$1.00 − .10 − .01] 89 cents per bushel. With both the Chicago price and freight rates known, it can readily be determined whether or not the full commission rate had been charged. But, if there is no official Chicago price, this is no longer possible. Suppose, for example, that there were no official Chicago price but that the "true" market price is still $1.00. By reporting a Chicago market price of, say $1.005, the bids to the country would be [$1.005 − .10 − .01] 89½ cents per bushel. Even though it appears that the full commission of one cent per bushel is charged, an effective commission of only one-half cent per bushel is actually levied.

Before 1913, market efficiency, antimonopoly aspects, and aid to commission men in relation to terminal elevator operators appear to have provided the dominant motives. After 1913, however, cartelization of commission rates appears to have provided the primary goal.

By 1913, *all* grain received in Chicago had become subject to fixed rates of commission. The efficiency effects that the Call Rule produced were no longer needed or were not as important. The extension of fixed rates to within-hours trading eliminated the effect of commission rates in increasing within-market trade relative to after-hours trade. Similarly, the fixed price provision for after-hours trade was replaced by a more flexible procedure under which new bids could go out "upon proper record being made of the same" [*Annual Report, 1913*]. Thus the Call Rule no longer had as much effect in moving trade from after to within market hours. After 1913 the Board maintained records of price and specification of all to-arrive bids.

It is ironic that the elimination of the fixed price provision in 1913 obviated the government's case while extending the relevant cartel, the one for commission services. Why this extension was delayed until 1913 is unclear. It may be that prior to 1913 efficiency considerations were paramount; perhaps political difficulties interfered in deciding the optimal structure of rates when two classes of dealers have different costs, since the optimal rate would have been higher for commission men than for terminal dealers owing to the lower costs of the latter. Since the relevant antitrust case involved fixed commissions rather than fixed grain prices, it is clear that the Call Rule applied not to a small part of the daily business but to the entire cash grain business in Chicago.

Couldn't one cheat on the fixed rate simply by offering more for grain? The Board addresses this question specifically in its rule changes for 1913 and 1925. During market hours members were "prohibited from bidding the country for grain to arrive at prices in excess of the last posted price less the following minimum charges: . . ." [*Annual Report* (1925), ch. 13, secs. 330–334 at 49]. During market hours, the high bid was posted and such bid "constitutes an open offer to buy, which may be accepted by any other member who may compel the bidder to take at least one carload . . ." [*ibid.*] The last posted bid for the day carried over after the close of the session. The 1913 and 1925 changes in the Call Rule, the last major changes, illustrate the concern of the Board that after-hours prices be flexible [*id.* (1914), p. 124]. After the close, members were prohibited from bidding higher than the last posted price except that:

A member who having made bona fide bids to *not less than five members* in the cash grain business in excess of any closing price may bid the country the price named in such bids less the regular charges. [*Ibid.*; emphasis added.]

A. Rate-Fixing: The Evidence

The evidence that commission rates were effectively fixed is of several kinds, both direct and indirect. The direct evidence concerns the activities of the call committee, the penalties for violation, and certain ancillary rules. Indirect evidence arises from the monopoly power of the Chicago market, and the existence of similar commission-fixing at other markets.

Direct Evidence

Records of the Call Committee. A variety of records provide cogent and direct evidence that a purpose of the Call Rule was to aid in maintaining fixed commissions for direct buying. Letters and the files of the Call Committee and its successor, the To Arrive Committee, show clearly that maintaining commissions for direct buying was not just the primary but the only task of these committees during the period before the Chicago Board of Trade case in 1918.[24] These committees policed fixed commission rates. The records of the Violation of Rules Committee of the Board of Trade are filled with enforcement cases and questions of the proper commission in questionable situations. The Call Committee was concerned with questions directly related to the proper commission such as whether or not premiums could be paid for grade changes (no), color changes (yes), who paid if the buyer insists on reinspection (depends on whether the buyer was right), and whether extra switching charges should be billed.[25] These files convey the impression that firms were anxious to check the correct procedure in complex cases so as not to violate the

commission rule. The array of detail considered by this committee indicates that the enforcement of commission rates was taken seriously.

Penalty for Violation. Such concern on the part of the firms over
obeying the commission rule is consistent with the penalty for violation.
The penalty for violation of the fixed commission rule was severe. The
commission rules of the Chicago Board of Trade provided:

> Any member who, or whose firm or corporation shall be convicted
> by the Board of Directors of a violation . . . making rebates in prices,
> by making any contract or observing any contract already made, by
> furnishing a membership in the Exchange, by giving any bonus, gift
> donation or otherwise shall purchase or offer to purchase any grain,
> seeds, provisions or other commodities consigned to him, them or
> it; for sale, or by rendering any other service or concession what-
> soever, with the intent to evade in any way directly or indirectly the
> regular rates of commission or brokerage established by the rule,
> *shall be expelled from the Association.*
>
>   . . . .
>
> The Board of Directors is authorized to offer a reward of not more
> than twenty-five hundred dollars to any person who shall furnish
> evidence that does convict any member, firm, or corporation of a
> violation of this rule. [*Rules and Regulations,* No. 14, Sec. 9]

The penalty for cheating on commission rates was obviously great and
the reward for informing was substantial. The power of the Board of Trade
to expel violators meant that Rule enforcement would be effective. To
be expelled meant losing the equity of one's membership right.

Other Rules. Additional evidences that commission-fixing was taken
seriously is found in ancillary rules aimed at closing off indirect methods
of cheating. For example, Rule 14, Sec. 7, of the Chicago *Rules* states:

> In addition to all the rates of commission prescribed by this rule,
> there shall be charged all legitimate expenses incurred in handling
> and caring for the property involved, including storage, insurance,
> inspection, weighing. Cost of sampling shall not be considered a
> charge against the property.

Interest was required to be charged on advances [*FTC Report,* Vol. III
at 49; Vol. II at 231] and freight and taxes had to be included in billings
[Vol. III at 40]. Gifts in any form were explicitly forbidden [Vol. II at
229–230]. Probably the rule that forbade solicitors of grain, working for

members of the Board of Trade, to operate on a percentage basis was aimed at reducing the incentive for the solicitor to give up rebates out of his own commission. Such rebates are well known in the insurance business, for example, where salesmen work on a commission. Chicago early adopted a rule to prevent brokers from securing member rates by buying into member corporations [Taylor (13), Vol. 2 at 1021].

Commissions at Other Exchanges. Commission rates were fixed at all important markets throughout the Midwest. Minimum rates for consignment were part of all exchanges. The seven largest primary markets—Chicago, Minneapolis, Milwaukee, Duluth, Kansas City, Omaha, and St. Louis—had minimum commission rates in effect for direct buying as well as consignment sometime after 1906 [*FTC Report,* Vol. II at 235–239]. Minneapolis had an apparently effective commission rule after 1906 [*id.* at 228]. Rates for only consignment business applied to the primary market, Peoria, and to the secondary markets of Buffalo, Baltimore, Philadelphia, and New York. Rates were also listed for Cincinnati, San Francisco, and Indianapolis but apparently were not enforced.[26] Moreover, there was at least some correspondence among Boards of Trade regarding each other's commissions charges.[27]

There is reason to think the minimum rates were effective. Elaborate rules existed for their enforcement. All but two primary markets, and some secondary markets, required that charges for both direct buying or consignment include "all legitimate expenses" in addition to the prescribed rates [*FTC Report,* Vol. II at 234]. Chicago, Milwaukee, Minneapolis, Duluth, and Kansas City explicitly forbade gifts in any form as a means of soliciting business [*id.* at 229–230]. Other exchanges usually maintained some general prohibition under which gifts would fall. In 1914 the Minneapolis Rules Committee issued an opinion that to keep the books of a country shipper without full compensation for this service was contrary to their commission rule [*id.* at 230]. Twelve exchanges with minimum rates explicitly forbade rebates of any sort. Penalties could be severe. In Minneapolis, at least as early as 1894, fines were required and censorship, suspension, or expulsion was possible for violation of a commission rule.[28] A Minneapolis firm was fined $1,000 in December 1910 for having rebated commissions [*FTC Report,* Vol. II at 229].

An additional problem in enforcement existed in North Dakota, South Dakota, and Minnesota, where the practice of financing country elevators by commission companies was common. Here the exchanges had to contend with a cheating problem in which the commission companies charged less than the market rate of interest. As with other rules, it is difficult to tell the extent of this manner of cheating. However, in 1902 the Minneapolis exchanges did fine two commission companies $500 each, one for loaning money without interest, and the other for offering to loan money without interest [*id*. at 231]. Most exchanges specified in one form or another that the receiver "charge the current rate of interest for any advances; provided always that the minimum rate of interest so charged be at the rate of five percent per annum."[29]

In Milwaukee and Omaha the provision to customers of free telegraph service was prohibited [*id*. at 231]. In Chicago, an attempt in 1901 by the smaller commission men to enforce a similar prohibition was defeated and for many years explicitly and until the present implicitly, "free telegraph and telephone communication" was allowed as not being in violation of commission rules.[30]

In addition, the various exchanges had, and in most cases have still, detailed regulations affecting the employment of solicitors for both cash and future business. Chicago, Kansas City, Minneapolis, and Duluth forbade solicitors from operating on a percentage basis [*FTC Report,* Vol. II at 238, 240].

Chicago was not the only market with a Call Rule. Milwaukee also "had call" just as at Chicago [*Sen. Doc.* 278 at 747]. Minneapolis attempted to deal with the problem of using direct buying as a method of cheating on commission at least as early as 1894. A part of the Minneapolis penalty clause reads:

> Any member charged with violating the rule relating to the established rates of commission, — by *purchasing any grain consigned to him for sale, where such purchase is made with intent to evade the established rates of commission, — shall be fined a sum not less than $100 nor more than $250.*[31] (Emphasis added)

Apparently, cash commission rates were difficult to maintain in the absence of restrictions on nonmarket trading. The Call Rule was an alternative to complete restriction less damaging to Chicago's competitive position in a time when this was slowly eroding.

The Call Rule was similar to these regulations and should be seen as one of a number of rules, though a very important one, designed to maintain minimum commissions. At that, the rule was less restrictive than rules with similar effects adopted by the exchanges in Kanas City, Omaha, St. Louis, and Indianapolis. These markets went beyond the Call Rule and *forbade* cash trading in consigned grain except during regular market hours [*FTC Report,* Vol. II at 250].

Indirect Evidence

Market Power. The Chicago market must have had some potential monopoly power in order for commission-fixing to be effective. Did the Chicago market (and other markets) have in fact such power? Brandeis implies not; he noted, "country dealers and farmers in practically every part of the territory called tributary to Chicago, had some other market for grain 'to arrive' " [*id.* at 18–23].

Even though Chicago's position as a cash grain market declined after 1900, it nevertheless remained the pre-eminent cash market for many years. As Table 1 shows, for the five-year period 1913–1917 Chicago was the largest receiver market in terms of the combined volumes of various grains. This was so in spite of the fact that receipts at Chicago declined absolutely after 1914 until the mid-1930s, and receipts as a percent of Illinois production showed a sharp downturn after 1913, the downturn continuing until the present. Table 1 indicates that Brandeis' judgment about the availability of other markets may have given insufficient weight to Chicago's prominent position.

A more detailed inquiry indicates that not only Chicago but other primary markets had some geographic monopoly. The most important of the primary markets in the period before 1920 were Minneapolis, Duluth, Milwaukee, Omaha, Kansas City, St. Louis, Chicago, Peoria, Indianapolis, Cincinnati, Detroit, and Wichita. There were also secondary markets, markets with less well-developed exchanges or trading associations but with physical facilities for receipt or shipment of grain. These included Toledo, Buffalo, New York, Philadelphia, Baltimore, Galveston, New Orleans, Portland, Los Angeles, and Seattle [*FTC Report* at 23]. In the 1913–1917 period, only 2 percent of wheat, 4.4 percent of corn, and 4.5 percent of oats were shipped from the country to secondary markets.[32] These markets generally received grain from primary markets. Thus they were complementary to rather than competitive with primary markets. Smaller markets existed in Des Moines, Sioux City, St. Joseph, Oklahoma City, Fort Worth, Cairo, and Memphis [*id.* at 24]. Table 2 shows the percentage distribution of the grain of each state by primary market. The tendency toward concentration of grain from different states in a few markets is evident. Well over half of all Illinois grain and of all Iowa grain went to Chicago. These two states were the two largest producers of grain by a significant margin at this time [*id.* at 38]. Table 3 illustrates regional market concentration in a simpler fashion: four states sent over 95 percent of their marketed grain to no more than two markets, and all but two states (Iowa and Indiana) sent nearly 80 percent or more to two markets.

These tables suggest, though they do not prove, the importance of transportation costs and the possibility of local monopoly positions for each primary market. If transportation costs define an important area of local advantage for each market, then Tables 2 and 3 understate the advantage, as they show market concentration by state rather than by transportation cost. The drawing power of the Chicago market, in fact, would be greater

Table 1. Average Annual Receipts in Bushels at Major Exchanges, 1913–1917

	Wheat	Corn	Oats	Barley	Rye	Total	Percent of All Market
Chicago	65,412	100,592	136,687	27,993	4,259	334,943	32.2
Minneapolis	120,151	9,366	30,446	33,171	6,882	200,016	19.3
Kansas City	55,612	20,422	9,712	1,084	375	87,205	8.4
St. Louis	34,209	18,586	23,758	1,883	518	80,152	7.7
Duluth	56,884	862	5,624	11,424	3,299	78,093	7.5
Milwaukee	8,062	13,666	28,153	18,840	308	72,031	6.9
Omaha	21,275	27,352	15,845	872	805	66,149	6.4
Peoria	3,079	23,843	12,779	3,001	468	43,170	4.2
Indianapolis	3,175	18,586	23,758	1,883	518	80,152	7.7
Cincinnati	5,955	8,502	7,014	855	649	23,007	2.2
Wichita	—	—	—	—	—	11,136*	1.1
Detroit	—	—	—	—	—	10,315*	1.0
Total	339,605	223,191	257,173	97,240	20,708	1,038,041	
Chicago as % of total by grain	19	45	53	29	21	32	

Note: Cincinnati, Duluth, Kansas City, Milwaukee, and Minneapolis show only local-billed cars. Chicago, Peoria, St. Louis, and the seaboard markets include local, through-billed, and reconsigned cars. Receipts for Omaha, Toledo, Indianapolis, and Louisville consist of cars inspected which generally means local and reconsigned grain. Except for St. Louis and Chicago, receipts at the major markets consist mainly of local-billed grain. It is well known that Chicago has the largest proportion of through-billed grain of any of the markets. Hence the omission of through-billed grain from other markets is not as serious as it would be from Chicago.

Chicago's position is somewhat diminished when the grains are weighed by price since during this period wheat prices were about 1⅔ those of corn, the next highest priced grain, except for rye, for which receipts were small. Prices were calculated from *FTC Report*, Vol. IV at 11. Nevertheless, during this period Chicago is clearly the leading grain market.

* Calculated from tables 7 and 21 of *FTC Report*, Vol. II at 23 and 40. Figures for individual grains cannot be calculated.

Source: Calculated from *FTC Report*, Vol. II at 18–23, 40.

Table 2. Market Distribution for States Leading in Grain Production, 1912–1917

State	Chicago	Minneapolis	Kansas City	Duluth	Primary Market* St. Louis	Milwaukee	Omaha	Peoria	Indianapolis	Cincinnati	Wichita	Detroit
Illinois	66.7	0.8	—	—	12.9	0.4	—	12.2	5.5	0.9	—	0.6
Indiana	21.6	—	—	—	0.1	—	—	—	39.4	27.7	—	11.2
Iowa	59.0	1.1	3.1	—	11.4	12.0	8.4	4.5	—	—	—	—
Kansas	1.6	0.9	81.6	—	0.4	—	0.3	—	—	—	15.4	—
Michigan	2.1	—	—	—	—	—	—	—	—	0.7	—	97.2
Minnesota	4.2	69.7	0.3	6.5	6.4	0.4	7.5	0.1	—	—	—	—
Nebraska	6.1	3.5	28.1	0.2	3.5	0.5	58.0	0.1	—	—	—	—
North Dakota	0.4	62.7	—	36.8	—	0.1	—	—	—	—	—	—
South Dakota	8.1	67.2	2.9	3.0	0.1	12.2	6.4	—	—	—	—	—
Wisconsin	11.3	2.4	0.1	—	0.2	86.1	—	—	—	—	—	—

Note: Percentages for Indiana, Kansas, and Michigan were calculated from data provided in *FTC Report*, Vol. II at 40 and 41. The relative weights of the various markets are based on survey of shipments by country dealers. These are probably less accurate than the weights used for all the other states, which were based on receipts of the Board of Trade, and thus the importance of the Chicago market is probably understated. Percentages for the other states were calculated from *FTC Report*, Vol. II at 23, 40, and 41.

* Corn, oats, wheat, rye, and barley.

Table 3. Portion of Grain to their Two Largest Markets, by State

Illinois	Indiana	Iowa	Kansas	Michigan
79.6	67.1	71.0	97.0	99.3
Minnesota	Nebraska	N. Dakota	S. Dakota	Wisconsin
78.9	86.1	99.5	79.4	97.4

for southern Michigan than for northern Michigan for those parts of Illinois closer to Chicago than to Peoria, and so forth. Unfortunately, shipments of grain are not given for units smaller than states or for different types of grain.

The importance of transportation costs, however, is subject to test. For Chicago, transport costs in 1916 from the "agriculture center" of each of the major grain-producing states shipping significant grain to Chicago were about 12 percent of the purchase price of grain of Chicago. This varies from a low of 5.1 percent in Illinois to a high of 18.3 percent in Kansas. A more exact test of the role of transportation costs is achieved by regressing the percentage of a state's grain going to market against transport costs from the "agricultural" center of the state to the particular market.[33] Treating states as points and using them for total across all major grains understates the true contribution of transportation costs.

Separate regressions were run for each of the nine states with the percentage of a state's grain going to each market as the dependent variable and the measures of transportation costs as the independent variables. Transportation costs to primary markets were all of the right sign and all significant at the 5 percent level, except for Iowa which was of the wrong sign but not significant.

The probability of 8 out of 9 coefficients being of the same sign when drawn from a random sample with an equal chance of either sign is 2 percent. Since the reasons for Iowa can be "explained away," the results are significant at better than the 1 percent level. The coefficients for transportation costs varied from 5.8 for North Dakota to 11.2 for Minnesota with the other results clustered around 9 and 10. Thus each one-cent per bushel increase in transportation costs to a particular market decreases the amount of grain going to that market by between 5.8 and 11.2 percentage points. The explanation for the Iowa results offers additional insights.

The regression results for Iowa occur because, although freight rates are lower from this state to Minneapolis, most of the state's grain, predominantly corn and oats, went to Chicago. As the leading producer of corn and oats, with 63 and 34 percent, respectively, Iowa shippers undoubtedly found higher prices for these grains at Chicago, which handled approximately eleven times the quantity of corn and nearly five times the quantity of oats handled at Minneapolis. The higher prices at Chicago reflected the concentration of corn and oats users in the Chicago area, even though Chicago handled less of all grains than Minneapolis (see Table 2).

To test this conclusion, comparison was made of the daily low price for No. 3 yellow corn for Minneapolis and Chicago during a specified period in the important shipping months (see Table 4).[34]

Table 4. Differences between Chicago and Minneapolis Price for No. 3 Yellow Corn for Selected Years
(cents per bushel)

	Absolute	*Percent of Chicago Price*
1914	4.40*	5.7%
1918	2.84**	1.7
1936	1.35	1.3

* Significant at 5% level
** Significant at 10% level

These differences indicate that prices for corn were consistently higher at Chicago, though the price differences were declining with time. These results not only explain the Iowa result but also indicate that if data or price differences between all markets for all grains were available, the power of the overall regression would certainly be improved. The above price differences also serve to suggest directly that the Chicago market had monopoly power with respect to corn.

An alternative way to assess the importance of transportation costs that also allows a test of price differences between markets is to run a pooled regression with dummy variables for states and markets. Because the dependent variable is a probability, both a linear and a logit specification were tried. The results and the linear specification are given in Table 5. Since the dependent variables are different in the two specifications, the R^2 do not provide a meaningful comparison of the two equations. Theil (16) and Theil and Mnookin (17) have used information theory to develop an elegant and powerful evaluation of the different specifications [see also Parks (11)]. If our predicted market shares for state i and market j are $\hat{W}ij$, and the actual market shares are Wij, the information inaccuracy of the predictions is measured by

$$ I = \sum_{1=1}^{n} Wij \ \log_e \frac{Wij}{\hat{W}ij} . $$

Table 5. Shipping Grain to Market
(Linear Equation)

Variable	Coefficient	t Value
Constant	1.01	8.01
Transport cost	.10	7.15
Illinois	.32	2.56
Kansas	.27	2.91
Minnesota	.14	1.52
Wisconsin	.01	0.14
Nebraska	.17	2.13
South Dakota	.23	2.48
Indiana	−.41	3.10
North Dakota	.31	2.99
Iowa	.04	0.50
Chicago	.20	2.83
Kansas City	.25	2.19
St. Louis	.05	0.57
Minneapolis	.18	2.11
Duluth	−.14	1.13
Omaha	−.13	1.18
Milwaukee	.21	2.10
Wichita	−.35	1.80
Indianapolis	−.04	0.27
Peoria	−.33	1.71
Detroit	.05	0.25
Cincinnati	0.95	1.52

Dependent variable is percent of grain from state i to market j.

$$R^2 = .75 \qquad R^{-2} = .53, \quad DF = 22$$

Note: The full coefficient for the dummy variables should be obtained by adding the constant to the regression coefficient. Iowa and Cincinnati were weighted (-1) so that the sum of all dummy regression coefficients adds to zero. Thus Iowa and Cincinnati results are obtained by adding the state and coefficients respectively and reversing the sign.

This produces the following levels of information inaccuracy for the two alternative specifications:[35]

	Information Inaccuracy
linear	1.07
logit	−7.72

The coefficients on the dummy variables can be compared to that of transport costs to give putative prices. Thus the dummies for market variables can be translated into price differences among markets. The relative prices are indicated in Table 6. Prices at Chicago were materially higher than most other markets, consistent with our argument that this market had market power.

B. Structure of Commission Rates

The demand for commission services is a function of both the demand and supply elasticities for grain at Chicago. This is shown in the figure below. Let D be the demand and supply for grain at Chicago. The optimum monopoly commission can be pictured as the rate T which will maximize area P_1P_2AB in the figure subject to a cost constraint.

Let total commissions be RQ where R is the commission rate and Q is quantity. Given C = marginal and average costs, profit maximization requires:

$$d\left(\frac{RQ}{dQ}\right) = R + Q\left(\frac{dR}{dQ}\right) = C \quad \text{or} \quad R = C - Q\left(\frac{dR}{dQ}\right). \tag{5}$$

Thus,

$$R = C - \frac{Q}{dQ}(dR_1 - dR_2) \tag{6}$$

where dR_1 is the change in demand price for grain and dR_2 is the change in supply price. Then, assuming fixed proportions:

$$R = C - \frac{P_1}{E_1} + \frac{P_2}{E_2} + C \tag{7}$$

where P_1 and P_2 are the demand and supply price for grain, and E_1 and E_2 are demand and supply elasticities for grain at Chicago. Where proportions are not fixed, we have Eq. (2) above, letting small q represent

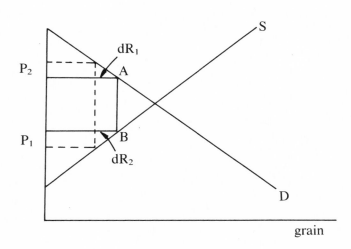

Table 6.   Imputed Relative Prices at Markets, 1913–1917

Price Differences	Cents per Bushel
Chicago*	100.00
Minneapolis	99.69
Duluth	96.59
Kansas City	100.20
St. Louis	100.50
Omaha	96.69
Milwaukee	100.00
Wichita	94.49
Indianapolis	97.59
Peoria	94.29
Detroit	98.40
Cincinnati	97.39

* Chicago standardized at 100 cents per bushel.

the quantity of commission services and large Q the quantity of grain:

$$R = \frac{q}{dq}(dR_1 - dR_2) + C, \text{ therefore } R = \frac{dQ}{Q}\frac{q}{dq}\left(\frac{P_1}{E_1} + \frac{P_2}{E_2}\right) + C;$$

$$\text{or,} \quad R = \alpha\left(\frac{P_1}{E_1} + \frac{P_2}{E_2}\right) + C \tag{8}$$

where α = the elasticity of the output of commission services with respect to the output of grain at Chicago.

In addition to the relationships of Eqs. (7) or (8) above, we might expect the commission rate per bushel to fall as the volume of grain bought and sold increased. The bid-ask spread for common stocks varies inversely with volume and represents a charge for commission services related to the holding time and the search costs. Search costs of commission men would also be lower per bushel for higher volume grain and both search costs and risks would be lower with volume for direct buying. Taking into account the effect of volume and the fact that P_1 and P_2 would not differ by much, we have the relationship of Eq. (9) to describe the structure of commission rates:

$$R = \frac{1}{V}\left[P\left(\frac{1}{E_2} - \frac{1}{E_1}\right) + C\right]. \tag{9}$$

A very approximate measure of elasticities is given by a measure (calculated by the author from figures in *Annual Reports* (1), 1870 through 1960, available separately as Appendix B) of the monopoly power of the Chicago market. This measure is the percent of Illinois grain received at

Chicago. This is multiplied by the amount of each grain produced in Illinois to give a measure that varies across grains and over time.

The most striking feature of commission rates is their near uniformity across grains and their stability over time. This suggests that uniform rates had value and that the costs of changing the rates were substantial. Given this underlying condition, Eq. (9) explains well the structure of commission rates.

The theory predicts that the commission rate minus marginal costs should be a positive function of price, a negative function of volume, and a positive function of market power. The difference between nonmember and member rates, the margin, is taken as a close approximation of the difference between nonmember rates and marginal costs. For the years before 1918 the margin is regressed on price, volume, and an index of market power and time for the 1906–07 period.[36] The results for direct buying are:

$$M = .094 + .0036P - .00068V + 1.55MP - .084T -$$
$$\quad (.146) \quad (.0012) \quad (.00092) \quad (.728) \quad (.043) \quad R^2 = 0.32$$
$$\quad DF = 15.0$$

For consignment we have:

$$M = .38 + .0012P - .0016V + .36MP - .091T$$
$$\quad (.084) \quad (.00061) \quad (.00063) \quad (.44) \quad (.027) \quad R^2 = 0.64$$
$$\quad DF = 15.0$$

All signs are as predicted. Price is significant at better than the 1 percent level in the direct buying equation and at better than the 10 percent level in the consignment equation. Volume is significant at better than the 5 percent level in the consignment equation but not significant for direct buying. The index of market power, MP, is significant at better than the 5 percent level in the direct buying equation but is not significant in the consignment equation. These results are generally consistent with the hypothesis that market power played a role in determining the structure of commissions at Chicago. The weak results for market power in the consignment market are probably a consequence of the crude nature of the market power index.

Although there is no significant variation in usual commission rates after 1916 there is some slight variation in minimum rates. Regressions of the minimum margin (minimum nonmember rates minus minimum member rates) against the above independent variables yield signs as predicted but insignificant coefficients except for the regression constant. The sample is small and variation is limited so the lack of significance is not surprising. The lack of significance of the market power index may well be also due to the fact that it is quite a crude measure.

The decrease in the cents per bushel rate and in the margin for wheat and rye in 1938 for consigned grain and the introduction of maximum rates in 1948 for both consignment and direct buying do not appear to be explainable in terms of changes in the price-volume ratio, nor by separate changes in price alone. These changes are, however, consistent with the decline in our measure of Chicago's locational advantage. Since this ratio had been declining steadily since about 1913, that must be regarded as a weak explanation. However, in the period after World War II, interior brokers, not members of the Chicago Board of Trade, began to become important factors in buying grain from the country and are reported to have been the primary reason for the elimination of rates for direct buying and for the demise of the Call Rule.[37] The power of the Chicago cash market may have declined in this period by more than our measure indicates.

Both the purpose and the importance of the Call Rule (or To Arrive Rule) are illustrated in the circumstances surrounding its demise. In the 1950s it was felt that the Rule was materially hurting members of the Chicago market vis-à-vis competitors. Considerable sentiment for elimination of the Rule arose and was met by substantial opposition. The Rule was first voted out on July 8, 1954, but was readopted May 23, 1955. Finally, in reportedly as tumultuous an election as had ever occurred on the Board, the Rule was again, and finally, eliminated August 8, 1955 [*Rules and Regulations,* 1954–56]. Following elimination of the Rule, the bulk of cash grain commission firms disappeared from the Board. Today, two or three such firms remain as an indication that the Call Rule attained for a time some measure of success in one of its purposes, the survival of commission merchants.

C. Summary

Evidence from records of the Board, from rules of the Board, from other markets, and from the structure of commission rates indicates that after 1913 commission-fixing was successfully pursued by the Board. A strong case can be made that enforcement of the minimum rates was the primary purpose of the Rule after 1913, and was fairly successful. Otherwise, how can one explain the considerable resources devoted to enforcement for a substantial period of years by a number of markets? The persistent devotion of resources to a similar goal over a period of years is consistent with meaningful policy.

Monopoly Profits

Earlier I argued that the member-nonmember rate differential would represent the monopoly differential if there were any relative financial

Table 7. Total Nonmember–Members Margin, 1906–1948, by Grain
(Present Value in Millions of 1975 Dollars)

Grain	Total Commissions	Total Member–Nonmember (differential × bushels)
Wheat	16.44	4.93
Rye	2.35	0.62
Corn	32.03	8.33
Oats	11.80	2.95
Barley	5.49	1.37
Soybeans	3.45	0.92
Totals	71.56	19.12

Note: Among a number of sources of bias in these calculations, the most serious is that of estimating the number of times grain was handled, and thus the number of commission charges borne by the grain. The net effect in undoubtedly to bias downward the estimate of commissions. Because of the difficulty of calculating freight rates and the frequency of their change, only rates at a single point in time were used. Since rates were generally decreasing, the estimates used were under-estimates for earlier than 1916 and overestimates after 1916. However, this source of bias is very small; a doubling of freight rates would reduce the estimates by less than 3 percent. [Estimates of handling turnover is from Appendix 1, *FTC Report*, Vol. IV at 83–132 (1920).]

advantage in dealing with fellow members. An upper-borne estimate of total monopoly profits can thus be calculated by multiplying the member-nonmember rate differential by the number of bushels of grain handled.[38] The results of this calculation are shown in Table 7.

V. THE EXISTING LAW

On June 28, 1974, the Board of Trade entered a consent decree with the U.S. Department of Justice by which the Board agreed to refrain from fixing any nonmember commission rates for futures trading involving contracts over and above a specified minimum number.[39] This minimum number of contracts decreased over time, beginning on September 4, 1974, at 24 contracts and dropping by September 4, 1977, to a minimum of four.

Minimum commission rates for cash grain, however, remain. Member and nonmember rates apply for the receiving and selling by grade or sample or both, of grains, hay, straw, seeds, provisions, and cottonseed and soybean oil. Rates also apply for the purchase or sale of warehouse receipts of shipping certificates for grains, lard, beef, broilers, plywood, silver, gold, or stud lumber. These rates apply for consignment and not for direct buying [*Rules and Regulations*, 1975].

Those impressed with the per se illegality of cartels would undoubtedly contend that these minimum rates are illegal [see Baxter (2)]. They would argue that if they were not illegal in 1918, which they probably were on the basis of Addyston [40] they would certainly have been illegal after *Trenton Potteries* in 1927.[41]

The argument for this position is less than compelling. Those who have fixed the price of commission services have done relatively well in avoiding per se illegality. First there is *Chicago Board of Trade* itself which is, arguably, an indirect justification for minimum rates, though the argument may not be very strong. Rather stronger is the effect of the *Silver* and *Gordon* cases.[42] The essential rule in *Silver v. NYSE* was that a prerequisite to antitrust liability is a finding that fixed commissions are not "necessary to make the Exchange Act work" [*Silver* at 357]. *Gordon* extended this to hold that the explicit responsibility of the Securities and Exchange Commission for reasonable commissions implied an antitrust immunity for these commissions under the *Silver* doctrine, as long as the SEC was in fact exercising its responsibilities: the lack of such immunity would interfere with the explicit responsibility of the SEC for setting commissions under the Act.

The question is whether the functions of the Commodity Futures Trading Commission (CFTC) are such that the *Silver* and *Gordon* doctrines apply to fixed commissions set by the Board of Trade. Although the CFTC's responsibilities are largely for the futures market, it has the responsibility for an orderly market and its jurisdiction extends to operations of the market, such as cash trading, which might affect the operations of the futures market. More importantly, Section 5a of the Commodity Futures Trading Commission Act of 1974 requires that:

> Each contract market shall — enforce by-laws, rules, regulations, and resolutions, made or issued by it or by governing board thereof — which relate to terms and conditions in contracts of sale— or relate to other trading requirements, and which have been approved by the Commission pursuant to Paragraph (12) of Section 5a of this Act.[43]

Paragraph (12) of Section 5a requires that "each contract market shall— submit to the commission for its approval all by-laws, rules, regulations and resolutions made or issued by such contract market,—" This section appears to mean, and has meant in practice, that all rules of exchanges doing a futures business are under jurisdiction of the Act and must be approved by the CFTC. The present law requires positive approbation of the Commission for both new and existing rules [*id.*, Sec. 5a, ¶8].

Thus, the Commission may well be in the same position with respect to minimum cash commission as was the Securities Exchange Commission (SEC) in *Gordon*. The Commission is given explicit responsibility for rules of the exchanges. One of these rules is a commission rule.[44] Not to provide antitrust immunity would be a failure to allow the CFTC to perform a function specified in the Act, and would therefore be a failure to allow the Act to operate. Nevertheless, there may be an important difference in the position of the CFTC and the SEC; the Department of Justice succeeded in including in the 1974 Act the requirement that:

> The Commission shall take into consideration the public interest to be protected by the antitrust laws and *endeavor to take the least anticompetitive means of achieving the objectives of this Act* — by issuing any order or adopting any Commission rule or regulation, or in *requiring or approving any by-law, rule or regulation of a contract market*—.[45] (Emphasis added)

But, the Department of Justice did not prevent the replacement of their suggested word "insure" by the word "endeavor." Moreover, Congress states explicitly that the above requirement "is not intended to constitute any procedural roadblock to the Commission; — and separate proceedings to consider antitrust matters are not required —."[46] Under current administrative law the "endeavor" requirement may mean little. Probably the Commission may follow its own dictates on substantive grounds as long as procedure provides a ritualized obeisance toward antitrust.

The Court said in *Silver* that "under the aegis of the rule of reason, traditional antitrust concepts are flexible enough to permit the Exchange sufficient breathing space within which to carry out the mandate of the Securities Exchange Act" [*Silver* at 360, n. 114]. They cited *Chicago Board of Trade*. Thus a bungled cartel case involving fixed commissions is invoked to justify antitrust exemption for just such commissions. The irony is that fixed commissions were probably more illegal in 1918, had the *Chicago Board of Trade* case been presented, than they are now, due in part to *Chicago Board of Trade*.

VI. IN CONCLUSION: THE DIFFERENCE IT COULD HAVE MADE

I have shown that the antipathy between warehouse dealers and commission merchants, both members of the Board of Trade, led to the Call Rule. This antipathy arose in part from nineteenth-century government regulations.

The case law arising from attempts to regulate aspects of the grain trade in the period between 1870 and 1920 shows two parallel and contradictory lines of development, one of which was clearly the main line. These two streams parallel the division in *Munn*. The split in *Munn* was profound.

Justice Morrison Waite was appealing to a longstanding regulatory tradition in English and colonial law that supported an extensive basis for regulation [Hughes (7)]. The "business affected with a public interest" doctrine was simply an excuse that was ultimately unsupportable.[47] Justice Stephen Field, in his dissent, appealed instead to the American constitutional attempt to limit governmental power, and to a regulatory hiatus in American between roughly 1800 and 1870 produced by a geographic and material growth too virulent for the confines of the detailed and extensive colonial regulations.[48] Field well recognized that the distinction of business affected with a public interest was untenable; the question was not one of public utility but the extent of the police power. Field saw correctly where *Munn* would lead, and he thought it was dangerous.

The difference of opinion evidenced by the U.S. Supreme Court in *Munn* was not coincidental. The difference was reflected also in the earlier decisions leading to *Munn,* such as the decision of the Illinois Supreme Court in *Munn v. People.* Here, the Court failed first to reach a verdict and did so in the next term in a split decision only because two members of the Court were replaced in the intervening period.

This basic difference in regulatory philosophy was seen also in grain trade cases subsequent to *Munn.* For example, in *Brass v. North Dakota* (1894),[49] the logical consequences of *Munn* were decidedly more apparent, and four dissenting justices now appeared compared with the two in *Munn.*[50]

I am suggesting the possibility that the decision in *Munn* was not inevitable. By the time of *Brass,* the Court had lost one of the dissenters in *Munn* (Strong) and a dissenter (Brown) in a case subsequent to *Munn* (*Budd v. New York,* 143 U.S. 517 (1892)]. Presumably with Strong and Brown the Court's decision in *Brass* would have been different. But, since *Brass* was essentially the same as *Munn* with the "public interest" element removed in that the business was of small size and no monopoly or fraud were alleged present, it makes the *Munn* decision seem more tentative. Had there not been a Chicago warehouse monopoly, had the warehouse industry been declining, had a state or Federal equivalent of the Sherman Act existed, had all or any of these existed, would the decision in *Munn* have been the same? Perhaps not. Possibly, I believe, though not probably, a line of decisions could have developed that would have slowed down the trend toward regulation.[51] Such an approach would have affirmed for a time instead the antiregulatory tradition to which Justice Field appealed. Probably such a tradition was not socially supportable ultimately, but it is interesting to speculate. Had the tradition developed in this way, perhaps *Munn,* and the Interstate Commerce Commission as it has existed, would be missing, and so also, as we have shown, would the *Chicago Board of Trade* case.

It is important to recognize that the Supreme Court's decision involved only the 1906 rule. The court did, in 1917 or 1918, ask about mootness but both sides insisted on going forward on the basis of the 1906 rule. Hence the Court had in view a much less intrusive rule (given the effects of commission-fixing in 1913) than the later rule.

The government not only did not present the commission-fixing case, its heart did not seem in the case it did present; its witnesses read in the record as witnesses for the defense. Certainly there are variations of ambivalence on the goverment's part. The case was strongly urged by the U.S. Attorney in Chicago, who had been lobbied by some, unfortunately unidentified, members of the Chicago Board of Trade. It was rejected several times by the Attorney General and the Assistant Attorney General for the Antitrust Division because there was no evidence of harm resulting from the restraint and the need for it in terms of making the exchange work seemed convincing. In 1913, the lame-duck attorney general authorized the suit partly because of a recent corner on wheat in Chicago which upset the country. The Democrats who took over were not willing to reconsider the case.[52]

Chicago Board of Trade did of course exist, but the decision presumably could well have been different. Suppose the case had been presented as one involving the fixing of commissions. If the decision had remained the same, a clear exemption would have emerged to the per se illegality of cartels. In this situation, the language of *Trenton Potteries* [273 U.S. 392 (1927)] may well have been different, given the Blackstonian tradition that "the current law has always been the law," and the current per se rule would be stronger.

A possible outcome is that, with the case properly presented, commission-fixing would have been found illegal, probably in 1918, but almost certainly after *Trenton Potteries*. In this situation, would Congress have felt the need to give the Securities and Exchange Commission, in Section 19(b) of the Securities and Exchange Act, the power of "fixing reasonable rates of commission, interest, listing and other charges"?[53] This speculation is consistent with the legislative history of the Act since clearly Congress's purpose was to prevent monopolistic commission rates from being charged [*Gordon,* n.117]. This is also consistent with the Maloney Act of 1938 prohibiting price-fixing in the over-the-counter market [Baxter, n.114]. Had this line of development been followed, as seems to me not unlikely, the per se rule would have been the stronger and, arguably, the position of antitrust vis-à-vis the regulated exchanges might also be stronger.

Justice Brandeis in *Chicago Board of Trade* probably made the correct decision on the evidence he had; grain prices were not fixed in a meaningful way. Even so, Brandeis appears to have been influenced ·by the beneficial effects of the Rule as shown in the *Record.* But it was not grain prices that were fixed. It was prices for commission services. Thus, the price-fixing that actually occurred may have been found illegal had the Court an opportunity to rule. As it was, the decision in Chicago Board of Trade contributed to some small weakening of per se illegality of cartels and may have contributed indirectly to the legality of fixed commissions on regulated exchanges, and to present exemptions of these exchanges from antitrust attack.

At least in part the Call Rule arose as an unintended consequence of the grain regulations that gave rise to *Munn* and the price-stabilizing regulations of the Interstate Commerce Commission. The fixing of commissions represented different motives and produced different effects. Initially commission-fixing enhanced the efficiency of the exchange, and it was this effect of which Brandeis was aware. Later, the primary effect and motive seem to have been the extraction of monopoly rents.

ACKNOWLEDGMENTS

This paper was begun while I was a Research Fellow in Law and Economics at the University of Chicago Law School, whose support I wish to recognize. The paper benefits from the experiences of this period and from association with, especially, R. H. Coase and John Peterman, and briefly, with Aaron Director. It also benefits from the interest of Jonathan Hughes and from some conversations with him. My original interest in the *Chicago Board of Trade* case as well as in the industrial organization field I owe to John S. McGee.

Conversations with Jordan Hollander and James William Rose, merchants of the Chicago Board of Trade, were useful and their help is appreciated. Conversations with some other Board members who wish to go unnamed were also helpful. Joel Mokyr, Douglass North, Jonathan Hughes, Sumner Marcus, Victor Goldberg, John Narver, and John McGee have read an earlier version of this manuscript and I have benefited from their suggestions. Dick Parks had helpful suggestions on the structure of regressions. Comments by Donald McCloskey were especially helpful, as were comments by George Stigler and other members of the Industrial Organization Workshop.

NOTES

1. *Chicago Board of Trade v. United States*, 246 U.S. 231 (1918). Hostility had arisen among farmers and consumers alike toward the Chicago Board of Trade and other exchanges. As shown in *U.S. v. Christie* [198 U.S. 236 (1905)] had shown earlier, futures trading was not well understood, and was widely regarded as a tool for manipulating grain prices, or at best a contrivance for legalized gambling. Frequent instances and allegations of sundry frauds by members of the Board of Trade combined to undermine confidence in the Board and heighten feelings of manipulation. The facts in the case at hand may have increased that feeling. I am indebted to the late Sumner Marcus for pointing out that the reasons this case was brought to court during this period themselves form an interesting question.

2. *Chicago Board of Trade* at 238. Brandeis was quoted, among other places, in *White Motor Co. v. U.S.*, 372 U.S. 253, 261–262 (1963) and cited in *National Assoc. of Window Glass Manufacturers et al. v. U.S.*, 263 U.S. 403 (1923), and in *Silver v. New York Stock*

Exchange, 373 U.S. 341, 360 (1963). In the *Window Glass* case, Holmes observed that "to determine the legality of an agreement requires a consideration of the particular facts," then cited *Chicago Board of Trade*. Peculiarly, both cases suffer from just such a failure to look at the particular facts [see Zerbe (20)].

3.   The more important features of this Rule, as it existed between 1906 and 1913, were:

A.   A board of directors is hereby empowered to establish a public "call" for corn, oats, wheat, and rye to arrive, to be held in the exchange room, immediately after the close of the regular session of each business day.

B.   Contacts may be made upon the "call" only in such articles and upon such terms as have been approved by the "call" committee.

C.   The "call" shall be under the control and management of a committee consisting of five members appointed by the president with the approval of the board of directors.

D.   Final bids on the "call" *less the regular commission charges for receiving and accounting for such property may be forwarded by dealers.* (Emphasis added.)

E.   Any transaction of members of this association made with intent to evade the provisions of this rule shall be deemed uncommercial conduct, and upon conviction such member shall be suspended from the privilege of the association for such time as the board of directors may elect. [From *Rules and Regulations of the Board of Trade of the City of Chicago* (3), Rule 4, Sec. 32, for the years 1906 through 1913, respectively; hereinafter *Rules and Regulations.*]

4.   The decision in this case should be regarded as anomalous in the line of decisions leading from *U.S. v. Addyston Pipe and Steel Co.,* 175 U.S. 211 (1899) to *U.S. v. Trenton Potteries,* 273 U.S. 392 (1927). Not all regard this case as anomalous. Some noted antitrust economists in conversations with the author agreed with the defense that what was at issue was simply a closing rule for the Board.

5.   *Munn v. Illinois,* 84 U.S. 113 (1876). The attempt to regulate public grain warehouses, given force in *Munn,* made it advantageous to become a private warehouse which required dealing in grain directly. The greater cartel policing power of the ICC caused railroads to seek special arrangements with the large terminal warehouses that gave these warehouses freight rebates. See Zerbe (22).

6.   Illinois and Chicago were the center of both the commercial system and of the regulatory effort [see Zerbe (21), pp. 178–180]. For other major exchanges in this period, see Table 1, *infra*.

7.   These line elevators competed with independent and later farm cooperative elevators for farmers' grain. The line elevator organizations became adept at setting up and running cartels at country points.

8.   The success of line elevators has been attributed to predatory pricing, but such a view stops short of the whole picture. Insofar as predatory pricing was used, it was simply a vehicle to give discipline to a country cartel, not to drive others out of business [Zerbe (21)].

9.   The success of country cartels led farmers to build, or more usually, to buy, country elevators which became farm cooperative elevators, as a means of breaking a country cartel. It is easy to show that for a cartel member to sell to farmers would be a mutually profitable exchange. Sometimes the farm elevator joined the cartel. For a time, however, the growth in farm cooperative elevators was stymied by boycotts from terminal exchanges organized by state grain dealers [see Refsell (12), pp. 11–13; Report of the Illinois Railroad and Warehouse Commission (8), pp. 24–28; and Warrall (19), p. 14. The effect of the boycotts was broken as firms began to specialize in buying from cooperative elevators and even to help organize new farm cooperatives [see Refsell (12), p. 8, and *Sen. Doc.* 278 at 26–35 (9) for testimony taken by the Interstate Commerce Commission, 59th Cong., 2d sess. (1907), at 26–35; hereinafter *Sen. Doc.* 278].

10.   Commission men were instrumental in securing passage of the Call Rule as indicated

by testimony taken by the ICC: "The rule was advocated by the smaller commission firms [because] they considered . . . they were not getting the amount of trade due them . . . and as business was slack, they were hunting a method by which they could get returns and established this rule, which I understand is similar to the one in force in Minneapolis" [*Sen. Doc.* 278 at 107]. Representative testimony asserts that "in a general way the smaller merchants on the Board of Trade and the country shipper were advocates of that Rule, and the larger interests were opposed to it" [*id.* at 146], consistent with the statement of George Marcy, president of the Armour Elevator Co. (a large company), that the Call Rule "was passed because it was reported around that I was opposed to it" [*id.* at 175].

11. Testimony in 1906 was that "the number of receivers and shippers . . . is not to exceed 15 percent of what it was twenty years ago" [William Warren, *Sen. Doc.* 278 at 220]. The trend cannot be determined by a direct count of members by listed occupation. A spot check of the *Annual Reports* (1) for three different years (1897, 1906, and 1927) shows that the categories used at the time do not sufficiently distinguish commission work to be useful. *Annual Reports of the Board of Trade* (1887–1927); hereinafter *Annual Reports*.

12. All of the grain in private warehouses was owned by the warehouse itself. The warehouses owned 90 percent of all grain received in storage in Chicago. *Central Elevator v. People,* 174 Ill. 203 (1898).

13. Testimony is that "it was . . . frequent practice of said elevator proprietors to agree among themselves each afternoon upon the prices which all should adopt in their bids to be sent that day to persons in the country for grain 'to arrive' in Chicago" [*Transcript of Record* (18) at 12; see also at 133–134, 138, and 143; hereinafter *Record*].

14. Representative testimony from *Record* at 138: "Before the call system he [a country shipper] was restricted to one particular line. . . . . It enabled the buyer to frequently penalize the seller in excess of the current market."

15. For testimony that the Rule shortened the working day see *Record* at 98 and 114–115. None of the witnesses indicated this was a major purpose of the Rule and Brandeis's stress on this point seems misplaced.

16. *Report of the Federal Trade Commission on the Grain Trade* (1920), Vol. III at 67, 69–70; hereinafter *FTC Report*.

17. All price figures are from the *Chicago Tribune* for relevant years.

18. I owe this point to George Stigler.

19. The elasticity of demand for commission services E_3 is $(R/q)(dq/dR)$ where R is the price of commission services. The elasticity of demand for grain E_2 is $(P/Q)(dQ/dP) \cdot E_2/E_3 = \alpha[(R/P)(dP/dR)]$ where α is the output elasticity of commission services with respect to the quantity of grain. α would be 1 if commission services were in fixed proportion to grain. Evidence from declining rate schedules by volume on the New York Stock Exchange indicates that α is less than 1. Since $dP/dR < 1$, and since R/P was about 1 percent, $E_2/E_3 < 1$ percent.

20. An alternative, comparative statistics formulation is that members of the Board wish to maximize net profits per bidder.

$$H = E(N, I) - C[N, I] \tag{1}$$

where N is the number of bidders, E the gross profit per bidder, C the cost of information per bidder, and I is the quantity of information. Assume, for simplicity, there are no cross effects; that is, that $E_{IN} = C_{IN} = 0$. The first-order conditions require that

$$H_N = E_N - C_N = 0 \tag{2}$$

and

$$H_I = E_I - C_I = 0. \tag{3}$$

These are the usual sort of marginal revenue equals marginal cost conditions. The second-order conditions require that

$$E_{NN} - C_{NN} < 0 \qquad (4)$$

and

$$E_{II} - C_{II} < 0. \qquad (5)$$

Consider an exogenous factor X decreasing information costs. Differentiate totally and solve giving:

$$\frac{dN}{dX} = \frac{-(E_{NX} - C_{NX})(E_{II} - C_{II})}{(E_{NN} - C_{NN})(E_{II} - C_{II})} < 0. \qquad (6)$$

The denominator is Eq. (4) multiplied by Eq. (5), which is positive by the second-order conditions, and the second expression in the numeration is negative by the second-order conditions. The sign of $\frac{dN}{dX}$ then depends on the sign of $(E_{NX} - C_{NX})$ which is positive. Thus both numerator and denominator are positive, implying that a decrease in information costs will increase the number of bidders. Similarly, $dI/dX > 0$.

21.   *Record* at 112. Before the Call Rule a "large number of people . . . were at a disadvantage. The Call rule changed that condition because the competition was in the open market."

22.   *John Dickinson v. Board of Trade,* Ill. App. 295, 299–302 (1904).

23.   See note 3, *supra, Rules and Regulations,* Rule 4, Sec. 32.

24.   These records are in files of the Commission Committee, the Call Committee, and the To Arrive Committee of the Board of Trade manuscript collection of the University of Illinois campus.

25.   Call Committee file, 1906–1913. For example, see letter from Lowell-Hart & Co., Dec. 20, 1907, and letter from William Eckhardt, Chairman, Call Committee, Feb. 11, 1908.

26.   *FTC Report,* Vol. II at 226. Maximum rates were established for some grains on some exchanges.

27.   Letter of April 28, 1923, from H. J. Smith, President, Kansas City Board of Trade, to John R. Mauff, Executive Vice President, Chicago Board of Trade, and re.urn letter of April 30, 1923, from Mauff to Smith. Copies of these letters were obtained from files of the Board of Trade, University of Illinois, Circle Campus.

28.   *FTC Report,* Vol. II at 229; General Rules, Chamber of Commerce, Minneapolis, Rule 4, Sec. 7, Twelfth Annual Report, Chamber of Commerce, Minneapolis, Dec. 31, 1894.

29.   *Rules and Regulations,* Rule 22, Sec. 5; Chicago and New York required a 5 percent mimimum rate of interest. Kansas City, Omaha, St. Louis, and Peoria had a 6 percent minimum. Milwaukee determined the rate to be charged the first of each month. Other markets required the "legal rate" in the state [*FTC Report,* Vol. II at 231].

30.   *Rules and Regulations,* Rule 11, Sec. 9g (1905).

31.   General Rules, Minneapolis Chamber of Commerce, Rule 8, Sec. 1.

32.   Calculated from Table 50, Vol. I of *FTC Report.*

33.   Data for the distribution of grain are taken from Table 7, Vol. 1, *FTC Report,* for 1912–1917. Data on freight rates are for 1916 for wheat only, from *FTC Report,* Vol. IV at 212–214.

34.   Collected from *Chicago Tribune* for fifteen days in July, August, and September for relevant years.

35.   For the linear model a few of the predicted $\hat{W}_{ij}$'s are negative. To handle this, an ad hoc procedure is adopted using the absolute value of $\hat{W}_{ij}$ and increasing W_{ij} by this amount. Thus if $W_{ij} = .10$ and $\hat{W}_{ij} = -.10$, we calculate: 10 log (20/10). This leaves the arithmetic distance between W_{ij} and $\hat{W}_{ij}$ as before. An alternative procedure is to reduce

each positive $\hat{W}ij$ by proportional amounts such that the total reductions add to the sum of the absolute value of the negative $\hat{W}ij$. The results of the two procedures are not very different from each other.

The linear specification is clearly superior. When the estimated and predicted values are of different signs the information inaccuracy measure cannot be directly applied because logs of negative numbers are not defined. An ad hoc procedure was used to "correct" for this and the results are insensitive to variations in the procedure. However, in a separate check, the linear and log equations were made directly comparable by defining a transformed dependent variable y^* where $y^* = y.c$ and c is the inverse of the geometric mean of the y's. Multiplying the sum of the squared residuals in the linear transformations by c allows a direct comparison with the log formulation. This yields 12.14 and 22.83 for the adjusted sum of the squared residuals for the linear and log forms, respectively. Again this confirms the superiority of the linear form and indicates that the higher R^2 for the log form does not point to the better specification.

36. Beginning in 1917 rates are a percentage of grain prices and after 1917 there is no variation in the "usual" rates over time or among grains except as determined by grain price differences. Before 1917 commission rates are given in cents per bushel. There is one set for direct buying and another for consignment.

When the nonmember rate is used as the dependent variable and member rates included as part of the independent variable the results are similar. For direct buying we have:

$$\text{NMR} = 0.087 + .0031P - .00050V + 1.1MR + 1.4MP - 0.87T$$
$$(.151) \quad (.0014) \quad (.0009) \quad (.176) \quad (.78a) \quad (.044) \ R^2 + 0.89$$
$$\text{DF} = 16.0$$

The theory, however, indicates the margin formulation is more appropriate.

37. Conversations with Jordan Hollander and other members of the Board of Trade.

38. An upper bound estimate of total monopoly profits can be estimated by calculating total member-nonmember rate differentials and multiplying by bushels of grain handled. The procedure used involved an estimate of the number of times grain was handled and thus the number of times the commission rates applied. For the years after 1917 in which percentage rates applied, it was also necessary to subtract freight rates from the price offered to the country. Freight rates were calculated on the basis of rates existing on January 1, 1916, for transport of grain to Chicago from the center of each of the 13 major grain states supplying Chicago. These rates by type of grain were weighted by the percentage of each type of grain furnished to Chicago by the sending state. Data are from *FTC Report,* Vol. IV at 212–215, and from Board of Trade *Annual Reports.* In this manner average rates were calculated for wheat, corn, and oats. Since relative rates for the different grains bore a fairly close relationship to the relative weights of the grains, the rates for rye, barley, and soybeans were estimated from those of the grains already calculated. These rates were as follows:

Average Freight Rates to Chicago on Jan. 1, 1916

Wheat	6.415 cents per bushel
Corn	5.774 cents per bushel
Oats	3.208 cents per bushel
Rye	5.987 cents per bushel
Barley	5.132 cents per bushel
Soybeans	6.415 cents per bushel

39. *U.S. v. Board of Trade of City of Chicago* Civil Action No. 71c 2875. [U.S. District Court for the Northern District of Illinois, Eastern Division, June 28, 1974.]

40. *United States v. Addyston, supra* note 4.

41. *United States v. Trenton Potteries, supra* note 4.

42. *Silver,* 373 U.S. 341, 360 (1963); *Gordon v. New York Stock Exchange,* 498 F. 2d 1303 (1975), *aff'd.*

43.   Commodity Exchange Act. See 5a, ¶8 as amended by Commodities Futures Trading Commission Act of 1974.

44.   The Commission had not, at least by late 1976, actually approved any rules of the Board.

45.   The Commodity Futures Trading Commission Act of 1974, 93rd Cong., 2d sess., November 1974, "Committee Consideration," at 118.

46.   *Ibid.* Statement by Chairman Talmadge on Consideration of the Conference Report on HR 13113, Oct. 10, 1974, at 3.

47.   For an eloquent statement that the *Munn* doctrine was untenable, see Dunbar (5).

48.   Justice Field notes: "No reason can be assigned to justify legislation interfering with the legitimate profits of business, that would not equally justify an intermeddling with the business of every man in the community . . ." [*Munn v. Illinois, supra* note 5, at 154].

"If this [the majority decision] be sound law, if there be no protection, either in the principles upon which our republican government is founded, or in the prohibitions of the Constitution against such invasion of private rights, all property and all business in the State are held at the mercy of a majority of its legislation" [*ibid.* at 140]; and "the doctrine of this Court . . . appear to destroy . . . the efficacy of the constitutional guarantee" [*ibid.* at 141].

49.   *Brass v. North Dakota ex rel. Stoesser,* 153 U.S. 391 38 Lawyers Edition.

50.   *Id.* at 405–410.

51.   An example of the two separate legal traditions in cases involving commission men is shown in *Payne v. Kansas* [248 U.S. 112 (1918)] on the one hand, in which the Supreme Court upheld as valid the licensing of commission men by the State of Kansas as not exceeding the powers of the states, and a Michigan decision on this subject in 1900. In contrast, in *Valentine v. Berien* [124 Mich. 684, 83 N.W. 594 (1900)] the Michigan court pointed out that, although the commission business has always had dishonest men, so also had every other branch of business. In vitiating licensure the court argued there was no more reason why commission men should be required to execute a bond for debts than any other merchants. In any case, the common law provided ample redress. This decision was more in the spirit of Field's dissent.

The legalistic approach of the commission men toward maintaining their business found expression in attempts to achieve licensure in several states. By 1918 five states licensed and regulated the business of commission merchants. Minnesota and Michigan enacted such laws in 1899, North Dakota in 1903, Washington in 1907, Nebraska in 1909, and Kansas in 1915. A licensing regulation was also adopted in Illinois in 1919 but exempted "grains which are classified into grades." [Revised code of North Dakota (1905), 2197; (1897), ch. 54, 1; R.C. (1899), 1738; (1903), ch. 56, 1; Laws of Nebraska (1909), ch. 66; Laws of Washington (1907), ch. 139; Kansas General Statutes (1915), ch. 371; Illinois laws of 1919, p. 15; Minnesota Laws (1915), ch. 379, secs. 1 and 7. See also *FTC Report,* Vol. III at 57–59.]

52.   I am indebted to Prof. Peter C. Carstensen (4) for this information. Prof. Carstensen indicates he believes Brandeis favored the Call Rule just because it assumed it did have cartel and protective effects.

53.   Securities Exchange Act of 1934, 15 U.S.C., Sec. 19b.

REFERENCES

1.   *Annual Reports.* (1887–1927) Chicago Board of Trade.
2.   Baxter, W. F. (April 1970) "NYSE Fixed Commission Rates: A Private Cartel Goes Public," *Stanford Law Review,* Vol. 22: 674.
3.   Board of Trade, City of Chicago. (1906–1913) *Rules and Regulations.*

4. Carstensen, Peter C. (May 18, 1983) Written communication, Law School, University of Wisconsin, Madison.
5. Dunbar, William H. (1895) "State Regulation of Prices and Rates," *Quarterly Journal of Economics,* Vol. 4: 305–332.
6. Federal Trade Commission. (1920, Vols. I, II; 1921, Vol. III; 1923, Vol. IV; 1924, Vol. VI) *Report on the Grain Trade,* Washington, D.C., Government Printing Office.
7. Hughes, Jonathan. (1976) *Social Control in the Colonial Economy,* Charlottesville, University Press of Virginia.
8. Illinois Railroad and Warehouse Commission, *Annual Report,* 1903.
9. Interstate Commerce Commission. (1907) Sen. Doc. 278, Testimony (Oct. 15–Nov. 23, 1906) in [the] matter of *Relations of Common Carriers to the Grain Trade,* 59th Cong., 2d sess., Washington, D.C., Government Printing Office.
10. Lurie, Jonathan. (1970) The Chicago Board of Trade 1974 to 1905, and the Development of Certain Rules Governing Its Operation [a study in the effectiveness of internal regulation], Ph.D. thesis, University of Wisconsin, Madison.
11. Parks, R. (October 1969) "Systems of Demand Equations: An Empirical Comparison of Alternative Functional Forms," *Econometrica,* Vol. 37: 629–650.
12. Refsell, Oscar N. (1914) *The Farmers Elevator Movement,* Master's thesis, University of Chicago.
13. Taylor, Charles. (1887) *A History of the Board of Trade,* City of Chicago. 2 vols.
14. Teisberg, Thomas. (1978) *A Bidding Model of the Federal Oil and Gas Lease Auction,* Ph.D. thesis, University of California, Berkeley.
15. Teisberg, Thomas, and Gaskins, Darius. (1976) "An Economic Analysis of Presale Exploration in Oil and Gas Lease Sales," pp. 241–258 in *Essays on Industrial Organization in Honor of Joe Bain,* ed. Robert Masson and John Qualls, Cambridge, Mass., Ballinger.
16. Theil, H. (1967) *Economics and Information Theory,* Chicago, Rand McNally.
17. ———, and Mnookin, R. H. (1966) "The Information Value of Demand Equations and Predictions," *Journal of Political Economy,* Vol. 74: 34–35.
18. *Transcript of Record of the Supreme Court of the United States.* (1916) "Board of Trade of the City of Chicago et al. v. United States," No. 370, October Term 1916.
19. Warrall, Tom. (1905) *The Grain Trust Exposed,* Lincoln, Nebr., Jacob and Co.
20. Zerbe, Richard O., Jr. (1975) "Antitrust Cases as a Guide to Directions in Antitrust Research and Policy," in *The Antitrust Dilemma,* ed. J. Dalton and S. Levin, Lexington, Mass., D.C. Heath.
21. ———. (1979) "Predatory Pricing for Threat and Cartel Maintenance," working paper, Department of Economics, University of Washington, Seattle.
    ———. (January 1982) "The Origin and Effect of Grain Trade Regulations in the Late Nineteenth Century," *Agricultural History,* Vol. 56: 172–193.

PRICE-FIXING AND THE ADDYSTON PIPE CASE

George Bittlingmayer

Agreements among competitors are governed by the per se rule against price-fixing, and this is widely justified by the belief that unrestricted competition promotes public welfare. A careful analysis of market equilibrium reveals, however, that the conditions necessary to assure the existence of a competitive equilibrium are rather stringent. In fact, under quite plausible circumstances—in particular, if demand varies and if there are economies of scale over some range—a competitive equilibrium may not exist. These conditions appear to characterize a great variety of industries, including the cast-iron pipe industry at the turn of the century. The price-fixing agreement in this industry served as background to Judge William Howard Taft's celebrated opinion in Addyston Pipe. *This article assembles evidence concerning the nature of costs in this industry and finds that the plants possessed some of the characteristics of a natural monopoly. A competitive market mechanism could not by itself provide the optimal output and ensure the recovery of costs. Moreover, not only the fact of price-fixing but also various details of the agreement can be interpreted as attempts to stabilize the market through private regulation. A central policy implication of the* Addyston *case is that the costs of the per se rule against price-fixing have*

Research in Law and Economics, Volume 5, pages 57–130.
Copyright © 1983 by JAI Press Inc.
ISBN: 0-89232-419-8

probably been greater than generally thought because this rule often forces
firms to find other, costlier solutions to the unavoidable problem of market
coordination.

INTRODUCTION

The first objective of this article is to demonstrate that the model of competitive equilibrium presented in economics textbooks, while a useful ab-
straction for some purposes, is seriously flawed as a representation of how
prices are determined in the short run in actual markets. Under fairly
realistic conditions, a competitive equilibrium may not exist in a market,
and the buyers and sellers must arrive at some other way of determining
who sells what to whom. Once this possibility is raised, it is by no means
clear that the more or less arbitrary prohibition of certain arrangements
implicit in the antitrust laws is desirable. Although I hope to show that
the widespread enthusiasm for unrestricted, competitive outcomes is not
based on a careful assessment of the issues, it should be noted that this
view has been expressed by a number of economists and is not nearly as
novel as it may appear. A considerable and largely uncontradicted economic literature that begins with Alfred Marshall, if not earlier, makes
essentially the same point. Unfortunately, this literature has been ignored
in the application of economics to antitrust, and analytic emphasis has
been placed instead on collusion that takes place among sellers who could
behave competitively if only they had the public-spiritedness to do so.

The second aim, and by far the major portion of this article, is a detailed
examination of the cast-iron pipe industry and the celebrated *Addyston
Pipe* case.[1] *Addyston* was the first significant antitrust case not involving
a railroad,[2] and it served as the background for Judge William Howard
Taft's highly regarded 1898 court of appeals opinion. The events in this
case are particularly intriguing because the six defendants and five previously unassociated producers merged, forming United States Cast Iron
Pipe and Foundry, while the case was on appeal. Fortunately, we know
a great deal about the industry and this particular price-fixing arrangement. A duplicitous cartel stenographer copied documents in the hope of
sharing any damage awards with buyers who used his evidence, and these
documents are part of the court record. Also, since the implications of
the Sherman Act of 1890 were unclear in the mid-1890s, not only the
cartel's communications but also the industry's trade journal, *The Iron
Age*, revealed much more than they would today. Study of this industry
is further facilitated because the industry employed a relatively simple
technology and because nearly all of its output was a particular homogeneous good, cast-iron hub and spigot pipe. The price each month of the

major input, pig iron, is readily available, and we have frequent quotes, both in the court record and from the trade press, of the price of the output. Finally, detailed monthly data on costs, output, and other relevant measures exist for a one-year period for five of the six plants that were defendants, and for several other plants as well. As a consequence of this wealth of information, it is possible to provide a fairly thorough account of events in the industry, including the cartelization and merger, and to illustrate in terms of this particular industry the difficulty that manufacturers in many industries often face because of the nature of costs.

The source of this difficulty is by no means as hard to explain as the sustained neglect of this topic might suggest. Imagine an industry composed of plants that incur lump sum costs at positive output rates, but for which these costs are zero if output is zero. Each plant has a fixed capacity beyond which extra output is very costly, and each plant's capacity constitutes a substantial fraction of the relevant market. The cement industry provides one example of this sort of situation, although numerous other industries share these characteristics. Under arbitrary rates of demand, it turns out that marginal cost-pricing will not allow firms to recover their costs, except in rare instances. A related result in the relevant formal models is that there is no competitive equilibrium. Of course we would like to know what sort of equilibrium does exist, but the failure of economics to answer this question does not change our conclusion about the feasibility of unrestricted competition. It is widely known that "nonconvexities" pose serious problems for competition, which suggests that it may be useful to study instances of noncompetitive behavior to see whether the necessary conditions for the existence of a competitive equilibrium are met. The evidence from *Addyston* leads to the conclusion that this is one instance in which they are not, and in which a policy that forced firms to price at short-run marginal cost would have had undesirable consequences. Although the per se rule against price-fixing almost certainly falls short of forcing such pricing behavior, this rule is still likely to be less beneficial than generally believed because a blanket prohibition of formal or explicit agreements among producers compels them to resort to other methods to stabilize their markets. Although this policy may decrease industry profits, the net effect on consumer welfare is unclear.

I. COMPETITION AND COSTS

This section discusses the nature of competitive equilibrium and argues that competition, as defined in the familiar market model, is not possible in many realistic situations. The fundamental reason for this is that marginal cost-pricing of the optimal output does not generally allow firms to recover their costs, and therefore does not automatically provide firms with the correct incentives from a social point of view. In particular, the sorts of cost conditions that are likely to thwart competitive outcomes are examined. This is followed by a discussion of the technology, costs, and structure of the cast-iron pipe industry at the turn of the century. Although the concern here is with a particular industry, the facts are similar enough to what one finds in many other situations to warrant a fairly detailed treatment.

A. The Existence of a Competitive Equilibrium

Large manufacturing plants and industrial cartels became a significant part of American economic life in the mid- and late nineteenth century. Although Adam Smith had observed a century earlier that the tradesmen of a particular industry seldom gather that the talk does not end in a conspiracy against the public, cartelization of major industries in the United States does not appear to have been widespread until this period. Steel, railroading, and a host of similar industries were marked by periods of collusion, as well as periods of intense competition, in the years following the Civil War. The adoption of regulation for some industries such as railroading, and the adoption of antitrust laws for commercial activity generally, are often attributed to these conditions. The antitrust laws did not, of course, eliminate collusion, and there is also a widespread belief that the great mergers around the turn of the century, which resulted in the formation of industrial giants such as U.S. Steel, had fundamentally the same goals as the trusts and pools [see Stigler (47) and Clark (14), p. 381]. Other practices, such as the basing point system and leadership pricing, have also been widely condemned, although some of these seem to be out of the reach of antitrust laws as presently interpreted.

The economists whose job it was to analyze these matters did not speak with one voice. One group condemned the cartels and noncompetitive behavior,[3] while the other claimed the necessity of some sort of defense against "cutthroat" and "ruinous" competition, without necessarily endorsing price-fixing.[4] This second group did correctly identify the crucial issue: whether competition and marginal cost-pricing can sustain the operation of an industry.[5]

Although the debate concerning competition continued through the 1950s, the fundamental questions concerning costs and the feasibility of competitive, marginal cost-pricing have become obscured.[6] One exception to this general observation has been the largely theoretical literature on the effect of "nonconvexities," or economies, on competition.[7] This literature has not been incorporated into the typical economist's bag of tools, however, and as a result, much thinking about competition is based on a fairly limited model.

Imagine the market for a standard, homogeneous good, and imagine that it is produced by plants that have identical U-shaped average cost curves. If there is a fixed schedule of demand, there will generally be no competitive equilibrium in this situation. Notice first that marginal cost in this case is discontinuous and scallop-shaped. Initially these scallops are large in amplitude, but they grow smaller as the number of firms increases. Notice also that for most rates of demand there will be an integer n such that if n firms operate and price at marginal cost, they will make positive economic profits, but if n + 1 firms operate, they will incur losses. So, with n firms operating, there will be new entry; but if a new firm enters and the firms compete, there will be losses and one firm will exit, returning us to the initial point.

It is not correct in this case to argue that a new firm will not enter because it knows that it will have an undesirable effect. Such behavior would be inconsistent with competition. The notion of recontracting provides a precise definition of competition, which is recognized in the theory of the core.[8] If we let firms and buyers recontract, then when only n firms are operating, the idle plant can make a mutually advantageous arrangement with some of the buyers paying a higher price. This is competitive behavior. If the firm does not enter, we have to ask what makes it choose zero profits instead of the higher amount that some feasible arrangement can provide.

These issues are pursued formally in the Appendix, but it is useful to consider an example that illustrates how competition may fail. Consider three people marooned on an island. Any one alone can sacrifice a day's labor and catch one fish, any two can work one day each and catch three fish by working as a team, and all three working together and sacrificing a day each can catch four fish. This example, which exhibits increasing followed by decreasing returns, has no competitive equilibrium. Any two (say A and B) can get an average of $1\frac{1}{2}$ fish, so that the gain to one of the two (call him A) is less than or equal to $1\frac{1}{2}$. C, the outcast, who can get only one fish by himself, can bribe A, offering a return in excess of $1\frac{1}{2}$ fish and so obtain more than one fish himself. But this returns us to the initial situation. The formal version of this example appears in the Appendix.[9]

B. Fixed Costs, Uncertainty, and Transportation Costs

The simple model involving identical U-shaped average cost curves and an arbitrary rate of demand, although it illustrates the basic principle, is unrealistic in some crucial respects. In general, a range of plant sizes is available. Furthermore, larger plants have lower average cost at full capacity than smaller plants, at least up to a point. Let us assume, however, to help demonstrate the issue at stake, that these economies are indefinite: larger capacity always implies lower average costs at the point of minimum average cost. If there were no transportation costs, and if demand never changed, the optimal response would call for a single plant.

But consider now the effect of uncertain demand. If plants can avoid some of the fixed costs of operation, that is, if some plant costs are zero at zero output but attain a large constant value at larger outputs, the optimal industry response will call for a collection of plants of varying sizes, so that the variable demand can be satisfied by changing the number of plants in operation. What is more, this collection of plants will be such that, for any particular realized rate of demand, it will not in general be true that the optimal response calls for all plants to be operating at minimum average variable cost, even taking Ricardian rents into account. If the different plants have the same minimum average variable cost (which might occur if long-run economies became negligible after some point), then there will in general be no competitive equilibrium for the same reasons mentioned in connection with the case where cost curves are identical. If larger plants have lower average variable costs, it may be the case that the optimal response calls for only the largest plants to operate. In that case, it may turn out that no idle plant can undermine the optimal arrangement based on a price equal to marginal cost of the optimally active plants. Nevertheless, marginal cost-pricing may not cover costs for these plants. On the other hand, if prices are high enough, small plants could disrupt the optimal allocation. In still other instances, when both some small and some large active plants are called for, one or more of the idle plants with lower average costs could undermine the optimal arrangement.[10] Again, this is quite aside from the question of whether marginal cost-pricing will cover all costs.[11]

The discussion so far has been based on the assumption that all plants are located at a single point. If there are transportation costs, it will usually be worthwhile to have plants at various locations, although by no means at points that minimize either the transportation costs of the final product or the costs of inputs. Some spots will have site advantages, and the extent of these site advantages plus transportation costs for the final product need to be taken into account. In many practical examples the net result will be a clustering of plants.

One has to admit that the resulting configuration of buyers and sellers is a far cry from the textbook case of perfect competition. In some cases, of course, the plants can support themselves by exercising "market power." But it turns out to be a simple matter to construct examples where this market power of individual plants is not great and plants actually face too much competition. In a very fundamental sense, this is the case of a natural monopoly, although we will indicate later why it is not correct to assume that some sort of regulation is necessarily called for.

C. Technology and Costs of Cast-iron Pipe Production

The turn-of-the-century cast-iron pipe industry, and many other industries besides, conforms fairly well to the cost conditions discussed in the last section. A brief discussion of the manufacturing process shows that this is so for fundamental technological reasons.[12]

Cast-iron pressure pipe was the primary product of the *Addyston* defendants, probably more than 90 percent of their total output on a value basis. It was used to transport water or gas under pressure. To make this pipe, molds and cores were fabricated by ramming sand into forms and drying the forms and sand overnight in a drying oven. The dried molds and cores were assembled and placed vertically, and molten pig iron was poured to form the pipe. After being removed from the sand and cleaned, the pipe was dipped in a hot coal pitch bath. Pipe specifications were fairly standard at this time, and a considerable portion of output produced during the winter months went to inventory that was later sold in small lots. In the Northeast, often, small pipes were sold in a closely followed spot market. However, another large fraction of output was made to order. Some cities had their own specifications, and demand for the larger sizes was unstable from year to year. Consequently, a full inventory of all pipe sizes would have been costly. The work was often awarded by means of a sealed bid auction if the buyer was a municipal government.

The pig iron was purchased from producers and not used directly from the blast furnace. Because iron gains strength from remelting, many municipalities required that the pipe be made this way; an underground rupture of a water main is, of course, a costly accident. The iron was melted in a cupola, which is a furnace in which the fuel and pig iron come into direct contact. Layers of broken pigs and layers of coke are alternated, and a fire is started at the bottom. Molten pig iron is tapped from near the bottom of the furnace, while waste material is taken off at a higher point. More coke and iron can be added until finally, after twelve to sixteen hours of operation, the cupola must be shut down and cleaned. Until 1909, when a continuous process for drying molds and cores was introduced, all firms were single-shift operations.

The data we have on plants of various sizes indicate that large plants enjoyed economies of scale. The cupola illustrates very nicely where these economies arose. First, the number of workers required to operate a cupola will, at most, expand in equal proportion to its diameter. Second, cleaning and relining costs and radiation heat loss will tend to be proportional to the surface area of a cylinder. As its radius is increased, the surface area increases in roughly the same proportion. Third, the hourly capacity of a cupola is directly proportional to its cross section, which increases with the square of the radius. Together, these facts imply the existence of economies of scale in the operation of cupolas. Since a single cupola could adequately serve a small or medium-sized plant, we can point to these factors as one source of economies.

There are, of course, other sources of economies at a foundry, some of which arise from the nature of inventory costs. Doubling the rate of output at a plant will not usually require that inventories of materials be twice as great. A simple explanation for this is that the cost of reordering is the same for a large or a small order, and that this leads to lower average ordering costs and lower average inventory costs at larger plants. Other economies can arise from the expanded scope for specialization in other parts of the manufacturing operation and from physical laws that come into play whenever tubes and cylinders are used.[13]

These arguments have been advanced to explain falling long-run average cost. What about short-run costs? The simple geometry of cost curves tells us, of course, that short-run average costs must decline at least as fast as long-run average costs. It may be useful, however, to mention some features of production that tend to make some short-run costs particularly insensitive to the rate of output. For a given plant there are in fact many items of expense that cannot be varied in equal proportion to changes in output. Examples of these are central office expense, property taxes, and the cost of utilities and repair and maintenance. In the case of pipe foundries, there are additional and somewhat more subtle reasons for declining short-run average cost. Going back to our description of the cupola, for example, it is evident that the daily start-up and shut-down costs are in large part independent of how much pig iron was melted. It is not surprising, therefore, to find that plants were rarely operated below 50 percent of capacity. The choice, at least at the larger plants, was either to operate fairly near capacity or not to operate at all.

This discussion of the nature of costs is supported by the monthly accounting data we have for eleven cast-iron plants for the year June 1905– May 1906. Table 1 provides average direct and indirect costs for this period, exactly ten years after the events described in the court case took place. Because we lack a better measure of capacity, the maximum observed monthly output of pipe, expressed in tons, is used. Average direct cost encompasses chiefly labor and fuel but also some miscellaneous expenses, while average indirect expense encompasses office expense, replacement of tools, repairs to machinery and buildings, insurance, taxes, and a variety of other outlays that have no strict relationship to current output. The most striking relationship is the negative association between

Table 1. Plant Location, Maximum Monthly Output, and Costs per Ton of Pipe
June 1905–May 1906

Location	(1) Maximum Monthly Output of Pipe (in tons)	(2) Direct Cost per Ton	(3) Indirect Cost per Ton	(4) (2) + (3)	(5) Cost of Iron	(6) Total Cost (4) + (5)
Addyston, Ohio	7,224	$4.597	$1.601	$ 6.198	$14.258	$20.456
Burlington, New Jersey	6,147	5.130	1.400	6.530	14.506	21.036
Scottdale, Penn.	5,848	4.638	1.083	5.721	13.963	19.684
Bessemer, Alabama	5,316	5.486	1.747	7.233	11.754	18.987
Anniston, Alabama	4,269	5.920	1.586	7.506	11.826	19.342
Cleveland, Ohio	4,034	5.159	1.281	6.440	14.143	20.583
Louisville, Kentucky	4,018	5.541	1.763	7.304	14.091	21.395
Chattanooga, Tenn.	3,740	5.364	1.055	6.419	12.037	18.456
Buffalo, New York	2,157	6.755	2.496	9.251	14.820	24.071
Columbus, Ohio	1,433	7.049	2.241	9.290	13.486	22.776
West Superior, Wisc.	776	7.146	5.332	12.478	14.589	27.067

Source: Calculated from the ledger of the United States Cast Iron Pipe & Foundry Company, 1905–1906.

65

Table 2. The Variation of Sales, Output, and Costs

	Coefficients of Variation		Correlation Coefficients	
Plant	Sales[a]	Output	Output and Direct Cost	Output and Indirect Cost
Addyston	.212*	.087	.428	.130
Burlington	.304*	.112	.911	− .500
Scottdale	.194*	.105	.550	.188
Bessemer	.129	.107	.841	.313
Anniston	.205*	.098	.718	− .258
Cleveland	.346	.237	.942	− .664
Louisville	.269*	.134	.860	− .343
Chattanooga	.254*	.073	.532	.575
Buffalo[b]	1.129	1.522	.996	.835
Columbus	.427*	.228	.889	.806
West Superior[b]	.853	.991	.991	.589

Note: An asterisk indicates that the coefficient of variation for sales is significantly greater than for output at the 5 percent level. Correlation coefficients for 12 observations with an absolute value in excess of .500 are significant at the 5 percent level.

[a] "Sales" formed part of a stock-flow calculation. New output was added to the previous end-of-month inventory and sales were subtracted from this sum to obtain the new end-of-month inventory. This implies that it refers to shipments, regardless of when the pipe was actually sold.

[b] These plants were shut down for several months and direct cost was zero then. Consequently, the correlations overstate the strength of the relationship between output and direct costs.

Source: Same as Table 1.

capacity and the two types of cost. The cost of pig iron would not, of course, be related to capacity, except through a somewhat more subtle connection. Larger plants might be able to get better prices on pig iron, although this does not appear to be a major factor.[14]

A complication arises in this investigation of economies because certain costs, most notably capital and inventory cost, have been neglected. In principle, these could offset the direct and indirect costs and result in the same average cost across plants of various sizes. Capital costs are unlikely to be this large, however. The total value of properties, plant, and inventories in May of 1906 for United States Cast Iron Pipe and Foundry was $26,029,238. At a 5 percent rate of return,[15] capital cost on this total is $1,301,462. If this is divided by the yearly production of 459,466 tons of hub and spigot pipe, it implies an average capital cost of $2.83 per ton. Yet the difference in direct plus indirect costs between large plants near the Pennsylvania-Ohio border (Cleveland and Scottdale) and the small plants in the same vicinity (Columbus and Buffalo) requires that capital costs at the large plants be approximately $3 higher to achieve a weighted average for the whole group of roughly $3. But this is implausible since it would imply nearly negligible capital costs at the small plants. Equally important, the assertion that there are no economies of scale has to contend with the fact that the smaller plants were located in the areas with more variable consumption. If small plants, with their obvious advantages in meeting uncertain demand and filling market niches, are just as efficient as large ones, we should expect to find them everywhere.

Economic reasoning not only suggests that costs are greater at smaller plants, but also that average costs at a given plant first fall and then rise as output is increased. It should be emphasized, however, that in practice we may not often find firms operating over the range of rising average costs. The basic reason for this is that the optimal industry response calls for slack capacity at most times. Slack capacity is the price we pay for being able to meet demand at peak periods at reasonable cost.[16] Transportation and service industries illustrate the most commonly observed instances of slack capacity, and our intuition provides some notion of why existing capacity is not fully utilized. Airplanes, trains, hotels, and restaurants typically operate with slack capacity, and yet we do not infer that this is not optimal.

The same has often been asserted for manufacturing plants, and considerable statistical evidence supports this view. Generally, researchers find marginal cost to be less than average cost. This was true of the cast-iron pipe industry, as Table 2 suggests. First, note that the coefficient of variation, which measures proportional variability, is much larger for sales than for output. This suggests that there was some minimum average cost of operation, because the best way of meeting variable shipments requirements if average cost curves are U-shaped is to use inventories as a buffer. Note that there are very good reasons why the plants and not the ultimate purchasers held a good deal of the fluctuating inventory, since it is more conveniently held at a central location than at various municipalities. It is also probably true that "consumption" of pipe, that is actual pipe-laying, was even more volatile than sales. This makes the relatively steady output at most plants even more impressive as evidence for the view that the plants had U-shaped average costs.

A second strand of evidence comes from the fact that output at the large plants was much better correlated with direct cost than with indirect cost. In fact, indirect cost is negatively related to output in several cases because repair and replacement was deferred to slack periods in the winter. This suggests that in addition to capital and inventory costs a certain amount of "out-of-pocket" expense was also not related to current output. On the other hand, labor and fuel costs tended to be very strongly related to output. But since significant capital, central office, and inventory expenses have been excluded, and since these probably do not change with output, we have good reason to believe that a large part of a plant's costs are uninfluenced by the level of current output.

D. Industry Structure

A central question in this analysis is the importance of each plant in its relevant market. The larger each plant is in the appropriately defined market, the more difficult it becomes to adjust to changes in demand by shutting down plants and the harder it becomes to find marginal cost-pricing schemes that cover even short-run costs. If plants are small relative to the market, changes in demand can be accommodated by shutting down plants, and the active plants can continue to operate fairly close to minimum average cost. On the other hand, if several plants are clustered together and serve the same market, the optimal industry response will often call for some or all to stay in operation, although at output rates short of minimum average cost. Note also that if plants are slightly dispersed, or if they make a slightly different mix of pipe sizes, we might have industry demand fall more than 25 percent from the point at which all four identical plants operate at full capacity, and still find that it is optimal for all four to stay in operation. Finally, shut-down and start-up costs can generate situations in which, even though current demand is low, the continued operation of plants remains desirable as long as the outlook for the future is optimistic.

The geographical distribution of plants in the United States during the time covered in this study is fundamental to an analysis of industry structure. Figure 1 gives the locations of the major operating plants from 1880 to 1920 and presents the information in a way that reveals the shift of plants from the North to the South. Also note the substantial increase in the number of plants, from 11 in 1881 to 26 ten years later. After a slight decline during the mid-1890s, the number increased again during the first decade of this century. Although there were at most 28 plants in operation at any one time, Figure 1 documents the activity of 43 plants in all. This indicates a substantial amount of plant turnover.

Until 1898, the year of the first mergers, all firms were one- or two-plant operations. Except for USCIP&F, the firm formed by the defendants, this remained the case for all other firms in the industry until the late 1930s. It should also be emphasized that a substantial number of nonspecialized iron foundries could make pipe at a slightly higher cost on a makeshift basis, and frequently contracts were taken by such local firms. These foundries could not, however, compete profitably on work for more distant points. It was also possible to convert other types of foundries to full-time cast-iron pipe production, as happened in several cases during the period of expansion following 1900.

Figure 2 shows the locations of the major plants in 1900, including the six *Addyston* defendants and the five other producers who formed USCIP&F in the 1898 and 1899 mergers. The geographic clustering of plants is apparent. One group of plants was located in eastern Pennsyl-

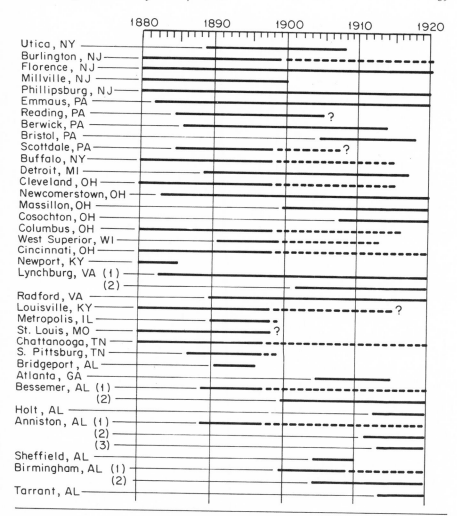

Figure 1. Locations of Major Cast-iron Pipe Plants, 1880–1920

Note: A dashed line indicates that the plant was owned by USCIP&F that year. A question mark indicates that the sources above say a plant was out of operation by that date (or perhaps earlier).
Sources: Noble (35), *passim*; Moore (32), *passim*.

vania and western New Jersey. A second group was located in northern Alabama and southern Tennessee, while a third somewhat more dispersed group was located in western Pennsylvania, Ohio, and along the Ohio River in Kentucky. Five other plants were located along Great Lakes water routes and the Erie Canal, and one was located in western Virginia. Table 3 provides the capacities of these plants and reveals that the large

⊛   Plants belonging to defendants in <u>Addyston</u>

✳   Plants included in United States Cast Iron Pipe & Foundry by 1900

●   Plants of major independent producers

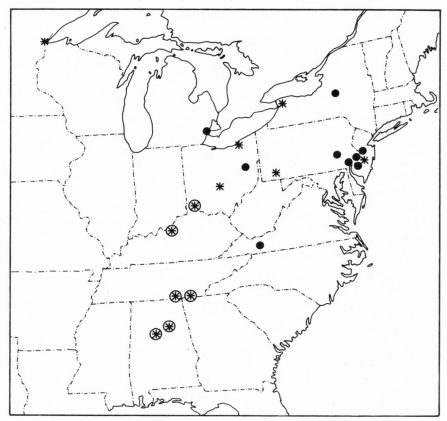

Figure 2.   Location and Ownership of Major Plants, 1900

plants were located predominantly in one of the three major producing areas. The small northern plants were the peak-load units in this market, as we might expect in an industry in which demand fluctuated more in the north.

One factor of considerable importance is the nature of transportation costs. Railroad regulation had begun just before the period covered in this study, and we find relative stability of rates because of the long-haul/short-haul clause. There was, however, considerable competition on the long distances, subject to the restrictions this clause provided.

Table 4 shows the railroad rates for mid-1893 per ton of pig iron for carload lots. (Pig iron and pipe were transported at nearly identical rates.) It is clear that average costs declined as distance shipped increased. For example, Louisville is about halfway between Birmingham and Chicago, yet the rate to Louisville is 65 percent of the rate to Chicago. Note also that the rates from Chattanooga and Birmingham to Chicago are nearly the same. Consequently, since the southern plants shipped nearly all their

Table 3. Major Cast-iron Pipe Plants
1900

		Daily Melting Capacity (in tons)	
Firm and Plant		1900	1896
U.S. Cast Iron Pipe and Foundry	2,625		
Defendants in *Addyston*	1,500		
Addyston: Cincinnati, Ohio		350	
Dennis Long: Louisville, Kentucky		250	
Chattanooga: Chattanooga, Tennessee		150	
South Pittsburg: South Pittsburg, Tennessee		100	
Howard-Harrison: Bessemer, Alabama*		300	
Anniston: Anniston, Alabama		350	
Included in USCIP&F, 1899–1901	1,185		
Lake Shore Foundry: Cleveland, Ohio		300	200
McNeal: Burlington, New Jersey		200	225
National Foundry: Scottdale, Pennsylvania		300	200
Buffalo: Buffalo, New York		150	100
Ohio: Columbus, Ohio		175	150
West Superior: West Superior, Wisconsin		60	75
Major Outside Firms	1,270		
Warren: Phillipsburg, New Jersey		275	200
Wood: Florence, New Jersey		300	400
Donaldson: Emmaus, Pennsylvania		100	
Utica: Utica, New York		80	50
Reading: Reading, Pennsylvania		140	125
Clow: Newcomerstown, Ohio		125	75
Penninsular Car: Detroit, Michigan**		100	
Jackson and Woodin: Berwick, Pennsylvania		75	75
Radford: Radford, Virginia‡		75	
Glamorgan: Lynchburg, Virginia			75
Shickle, Harrison & Howard: St. Louis, Mo.			75

* Closed temporarily in 1900.

** Joined in Southern Car and Foundry, *Directory, 1901*, p. 143–144.

‡ Owned by Virginia Iron, Coal and Coke and leased to Glamorgan Pipe and Foundry of Lynchburg, Virginia, *Directory, 1904*, p. 177.

Sources: Directory to the Iron and Steel Works of the United States, various issues; *Transcript of Record*, note 12, at 36–37; Noble, note 12, *passim*. Three small foundries in Texas, Colorado, and Oregon are omitted.

Table 4.   Freight Rates from the Southern Pig-iron Producing Areas,
May 1893
(dollars per ton of pig iron)

To	From	
	Chattanooga, Tenn.	*Birmingham District*
Addyston, Ohio	$2.25	$2.75
Buffalo, N.Y.	3.90	4.40
Chicago, Ill.	3.60	3.85
Council Bluffs, Iowa	5.00	5.00
Detroit, Mich.	3.60	3.85
Grand Rapids, Mich.	3.85	4.10
Louisville, Ky.	2.25	2.50
Memphis, Tenn.	2.00	2.00
Milwaukee, Wisc.	4.00	4.25
Omaha, Neb.	5.00	5.00
Pittsburgh, Pa.	3.90	4.40
Richmond, Ind.	2.95	3.20
St. Paul, Minn.	5.14	5.39
West Superior, Wisc.	5.29	5.54

Source: Iron Age, May 18, 1893, p. 1130.

output to other parts of the country, plants at the two shipping points can essentially be thought of as having been at one location. These railroad rates also indicate that firms that were located only one or two hundred miles away were at a disadvantage amounting to $2 or more per ton. Since we note that the cost of production was only $7 to $12 per ton (excluding the cost of pig iron), location was likely to play a large role in determining which was the best plant to fill an order. This naturally raises the possibility that a firm would charge a higher f.o.b. price to local purchasers if there were no competitors nearby.

II. THE ASSOCIATED PIPE WORKS AGREEMENT AND THE FORMATION OF UNITED STATES CAST IRON PIPE AND FOUNDRY

We now turn to a detailed description and analysis of events in this industry, keeping in mind our earlier remarks about competition and the nature of plant costs. While certain aspects of the cartel agreement are well known, an extensive economic analysis of this case has not been made.[17] Evidence concerning earlier attempts at cartelization and merger, as well as events in later years, is also presented. It should be kept in mind that there are in any market substantial "market imperfections" that put some distance between an actual market and our theoretical models, which are characterized by pervasive instability. These imperfections are not, of course, necessarily undesirable or avoidable except when judged against an abstract and unobtainable ideal. They result from the costs of using markets and from some inevitable degree of product differentiation. There are times, however, when these imperfections, which may be thought of as market frictions, are slight, and the major conclusion of our model—that there can be too much competition—is upheld. This is likely to occur when demand is slack, and our investigation indeed confirms that an alternative to independent operation of the plants was sought during lean years, especially in the 1890s.[18]

A. Boom and Bust in Cast-iron Pipe

Cast-iron pipe is a prime example of a capital good the demand for which is sensitive to general business fluctuations. Although the second half of the 1880s were good years, especially for the cast-iron pipe industry, there had been contractions in the late 1870s and early 1880s. The industry, which at that time was located primarily in the Northeast, had responded to these contractions by attempting to form a pool of manufacturers. At the first attempt, in 1879, participants agreed that a pool should have four aims:

1. To devise some method to secure more remunerative prices.
2. To divide the work or assets realized for the letting of the work on a basis equitable to all.
3. To prepare uniform specifications under which we shall all pledge ourselves to bid at public auctions.
4. To prevent the expansion of present shops or the building of new ones.[19]

This attempt failed because one firm, the Warren foundry in New Jersey, refused to take part.[20] A similar effort, in 1892, failed because a few concerns opposed the effort or failed to join. It should be noted at the outset, however, that these failed attempts at cartelization do not mean that there were no local understandings or that some sort of less formal, even tacit, collusion did not take place.

The circumstances that made a cartel desirable to some members in 1879 did not long endure. We have already noted the substantial increase in the number of plants in operation during the mid- and late 1880s. The extent of the increase in demand that resulted in this new construction can only be guessed at, since figures on total industry output are hard to come by. The amount of new water pipe laid down during the late 1880s in Chicago must have been considerable, however, to provide the astounding increase in pipe-in-use (measured by miles of pipe in service) recorded for the year 1890 in Figure 3. This increase in demand was not confined to Chicago, but seems to have covered the whole eastern half of the United States.

By the early 1890s, however, the boom in water pipe was over. The

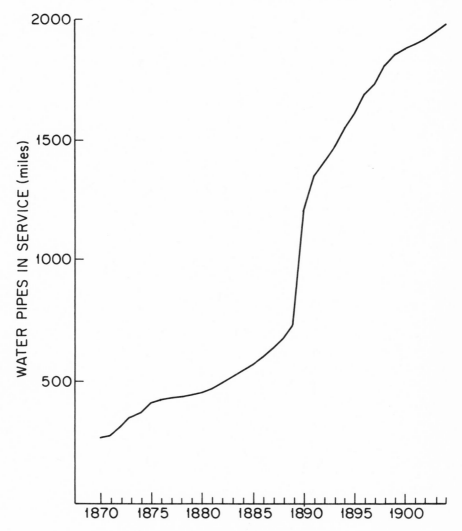

Figure 3.   Miles of Water Pipe in Chicago, 1870–1904
Source: Fifty-fifth Annual Report of the Chicago Department of Public Works, 1930, p. 74.

new Anniston plant, built in 1889, went bankrupt eighteen months later [Moore (32), p. 20]. In February of 1892 the *Iron Age* reported that "the manufacturers of cast-iron pipe are just now passing through the vale of adversity."[21] By the end of the year, trade reports predicting a consolidation of firms in the business began to circulate. In December it was rumored that two groups had been formed, one in the East, the other in the "West," that is, Ohio and the South, "the ultimate object being to fuse the two groups into one large concern, which is to manufacture and distribute the product for the whole country."[22] Two weeks later this intelligence was changed. The eastern shops had not proceeded very far in their plans. The western shops denied the merger, but *Iron Age* stuck to its story, and backed it up with the details concerning the identity of the negotiating parties (nine firms including all six of the *Addyston* defendants) and the news that the new firm would offer stock to the public. It also noted that the western producers had met with the eastern producers to discuss the prices on some large upcoming contracts.[23]

B. The Associated Pipe Works Agreement

This merger attempt failed and little is known concerning what measures the various firms were compelled to resort to. From the court record we know that the four southern shops located in Tennessee and Alabama operated a cartel in 1894, although it may have been formed earlier [*Transcript of Record* (53), p. 8; hereinafter *Record*]. In December of that year the Southern Associated Pipe Works allowed the two Ohio River firms (Louisville and Addyston) to join them, and modified rules for the association were drawn up. Although key features of the agreement were changed several months later, it is instructive to consider the main features of these rules. Each shop was given exclusive rights to certain cities, usually but not always those close by (Table 5 has the details), and a schedule of "bonuses" was established which indicated how much was to be paid into the common fund for every ton of pipe shipped to various points in "pay territory." The schedule seemed designed to conform to a limit-pricing notion. Since water transportation was cheaper than rail, North Carolina, South Carolina, Florida, and coastal points in Georgia and Texas had bonuses of only $1 per ton. Wisconsin, Kansas, Montana, Minnesota, Illinois, Indiana, Iowa, and the interior of Georgia had $2 bonuses. Nebraska, Oklahoma, and Louisiana had $3 bonuses. The fact that the bonus was higher for Louisiana than for Kansas and Wisconsin was probably due to the influence of competitors in northern Ohio. Ohio itself had a $1.50 bonus. Pennsylvania, Virginia, and states in the Northeast, called "free territory," had no bonuses, while reserved cities had bonuses of $2.

Table 5.   Reserved Cities for Members of the Cartel

Firm Location	Reserved Cities
Addyston, Ohio	Cincinnati, Ohio
	Covington, Kentucky
	Newport, Kentucky
Louisville, Kentucky	Louisville, Kentucky
	Jeffersonville, Indiana
	New Albany, Indiana
Anniston, Alabama	Anniston, Alabama
	Atlanta, Georgia
Chattanooga, Tennessee	Chattanooga, Tennessee
	New Orleans, Louisana
Bessemer, Alabama	Bessemer, Alabama
	Birmingham, Alabama
	St. Louis, Missouri
South Pittsburg, Tennessee	Omaha, Nebraska

Note: The plants are referred to by the name of the city in which they were located, following the practice
        of the successor firm, United States Cast Iron Pipe and Foundry. Addyston is near Cincinnati.
Source: Transcript of Record, p. 66.

How was the bonus fund divided? It was explicitly set forth in the
agreement that this fund would be divided on the basis of plant capacity.
The bonuses on the first 90,000 tons shipped to any territory were divided
six ways; the bonuses on the next 75,000 tons five ways, with the smallest
plant (South Pittsburg) dropped; those on the next 40,000 tons four ways,
with the two smallest plants (South Pittsburg and Anniston) dropped; and
those on the next 15,000 tons were divided among the three largest plants
only (adding Chattanooga to the dropped firms). If tonnage was in excess
of 220,000 tons, the "reserve fund" beyond that amount was allocated
to the plants according to the proportion of excess tonnage that each firm
had shipped to pay or free territory. The settlements were made twice
each month, which implies that the small plants received their shares
during the first part of each year.

The agreement also contained explicit reporting requirements. All orders, whether from pay or free territory, were to be reported daily, and
summary reports of shipments were to be made twice each month. Carbon
copies of all reports received were to be sent to all members of the cartel,
together with a statement showing net bonus payments due from one firm
to another. A record of all existing orders at the time the agreement was
entered into was to be filed with the cartel, and only these orders would
be exempt from the bonus payment. Furthermore, existing quotations
were to be withdrawn unless firms were willing to pay the bonuses on
these amounts. The agreement also required that an auditor check all
firms' books each month, and stipulated that each firm's representative

at a public auction was to send to the auditor a list of bids and bidders. In addition, any information about work undertaken by firms outside the association was to be submitted to the auditor. [*Record* at 64–69]

Apparently, the system of fixed bonuses did not work well. Only five months later, on May 16, 1895, the members met and considered the following resolution concerning work awarded through public auctions.

> Whereas, the system now in operation in this association of having a "fixed bonus on the several states" has not in its operation resulted in the advancement in the prices of pipe anticipated, except in the "reserved cities" and some further action is imperatively necessary in order to accomplish the ends for which this association was formed. Therefore, be it resolved. That from and after the first day of June that all competition on the pipe lettings shall take place among the various shops prior to the said letting. To accomplish this purpose it is proposed that the six competitive shops have a "representative board" located at some central city to whom all enquiries for pipe shall be referred, and said board shall fix the price at which said pipe shall be sold, and bids taken from the respective shops for the privilege of handling the order, and the party securing the order shall have the protection of all the other shops. [*id.* at 70]

The crucial change proposed in this resolution was that prices be fixed in advance and that firms be allowed to bid for the work by offering higher bonuses. The "protection" referred to was the submission of false bids above the price that the highest bidder in the association's internal auction was committed to charging. Eleven days later, a new meeting was held at which this resolution was adopted, and the provision was made for sales not made through public auctions. In the case of "special customers," the price and bonus would be established by the committee of six representatives to reflect prices and bonuses generally prevailing at that time. On other work the minutes simply state that "bonuses shall be fixed by the committee." Again, existing quotations were recalled and new prices and bonuses on such work were established by the committee [*id.* at 71].[24]

The new system of internal first-round auctions proposed in May 1895 and apparently aimed at remedying the problem of low prices was in fact implemented. The bonuses collected on the first 220,000 tons shipped were still allocated on the basis of capacity, although on December 20, 1895, the agreement was changed so that the first 220,000 tons shipped to pay territory—which included all states west of Pennsylvania, south of Virginia, and east of the Rockies—rather than shipments to all destinations, formed the basis for the allocation [*id.* at 72–73]. This was proposed by the firm located in Bessemer, Alabama, and may have been the response to, or anticipation of, the acceptance of work outside pay territory by member firms along the Ohio River. Depending on how much work was done there, the bonus fund on the first 220,000 tons would have been watered down. All firms but Addyston, which was "not prepared to vote," supported the resolution.[25]

How much of the work of the six firms was taken by the reserved cities? A good deal of work went abroad, to the Northeast or to the Plains States and Far West. In 1895 one-half of the cartel's output went to Illinois [id. at 73]. The 1890 census figures provide data on the number of people in each state living in cities with 25,000 or more inhabitants. Using these figures, it can be calculated that the reserved cities accounted for 47.7 percent of the total inhabitants in such cities in their respective states. In Louisiana, only New Orleans had a population over 25,000, while in Indiana inhabitants of the reserved cities accounted for less than 10 percent of the urban population. Towns smaller than 25,000 did have waterworks, and at least half of the cartel's output went to states without reserved cities, so we can be sure that reserved cities accounted for less than one quarter of total cartel output.

Something of the method used by the cartel to allocate its gains can be learned from Table 6, which presents the net settlements between firms during the first three and one-half months of the year. The striking feature in these settlements is that some firms, namely Bessemer and Louisville, were very big net losers, at least as far as the bonus fund goes, while Chattanooga, South Pittsburg, and Anniston were net winners. The fact that these small plants appear to be net winners is not surprising, however, because the system called for small plants to be reimbursed early in the year, as mentioned above. Other factors also played a role, although it is difficult to say what weights we should give them. What we can say is that a firm that received a large (positive) net settlement in the first part of the year did so because (1) it did relatively little work, (2) it did relatively little work in pay territory, or (3) the jobs it bid on had low bonuses. Small plants would have negative net settlements if they took work in pay territory once a certain aggregate tonnage was reached. The Addyston plant, located in the Northeast and close to nonmember plants, was better situated to take low bonus work in Ohio and Pennsylvania; yet its *share* of the fund was not affected, and so it received a positive bonus settlement. Shops located closer to the heart of pay territory paid out more than they earned in the way of bonuses. Louisville, a few hundred miles down river from Cincinnati, was a small net loser. Bessemer, even farther south, was the big net loser.

An additional factor seems to have been plant cost conditions; it should probably be expected that firms with low marginal cost would bid more

Table 6. Net Bonus Settlements between Plants, Early 1896

| | January | | February | | March | | April | January 1 to | Cartel Assigned |
	1/1 to 1/15	1/16 to 1/31	2/1 to 2/15	2/16 to 2/29	3/1 to 3/15	3/16 to 3/31	4/1 to 4/15	April 15	Capacity*
Addyston	+1,159	+312	+2,392	+2,708	+1,387	+589	-2,662	+5,925	45,000
Anniston	+1,173	+1,475	+1,818	+2,150	+589	+181	+715	+8,101	30,000
Bessemer	-882	-2,685	-6,295	-8,534	-1,773	-3,958	-4,261	-28,388	45,000
Chattanooga	-2,016	+213	+2,265	+3,147	+1,635	+3,188	+4,630	+13,062	40,000
Louisville	-52	+41	-1,627	-1,218	-1,721	-1,554	-1,126	-7,257	45,000
S. Pittsburg	+619	+645	+1,449	+1,747	+1,061	+850	+2,663	+9,034	15,000

Note: + means a net positive settlement or gain that month, − means a loss.
* "Cartel Assigned Capacity" formed the basis for the bonus fund settlements.
Source: Transcript of Record, pp. 98–99.

79

to obtain a contract and contribute more than their share of the bonus. The Chattanooga management was very happy, in fact, to let the Bessemer plant take work in early 1896 that, after bonus and freight were paid, netted only $12 per ton. In a letter to its cartel representative in Cincinnati, Chattanooga management instructed him to accept no work that would not provide at least $14.25 for the smaller and $13.00 for the larger sizes at the shop gate after bonus was paid. Chattanooga's share of the bonus was secure in any event, and it looked to work in free territory to provide some extra return [*id.* at 94]. In fact, it seems to have been able to get at least $13 in free territory.[26] This policy may very well account for its large net settlement. Although one might object that there is no good reason why Chattanooga should get work in free territory at a higher net price, it is quite likely that variations in output were more expensive at the larger plant and that fixed costs were a larger fraction of costs. If work in free territory was more sporadic, there is no necessary inconsistency. Furthermore, as the year progressed, the smaller plants no longer received bonus payments. Consequently, the larger plants could expect to receive a larger incremental share for work in pay territory.

It should also be noted that the curious method of dividing the bonus fund had a predictable effect. By the rules of the agreement, if there was a bad year—say, only 90,000 tons were shipped to pay territory—then each of the six firms, large and small, got only one-sixth of the bonus fund. Clearly, the large firms might be unhappy with this arrangement of business conditions turned sour. It comes as no surprise, then, to learn that the Addyston plant, the largest of the six plants, sought a readjustment in December of 1895. It predicted that in 1896 total cartel tonnage would be only 195,000, in part because bonuses were now calculated on the basis of shipments to pay territory rather than net shipments to all territories. Accordingly, it suggested a decrease from 220,000 to 200,000 in the tonnage forming the basis for the division of the bonuses, with the relative allocations to remain unchanged [*Record* at 90–92]. No evidence exists that this suggestion was adopted. This may be explained by the cartel rule that five out of six firms had to support motions for changes in the agreement for those motions to pass.

C. Discovery of the Agreement

The system of internal auctions and reserved cities was in effect in February of 1896 when the Anniston, Alabama, works submitted a bid of $24 per ton to the city of Atlanta, its reserved city, on a small order of only 375 tons. This bid was duly protected by other members, but was underbid by a New Jersey firm whose representative was in town. "In reply will say," wrote the vice-president of Anniston to one of the other

firms, "we believe we made a mistake in trying to get $24.00 for pipe and
$2\frac{1}{2}$ cents for specials, but there would have been no difficulty in this respect
had we not run up against R. D. Wood & Co.'s man there putting in his
bid for hydrants, and he also put in a bid for the pipe and specials at the
last minute" [*id*. at 84].

Nor can it be doubted that the price was high. The January 30, 1896,
issue of the *Iron Age* reported that Anniston had bid $21.50 per ton in
Jacksonville, Florida, for 4,100 tons of pipe. The Bessemer shop, which
had protected Anniston in Atlanta with a higher bogus bid, won that
contract at $19.20. Since the freight rate from Anniston to Atlanta was
only $1.60 per ton, the Anniston shop bid more per ton, net of freight,
for work to be delivered to Atlanta than it did for work, including freight,
for Jacksonville.[27] A curious detail about the Jacksonville bid was that
the Chattanooga management thought it was too low.

> It is useless to argue that Howard-Harrison Iron Co., Cincinnati and
> other shops, who have been bidding bonuses or six and eight dollars
> per ton, can come out and make any money if they continue to bid
> such bonus. In the case of the Howard-Harrison Co., people on
> Jacksonville, Florida. [*sic*] The truth of the business is they are losing
> money at the prices they bid for this work. [*id*. at 93]

Work in the Northeast at that time was being let at $17 to $20 per ton,
even on small lots. The Anniston and Chattanooga plants themselves bid
$20.00 and $20.62 for work in Boston during the early part of 1896.[28] Since
freight was at least $5, the price at the factory gate was at most $15. Later
that year, a "southern shop" bid $21.12 per gross ton ($18.86 per net ton)
on a contract at Lawrence, Massachusetts. *Iron Age* speculated that the
southern firms must have had some cheap sources of pig iron, since freight
charges left only $12.15 at the shop.[29]

Other evidence that the cartel's prices were discriminatory, in that they
charged more to people close by, comes to light in a letter to a contractor
(it seems) in New Orleans. The South Pittsburg works had quoted a much
lower price f.o.b. New Orleans on an inquiry for a lot of pipe that was
to go ultimately to South America than on an identical lot going to New
Orleans itself. Anxious to avoid any misunderstanding, South Pittsburg
sent off a letter dated May 10, 1895, which included the following.

> We cannot furnish this pipe for New Orleans consumption. It's true
> that the transaction looks all right on the face of it, but we could
> never explain it satisfactorily and it would result in breaking up an
> arrangement, which is bringing to us as well as others considerable
> more profit than we would reap if this arrangement should be broken.

The parties that I refer to, as your Mr. Marrion well knows, will watch every movement made in New Orleans so far as the purchase of pipe is concerned, and for this reason we would greatly prefer not to run any chances. [*Record* at 41]

The suspicion in Atlanta that there was a cartel among the four southern shops had some interesting consequences. The Chattanooga works complained that the system of reserved cities was undesirable since the fact that a particular city's orders were always filled by the same firm was proof to the city that a combination existed. They also appear to suggest that this system had inefficiencies insofar as they were denied work, sometimes of considerable magnitude, of the type that had often fallen into their hands before the combination existed (or at least before "reserved cities" existed—we don't know how long or in what form the southern shops had been operating their cartel). Chattanooga also suggested that a "proper talk with R. D. Wood & Co. would result in a better understanding between us" [*id.* at 87].

The water commissioners of the city of Atlanta threatened that if they discovered a combination none of the southern shops would get another order, but in the meantime they rejected all bids and asked for new ones from the same local firms accused of price-fixing. Writing to Chattanooga, they inquired "if it is not possible for a lower bid to be made from those who are so near this point, you might say, right at our door" [*id.* at 84].

The Atlanta board of water commissioners did initiate an investigation into the question of whether any legal action should be taken. J. E. McClure, who had been the cartel's stenographer during 1895 and 1896, began in March of 1896 to contact various municipalities in pay territory with the aim of receiving some compensation for his efforts. He had assiduously and secretly copied dozens of letters, telegrams, and cartel minutes, and promised to provide his copies to the cities he contacted, among them Booneville, Indiana, and Omaha, Nebraska, if they split any damages with him. McClure also contacted the Atlanta officials, who reviewed his evidence but declined to press charges. In doing so, they argued for the importance of the following points:

1.   The outcome of the sugar case, *E. C. Knight,* indicated that a suit filed against the pipe companies was not likely to succeed.

2.   The common law on cases such as this was ambiguous.

3.   Georgia law granted relief only if purchasers made an effort to award their trade to other parties; i.e., Atlanta had not made an effort to shop outside the combination.

4.   The references in Chattanooga upon whom McClure had relied to provide letters of recommendation repudiated him once they found out

what he was up to. The testimony and evidence of their chief witness was therefore likely to be questionable.

The unanimous opinion of the water commissioners was not to bring suit, although their lawyers had argued that they should [*id.* at 169–174].

In addition to contacting the various city officials, McClure also seems to have attempted to blackmail the cartel. In their demurrer the defendants claimed that they had "persistently refused to be blackmailed by all parties claiming to have secured copies of private letters and agreements alleged to have been stolen from them" [*id.* at 35]. Although McClure is not mentioned, he appears to be a likely candidate.

The city of St. Louis also refused to prosecute, although for slightly different reasons than Atlanta's. The City Counselor, although declining to submit an affidavit on behalf of the defendants, did express a willingness to supply testimony on their behalf "at any time it may be desired, and sought in the regular legal methods." In a letter to the vice-president of the Bessemer firm, who had solicited an affidivat, he indicated that he too was suspicious of McClure and that the city had been reluctant to become involved with him. McClure had written to the mayor of St. Louis in March of 1896 and visited there in May. The second reason, besides McClure's character, that purportedly led the city to decline involvement in the matter was that it could and did reject bids that were too high:

> We have competent engineers who keep posted as to market values, and whenever bids do not come within the amount estimated by them for the doing of public work . . . the board rejects the bids and readvertises . . . we do not feel that the city has been or can be defrauded by any combinations that may be made between manufacturers, for whenever any such attempts are made the city protects itself by refusing to agree to pay the prices bid, and by continuing to readvertise for bids until the prices come within the estimated cost of the work. [*id.* at 256]

It is also interesting that the firms were accused by the government of maintaining their conspiracy in defiance of the restraining orders that were issued.[30] An odd detail that also emerges at this point is that by February of the next year (1897), the city of Atlanta had again solicited bids. Although Atlanta had bought pipe from the Anniston plant in April of 1896, none of the defendants wanted, or perhaps none was permitted, to provide pipe the following February. The firms that did participate in the bidding were located in Lynchburg, Virginia (the low bidder), Florence, New Jersey, Berwick, Pennsylvania, and Columbus, Ohio.[31] This is surprising when we remember that there are at least four plants, all four of them defendants in the case, who were located much closer. Two years later, however, in February of 1899, the low bidder on an Atlanta contract was American Pipe and Foundry, the firm formed by the merger of those same four plants.[32]

D. Cartelization in Related Industries and Sources of Supply

It should be noted that cast-iron pipe manufacturers were not the only producers of iron and steel products to be involved in price-fixing arrangements at this time. The southern pig-iron producers also had an agreement and this was well known. For example, the trade press reported in December of 1895 that a large southern producer had sold 10,000 tons to "pipe works in Tennessee" (the Chattanooga and South Pittsburg shops are the only ones we know of) at 50 cents below quoted prices, or so it was charged. "Others claim that 'full' prices were obtained. Since the placing of this order, however, the information comes that the largest Southern furnaces have reached an understanding by which prices will hereafter be maintained."[33] One month later, trade reports indicated that some suspicion existed among these pig-iron producers. One firm had committed itself to a contract at a price below prevailing prices, claiming that a mistake in the telegrams had resulted in that low price. Unfortunately, the buyer, a large northern pipe producer, accepted before it could be withdrawn. "Whether this explanation is correct or not seems to make little difference. It has resulted in unsettling confidence and subsequent sales have been made on a lower basis, at least 25¢ per ton under the level recognized by the furnaces, and in some instances even lower."[34]

Given that the producers of pig iron were operating a cartel, what can we say about the way the pipe works purchased their pig iron and the prices they paid? Very little can be known a priori. As large consumers, they had a substantial incentive to induce their suppliers to shade prices, and the relative stability and size of their requirements might lead us to expect that they got lower than "prevailing" or openly quoted prices. On the other hand, it is probably more difficult to hide from other cartel members such large orders made at reduced prices. Furthermore, if the cartel of pig-iron producers was formed for the same reasons as those we propose for the cast-iron pipe cartel, then the pipe producers, who numbered among the furnaces' steady and sizable consumers, would not have eagerly sought to initiate and sustain cutthroat competition among their suppliers. Considering their interests as a group and over time, it was to their benefit if prices enabled producers to cover costs. At the risk of belaboring our theme, these prices were not necessarily marginal costs.[35]

Speculation aside, we can establish that the pipe plants contracted for large lots of pipe at a time and received these contracted amounts in sizable shipments, sometimes dividing the whole contracted amount into two or three shipments several months apart. This much is clear from the trade reports as well as the monthly plant data on which our results in Tables 1 and 2 are based. Orders of 5,000 to 10,000 tons were common, which would have provided for one to three months' operation of a plant.[36]

The tonnage of these contracts depended on expectations about prices. In January of 1896, many observers predicted that prices had bottomed out. This turned out to be false; prices fell almost $2 more very soon. Regardless, the Bessemer cast-iron pipe plant took delivery of 18,000 tons at prevailing prices that month, a decision which the trade press attributed to these expectations.[37] The next week, the "various interests at Anniston" also bought a large order on the belief that prices could go no lower.[38] The "various interests" turned out to be "one Pipe concern."[39] The total amount was purchased in three lots by the Anniston plant from three separate furnaces in Birmingham. For all six plants in the Associated Pipe Works cartel, the main sources of supply were the plants located in northern Alabama, primarily Birmingham. The foundries at Louisville, for example, got about 95 percent of their supplies from the southern pig-iron producers.[40]

E. The Two Mergers in Cast-iron Pipe and the Merger Wave

The defendants won their first trial on charges that they had violated the Sherman Act. This decision was appealed to the Court of Appeals for the Sixth Circuit, which reversed it. The opinion written by Judge Taft held that the attempts by the defendants to establish the reasonableness of the prices they agreed to charge was not at issue;[41] rather, the fact that they had agreed on prices, regardless of how high or low they may have been, was a violation and indicated intent to monopolize. This decision was appealed, but the Supreme Court affirmed Taft's decision in 1899.[42]

In May of 1898, however, four of the six defendants merged. In the month following the initial consolidation, *Iron Age* reported that an attempt was also under way to consolidate all the shops "west of the Alleghanies, north of the Ohio and east of the Rocky Mountains."[43] The following February it was reported that "no marked progress has been made in the effort to consolidate the Cast Iron Pipe business. The options on some of the plants expire on February 15, while in the case of some concerns no options have been secured."[44] This issue also predicted better prices and expanded business for the upcoming season. A week later *Iron Age* reported that the consolidation had taken in more members.[45] At this point USCIP&F consisted of all six defendants and five outside firms.[46]

One issue was clearly on people's minds at this point: whether there would be rivalry between the consolidation and the remaining independent firms.

> As yet no opportunities have presented themselves to test the attitude of the consolidation of [toward?] the outside interests in the matter of competition for business nor will the Brooklyn order for about 3,000 tons, to be let tomorrow, throw any light on the situation because the contractors will do the bidding.[47]

The situation in the cast-iron pipe industry at this point was analyzed in early April by P. D. Wanner in an address to the Foundrymen's Association.[48] Wanner chronicled the history of the industry, noting that although business had been good in the 1880s, the boom had resulted in overexpansion. He also recalled that in 1879 producers had responded to poor business conditions by attempting to form a pool, but that this attempt had failed because one firm had refused to take part. Pressing his point, he added that a similar effort in 1892 had failed because a few concerns had opposed the effort or failed to join.

Considering this record of plans gone awry, Wanner welcomed the move to consolidation. Since cast-iron pipe was expensive to transport, he thought it sufficient that there be only regional consolidations. What the aim of such mergers would be was clear to Wanner:

> This [consolidation] and all governments were created and upheld by necessity. It will be so with both all trade or manufacturing interests in the future. It has been truly said that business is war, and to make it a success warlike methods will have to be restored [sic] to, and success will be on the side of those who have the largest guns or aggregation of capital; in other words, a combination of the greater part of the trade will be able to dictate prices and a line of behavior to those outside, or crush them. It is no longer the survival of the fittest, but of which can hold out best and longest. [Iron Age, April 13, 1899, p. 8]

The next report of activity occurs one month later, when it was noted that "efforts are being made to reach an agreement with the outside shops in the East."[49] Comments on these efforts unfortunately remained sparse. During the same period the price of pig iron moved up to very high levels and business slacked off as a result. One southern town even considered using wooden pipes, which was the standard practice in some parts of the West.[50] In early 1900 it was reported that "there are indications of a struggle between the Eastern independent shops and the consolidation."[51] Business for the midwestern and southern shops picked up over the next few months, but competition between this group and the eastern shops was considered to be sharp. By June of 1900 business was so bad that at least six foundries in the Northeast closed down in the middle of what was normally the peak season.[52]

Two months later competition was still keen between USCIP&F and the independents, and it was reported that "invasion of territory is general. Eastern shops have taken good orders in the Central West and in the Northwest. The result is that the market is very irregular."[53] Data on prices supporting the view that this was a period of unusually low pipe prices, taking into account the price of iron, are presented in the next section.

Perhaps only by coincidence, the firms in a related industry, cast iron *soil* pipe manufacture, were among those firms that merged in 1899. Soil pipe is used to carry off waste or to conduct water not under pressure. Although it does not have to meet the same standards as water pressure pipe, it was manufactured the same way. In July of 1899 the firms of this industry merged and formed the Central Foundry Company. The expectation was that the promoters "would have a free and undisputed field in which they could control the market for Cast Iron Soil Pipe and Fittings. . . . It was explained that with the control of all the plants new prices would be announced and new regulations as regards shipments and freight allowances would be made, which would leave considerable profit to the interested parties."[54] New firms entered almost immediately, however. The response of Central Foundry was not to lower prices, but rather to maintain its original prices and to refuse to sell to jobbers who did not buy all their soil pipe from it. This policy failed, and the new firms were soon able to provide complete service to the jobbers. The response of the Central Foundry Company at this late point was warfare; it now reduced its prices with the idea, it was claimed, of driving the newcomers out of the business. Whether this was in fact the aim is open to question; in any case, the result was that in December of 1900 the consolidated firm and its new rivals formed a pool.

The details of the soil pipe agreement were remarkably similar to those in the case of water pipe. A percentage of receipts would be paid into a pool, and the pool was to be divided among the firms. The plants were located primarily in Alabama, the New York-Philadelphia area, and Indiana and Ohio, much as in the case of water pipe. All firms in the country were party to the agreement. We see here, then, a simultaneous merger in a closely related industry; a similar struggle between the major firm and the rest of the industry; and, in addition, the resolution of this struggle by means of a cartel arrangement. This agreement was made more than a year after *Addyston* reached the Supreme Court, and yet was publicized in the trade press.[55]

F. New Construction

Among the curious acquisitions of the cast-iron pressure pipe consolidation at this point were the small plant at West Superior, Wisconsin, and an idle unit located at Metropolis, Illinois. The plant in Illinois was built at the very end of the water pipe boom in the 1880s and was closed shortly afterwards. According to one source [Noble (35)], it was bought by the consolidation in 1899 but never operated. Exactly why this was done is unclear. The firm also announced in early 1899 that it was going to build a new plant at Bessemer, Alabama, but it appears that this plant was never built.[56] H. C. Frick, who had consolidated nearly all the coke ovens near Connellsville, Pennsylvania, at that time the country's major coke-producing area, had in June of 1898 announced plans to build a plant in Chicago.[57] These plans were also apparently never carried out.

Two operations were started up in 1900, however. One of these was erected in Massillon, Ohio. The other, more important, plant was constructed by J. K. Dimmick at Birmingham, Alabama. Dimmick had been owner of the Anniston plant and was one of the chief architects of the cartel. In 1898 he assumed the position of general manager with U.S. Cast Iron Pipe and Foundry before quitting to start his own firm. Several other operations were established in the next few years. A new plant was built at Lynchburg, Virginia, in 1902, and a soil pipe plant built in 1899 at Bessemer was converted to production of pressure pipe in 1903 [Noble (35), pp. 79–82].

The acquisition by USCIP&F of an idle plant smacks of capacity restriction, but other explanations are possible. For example, the plant may have been bought for its equipment. The particular circumstances also raise the possibility that the purchase was a mistake. The consolidation, as did H. C. Frick, may have thought that industry capacity should be expanded in Illinois, but these plants could have been rendered unprofitable, either by the establishment of new producers elsewhere or perhaps by some more general economic turn of events such as changes in pig-iron prices across regions. In particular, the sharp rise in iron prices in 1899 and 1900, which is generally attributed to the depletion of the Mesabi range in Minnesota, would naturally result in a tendency to favor southern locations.

It is also noteworthy that of the original twelve plants owned by USCIP&F in 1899, ten were still in operation in 1910, but only six by 1915. During this time the firm had acquired only one new plant, that of J. K. Dimmick, its former general manager who had set up his own firm in 1900. While complete figures on capacity are not available, it would appear that USCIP&F's share declined over this period. It is not clear, however, to what we should attribute this decline, since the boom of 1905 resulted in a radical restructuring and expansion of the industry. Whatever the classical monopoly gains to USCIP&F might have been before this time, they were surely brought to a negligible level in 1905. This makes it unlikely that the erosion of market share was due to gradual entry generated by an existing monopoly.

Who constructed and operated the new plants? For the most part it seems to have been the foremen, clerical workers, and managers of existing firms. The careers of two of these people are summarized here. In May of 1906 the American Cast Iron Pipe Company began operations at its newly constructed plant. This firm was founded by Charlotte Blair and her brother. Miss Blair had started in the cast-iron pipe business as a stenographer with the Radford Pipe Co. of Virginia. She later worked at the Anniston Works while it was owned by J. K. Dimmick and became the first Alabama woman to serve on the directorate of a corporation. The plant's manager, Edwin Linthicum, began with Dimmick as Anniston's telegrapher, and rose by rapid steps to become that plant's manager in 1898. In 1905 he took up his position with the newly formed American Cast Iron Pipe Company, from which he resigned in 1908. In 1913, when business began to pick up again, he organized the National Cast Iron Pipe Company and served as its vice-president and general manager. The lesson in this brief history of two careers is that it was an easy matter to find qualified managerial personnel for industry expansion.[58]

G. Prices and Cutthroat Competition

The major factor influencing the price of cast-iron pipe was the price of pig iron. By subtracting one from the other we obtain a gross margin, which could in principle be used to determine whether firms were charging more than their costs. This is, of course, not the same thing as determining whether they fixed prices. Unfortunately, the one long series we have for prices at a single location is not for the South but rather for the Delaware Valley in the East. Although trade reports suggest that cartel activity in other areas had an effect in the East, we would not be on safe ground if we attempted to find evidence of it in an overly generous margin near Philadelphia. As the history of the cast-iron pipe cartel suggests, collusion in the South and Midwest could very well mean *lower* prices in the East.[59] Our fragmentary evidence from the court documents indicates that the cartel did charge high prices in certain instances, but that buyers could and often did seek more favorable terms. The general impression is that prices may have been somewhat above average costs in some cases but rarely by more than one or two dollars per ton, and that alert buyers (generally the private buyers) were likely to do better than those who placed their faith in competition. In any event, it should be clear that a

finding that high prices were charged by the cartel would not undermine
the central proposition that collusion of some sort was necessary. On the
other hand, the finding that prices were too low to cover even short-run
costs indicates a serious failure of competition and might provide a justification for collusion. So, while we cannot provide a complete account
of the returns in this market, a single price series can be used to answer
the question of whether there was cutthroat competition in at least some
areas. For our purposes cutthroat competition will be taken to mean pricing at marginal cost in an industry where marginal cost-pricing will not
sustain its operation.

Figure 4 presents the price of pig iron and the price of pipe from which
our gross margin is calculated. The longer price-of-pipe series represents
prices at the Delaware River foundries in New Jersey and eastern Pennsylvania. These prices are usually greater than the prices (at the factory
gate) quoted on large municipal contracts, but are less than the spot prices
for small orders. Monthly data from which this series is compiled are
available beginning with 1902, and these monthly figures (e.g., $23.25,
$25.00, $25.00, $24.75, for the first four months of 1902) suggest that the
basing point system or some other quotation method was used for part
of this period. Actual delivered prices on municipal contracts tend to be
consistent with this series, however. Although the contract prices are
about $2 to $4 higher, this is easily explained by the freight rates.

Two pig-iron series are used in Figure 4 because the price of gray pig
iron at Philadelphia is available only from January 1900. We see, however,
that the figures for Southern No. 2 foundry at Cincinnati closely match
this series, being only slightly higher in some years and slightly lower in
others. Since the Cincinnati series has more variability it might in fact be
a better measure of transactions prices, although other explanations are
possible. On average, however, these figures turn out to be very accurate.
We know this because we can check them against USCIP&F's own ledger
for June 1905 to May 1906. The average cost of iron for these twelve
months for the Burlington, New Jersey, plant was $14.51; Philadelphia
gray forge for those same twelve months had an average price of $14:32
per net ton. Similarly, the Addyston plant paid $14.26 per ton for its pig
iron, and Cincinnati No. 2 foundry iron had an average price of $14.10
per net ton for that period.[60]

The calculations of the gross margin per ton of 2,000 pounds are presented in Table 7 using both current dollars and 1906 dollars. The most
striking feature of these figures is that the difference between the price
of pipe and the price of pig iron hovered roughly between $9 and $13,
during good times and bad. There is one exception, however, at the end
of the 1890s. In 1899 the margin was only half of what it was in better

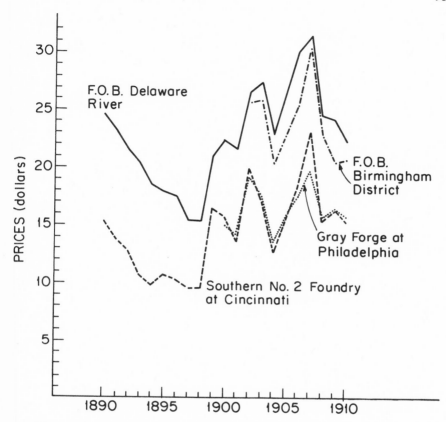

Figure 4. F.O.B. Prices of Cast-iron Pipe, Delaware River and
Birmingham, and the Price of Pig Iron, 1890–1916

Note: All figures are averages of monthly data.

Sources: Southern No. 2 Foundry Pig Iron at Cincinnati; *Iron Age,* March 30, 1912, p. 1351. Gray forge
at Philadelphia; *Iron Age,* January 2, 1913, p. 49. F.O.B. Delaware and Birmingham pipe prices;
United States Pipe & Foundry Co., *Price History & Price Index of Cast Iron Pipe* (no date).

periods. How is this explained? Recall that industry reports characterized
the end of 1899 as a period of struggle between the consolidation and the
rest of the industry.

What constitutes a remunerative gross margin? Our detailed plant-cost
figures in Table 1 for 1905–06, a relatively good period, indicate that labor,
fuel, and repair and replacement costs (together called "direct and indirect" expense and constituting out-of-pocket or "particular" expenses
only) amounted to between $6 and $8 for large northern plants. Another
$5 to $7 was left in most years to provide a return to capital, and to cover

Table 7. Gross Margin for F.O.B. Delaware River Prices per Ton of 2000 Pounds

	Gross Margin in Current Dollars		Gross Margin in 1906 Dollars	
Year	Using Cincinnati Iron Prices	Using Philadelphia Iron Prices	Using Cincinnati Iron Prices	Using Philadelphia Iron Prices
1890	11.16		12.36	
1891	10.74		11.93	
1892	10.05		11.96	
1893	11.10		12.92	
1894	9.60		12.44	
1895	8.25		10.48	
1896	8.45		11.31	
1897	7.07		9.43	
1898	7.03		9.00	
1899	6.37		7.58	
1900	8.45	8.94	9.36	9.90
1901	9.48	8.87	10.64	9.96
1902	8.77	9.18	9.23	9.66
1903	12.31	11.97	12.83	12.48
1904	11.55	10.56	12.00	10.97
1905	12.64	12.46	13.05	12.86
1906	13.73	14.46	13.73	14.46
1907	10.89	13.92	10.37	13.26
1908	10.81	10.56	10.67	10.43
1909	9.68	9.64	8.88	8.84
1910	9.45	8.95	8.31	7.87

Note: The wholesale price index is used to obtain the margins in terms of 1906 dollars.
Sources: Same as Figure 4.

selling expense and inventory cost. But in the lean years, 1897 to 1900, say, the gross margin was not very far above the figures for direct and indirect expense, leaving very little for the other items mentioned.

Were the prices equal to marginal cost? Indirect and direct expense probably contained some fixed element so that their average values would not reflect their contribution to marginal costs. However, some other items that also constitute a marginal expense are not included in the measures of direct and indirect cost. What this means is that estimates of marginal cost derived from direct cost items capture only part of marginal cost. These estimates, derived from plant cost data, range from $2.50 to $7.00 per ton, with a fairly solid tendency for the higher figures to be associated with the smaller plants.[61] For some plants, then, it seems that prices were at marginal cost.

These low prices, as well as the events in the cast-iron soil pipe industry described above, are by themselves consistent with at least three explanations, although in general I think they stem from a difference of opinion on the part of producers. First, such conditions suggest short-sighted, "destructive" competition that comes from the failure of at least one player to realize that this policy is inconsistent with the long-term welfare of all the participants in the market. In short, it is what the naïve theory of competition requires competitors to do. Clearly, the market structure and outlook that would promote this situation are unlikely to endure very long. Second, pricing to marginal cost when such prices will not allow firms to recover costs may be an instance of predation, that is, a deliberate attempt to drive out competitors by inflicting losses on them. The difference of opinion here is clear. If there were no difference, the potential victim would clear out early and cut his losses short. Third, such pricing tactics may represent attempts to discipline competitors, where again, the mere threat of effective discipline would be enough if the prospective students required no lessons. The last two alternatives are both instances in which one or more members to an agreement find that the gains from breaking faith are greater than the gains from observing the agreement, based, naturally, on what they believe to be true. Unfortunately, I see no way of distinguishing these three cases by outward appearances. A decisive judgment in any particular case would require a knowledge of the "objective" conditions, as well as a knowledge of what various players believe to be true. Nor can we judge by results. A struggle that results in reconciliation is consistent with a failed policy of predation, as well as a successful disciplinary action. A bankrupt victim could imply successful predation or a slow-to-learn student.

H. Performance of USCIP&F

The consolidated firm turned in only a mediocre performance during the first fifteen years of its existence. United States Cast Iron Pipe and Foundry made three successive quarterly dividend payments on preferred stock beginning December 1899, but passed payment in September of 1900. Payment on preferred stock was resumed in 1902. Later that decade, between 1904 and 1908, the stock's value rose and payment of dividends on common stock was made in 1905, 1906, and 1907. In fact, the firm surprised some observers by maintaining its dividends (on preferred stock) during the 1903–04 slump at a time when firms in related industries were doing poorly.[62] It was also noted that the 8 percent payment on preferred stock in 1905 was the highest allowed by USCIP&F's charter. But the firm's fall from this position was fairly rapid, as Figure 5 shows. Certainly, when judged by the performance of an index of stocks of industrial firms, the consolidation's success, relative to its position in 1902, was fleeting. By 1910 its value had dropped to the point where one would

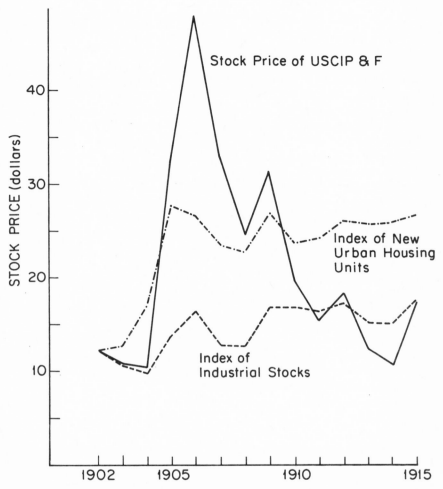

Figure 5.   Common Stock of USCIP&F and Index of Industrial Stocks
Sources: National Industrial Conference Board, *Mergers in Industry* (1929), p. 62; *United States Historical Statistics, Colonial Times to 1970,* Series X496, p. 1004, and Series N162, p. 640.

have done no better by investing in USCIP&F in 1902 than by investing
in the basket of industrial stocks. Other indications of the firm's financial
health are consistent with this picture. In 1915, for example, its bonds
had Aa ratings and its preferred and common stock were rated Caa and
D.[63] Certainly the merger seems not to have resulted in a successful long-
term monopoly, if that indeed was its aim. The extraordinary record of
entry and geographical movement would have made long-term monopoly
unlikely.

To what should we attribute the remarkable rise in the value of USCIP&F stock following 1904? The value of the stock in 1902 should, of course, incorporate any expected monopoly gain. If stock prices do reflect the value of expected future earnings, deviations of the price of the stock from the market average might reflect new views about whether the firm would reap a large or small part of any prospective monopoly gains. The value of the firm did rise relative to the industrial stock index during the period of 1904–06. As it happens, four new plants, three of them in Alabama, were constructed in 1905, suggesting that rents to industry capacity during a business boom and not monopoly determined changes in the value of USCIP&F stock. New competitors would mean declining, not rising, monopoly returns. This explanation gains support from the data on new urban housing, which are also included in Figure 5. Notice the remarkable burst in this series in 1904 and 1905. This measure provides a good indication of the state of economy-wide investment in urban housing-related capital and, what is more, probably gives a good idea of the demand for water pipe during this period. Once demand reached its new higher level, a revision of expectations could easily have caused the drop in value. For the years 1898 to 1902 we have only to look at the gross margin figures in Table 7 to see that the situation was even worse than in the years 1902 to 1910, when USCIP&F's stock price managed only to stay even with the market average. The stock price figures then, say little on the question of monopoly or competition, but do reveal the industry's sensitivity to demand conditions.

This sensitivity showed itself most strongly in the months of October through March during the years 1902 to 1908. Table 8 summarizes the evidence on yearly highs and lows for common and preferred stock, and indicates that fully 12 out of 28 highs or lows (26 if we discard the lows at the stocks' introduction to the exchange) occurred in the months of December and January. Why was this? These were the months during which cities made their plans for expansion in the coming year, and as commitments were made the value of the stock price changed to reflect this news; that is, movements were most likely during these months. Note that one alternative explanation cannot be supported by the data. It might be argued that a rising price level over this period or other trend-related factors caused the stock price to peak systematically at the end of the year and bottom out at the beginning. It happens, however, that the first and last three months each have roughly equal numbers of highs and lows. Might it be possible that this regularity will show itself in other similar data?

While we can satisfy our curiosity about prices, the behavior of stock values, and industry entry and structure, any regularities we observe are not consequential for our hypothesis, which addresses itself to a more

Table 8. Frequency of Yearly Highs and Lows of Common and
Preferred Stock by Month, USCIP&F, 1902–1908

Month	Preferred		Common		Total Yearly Highs and Lows
	Highs	*Lows*	*Highs*	*Lows*	
January	2	2	2	1	7
February	1				1
March		1	1	1	3
April	1				1
May*		1(0)		3(2)	4(2)
June					0
July					0
August	1				1
September	1			1	2
October		1	1	1	3
November		1			1
December	1	1	3		5

* A bias is introduced for May because these shares were introduced to the stock exchange in May 1902
and had their yearly lows then. Corrected figures are in parentheses.
Source: Gibson's Manual, p. 333.

fundamental question. Over the long term, looking at good times and bad,
this industry doesn't seem to have offered extraordinary profitability. It
is true that there is a record of collusion, not only among the southern
firms, but also in the East. In addition, after the consolidations of 1898
and 1899 this industry appears to have been one of the many that adopted
a basing point system, with Birmingham and the Delaware River foundries
serving as the two basing points. How do we reconcile the evidence of
easy entry and substantial turnover of firms with the evidence of collusion? Our explanation is that the two strands of evidence are not incompatible under plausible cost conditions. Even if collusion is demonstrated,
it will not necessarily be true that the primary motivation for this collusion
is the desire for classical monopoly gains.[64]

III. MARGINAL COST-PRICING
AND THE AIMS OF COLLUSION

Section I presented cost data based on accounting records which indicated
that plant costs contained a significant element that was unrelated to current output and that marginal cost was usually less than average cost,
even in a very good year. That this may be optimal bears some emphasis.
However, these conditions can result in situations in which marginal cost-
pricing fails to cover costs, even all short-run costs, and in which periods

of intense competition, such as those that occurred in this industry, turn out to have damaging consequences.

Three other sources substantiate the view that marginal costs were below average costs; the record of f.o.b. prices for work done outside of pay territory, f.o.b. prices net of "bonus" payments for work destined for the Midwest, and accounts of industry conditions that appear in *Iron Age*. This section examines this evidence in conjunction with an analysis of the purpose of collusion and merger in this industry. Finally, we turn our attention to an analysis of the costs and benefits implied by different solutions to the problem of market instability.

A. Marginal Costs and the Bonuses

It turns out that the prices received by members of the cartel do sometimes provide information about marginal costs. To see why this is so we must first summarize some aspects of the cartel agreement. Recall that after December of 1895, the price on any order placed with the firms outside certain reserved cities but in pay territory (areas to the south of Virginia and west of Pennsylvania) was fixed by a committee representing the six producers. The work went to the member who bid highest in an internal auction. The difference, or "bonus," was placed in a fund that was divided among the six firms on the basis of plant capacity. Although the price to buyers was not the marginal cost, in the course of the bidding the net price to the firm would be driven down to near that value. The net price was not exactly equal to marginal cost since a firm could expect to get back a fraction of the bonus (the precise amount depending on cumulative cartel tonnage), provided that the cumulative tonnage had not reached 220,000. On the other hand, all work outside of pay territory had to net *at least* marginal cost since it did not result in a bonus payment.

In passing it may be noted how nicely this system provides support for the hypothesis that firms could not cover all costs with marginal cost-pricing. The possibility of too much competition arises when certain costs are primarily associated with a plant's capacity and not with its level of output. Both kinds of cost must be covered, and the bonus fund arrangement provided assurance that there would be some contribution to fixed costs. Moreover, not only was price-cutting prohibited, but competition among the firms was channeled in a way that allowed those firms wanting work the most the opportunity to get it. While a simple scheme of geographic division could have established substantially the same protection against cutthroat competition, it would also have led to inefficiencies since the demand across areas is not perfectly correlated. Interestingly, the system by which the cities awarded contracts, namely, sealed bidding, also influenced the form of the agreement. William Vickrey (57) has shown that a sealed bid auction is less likely to result in optimal allocations in a market than a standard auction. The cartel's procedure removed this source of inefficiency.

Table 9 presents calculations of the net price to southern firms for pipe contracts recorded in the cartel minutes of February 14, 1896. This price represents delivered price less freight and bonus. It cannot be determined from the minutes of the meeting which shops filled these orders, but this is of no great importance. First, most of the orders were for buyers in Chicago or St. Louis, and the freight rates from the shops would not have differed by more than a dollar or two. As we saw, freight costs per mile decreased with distance. Second, the price of pig iron at Louisville and Cincinnati, where the two northernmost shops were located, was governed by the price of pig iron prevailing in Birmingham, Alabama, the difference being the freight rate for pig iron between the two points. The southern shops did often fill orders to the north and west of Louisville and Cincinnati, and the use of the Chattanooga freight rates probably introduces no sizable error even if the orders were filled by the two Ohio River plants. Using the average value, we have an estimate of the net gate price, our first measure of marginal cost, of $13.28 for February 1896.

We gain confidence in this estimate by looking at the calculations made by the Chattanooga firm on the net gate price it and the nearby South

Table 9. Estimates of Net Price to the Southern Shops, Various Destinations, February 1896

Buyer	Delivered Price	Bonus	Amount (tons)	Pipe Diameter	Freight[a]	Net Price
Chicago Gas Co.	$22.00	$5.00	7,000	6"–8"	$3.60	$13.40
Chicago Gas Co.	21.50	5.00	10,000	"larger"	3.60	12.90
Calumet Gas Co.	23.50	5.00 ⎫		4"	3.60	14.90
Calumet Gas Co.	22.50	5.00 ⎬	1,500	6"–8"	3.60	13.90
Calumet Gas Co.	21.50	5.00 ⎭		"larger"	3.60	12.90
Louisville Water Co.	22.50*	6.50	NA	4"–8"	2.25	13.40
LaClede Gas (St. Louis)	25.00**	5.65 ⎫		4"	3.25	15.10
LaClede Gas (St. Louis)	24.00**	5.65 ⎬	3,248	6"–12"	3.25	14.10
LaClede Gas (St. Louis)	22.75**	5.65 ⎭		16"–20"	3.25	12.80
St. Louis Water	24.00#	6.50	2,800	3"–12"	3.25	13.85
CRL&PRR (Chicago)	22.35	7.50	##	NA	3.60	11.25
CB&Q (Chicago)	22.35	7.50	##	NA	3.60	10.95
Indianapolis Water Co.	20.70	4.20	1,000	NA	3.25	13.25
					Mean =	$13.28

[a] Freight rates for pig iron from Chattanooga, *Iron Age*, May 18, 1893, p. 1130.
* Drayage of 35 cents included.
** Drayage of $1.00. This contract was taken by the Bessemer, Alabama shop.
# Drayage of 40 cents included.
Indicates "year's supply."
Source: Transcript of Record, p. 75. All figures are for February 1896 deliveries.

Table 10. Estimates of Net Price at Shop for Orders Taken by Chattanooga and South Pittsburg, March–April 1896

Destination of Order	Net Price at Shop
Peabody, Massachusetts	$13.75
Lockhaven, Pennsylvania	13.45
Clifton Springs, New York	12.57
Wytheville, Virginia	13.50
Troy, New York	14.00
Allegheny, Pennsylvania	13.25
Syracuse, New York	13.50
Malden, Massachusetts	14.40
	Mean = $13.55

Source: Transcript of Record, pp. 88–89.

Pittsburg plant received, which appear in Table 10. These were calculations of net price on orders going to free territory, areas in which the pricing agreement did not apply and which were excluded from the bonus scheme. The average for these figures was $13.55, or 27 cents higher than our estimate of marginal cost for work in pay territory for orders taken one and two months earlier. Both of these estimates are for early 1896 and for substantial orders.

We have another, independent estimate of marginal costs for this period. Since the estimates from Tables 9 and 10 are for the southern shops, it makes sense to attempt a comparison of these estimates with estimates from the three southern plants for which we have data covering June 1905 to May 1906. These are presented for the Anniston, Bessemer, and Chattanooga plants in Table 11, and, it should be emphasized, apply to the very good conditions prevailing in 1905–06, and not to the much poorer conditions of 1896. They are also calculated for direct (mainly labor and fuel) costs only and so are likely to exclude some components of marginal cost. Direct costs may also contain some fixed costs, and, in fact, average direct cost is greater than marginal direct cost, indicating that this was the case. Finally, to make our estimates here comparable to the ones in Tables 9 and 10, we also need to add the cost of gray forge iron. The following prices were quoted for Birmingham, Alabama, in *Iron Age* at the indicated dates:

$9.75 --------------------------- January 2, 1896
$8.00 --------------------------- February 6, 1896
$7.50 --------------------------- March 5, 1896
$6.50–6.75 ------------------- April 2, 1896

Since Birmingham was the center of the southern iron trade, these prices were probably a little below those prevailing for the three plants in Table

Table 11. Estimates of Average and Marginal Costs in 1896 for the Three Southern Plants Based on 1905–1906 Data

	(1)	(2)	(3)	(4)	(5)	(6)	(7)
		Costs in 1905–1906				Estimates for 1896	
	Maximum Observed Monthly Output	Average Direct Cost	Average Direct and Indirect Cost	Estimate of Marginal Direct Cost	Range of Iron Costs, Feb. through April	Estimated Range of Average Costs, Early 1896 (3) + (5)	Estimated Range of Marginal Costs, Early 1896 (4) + (5)
Anniston	4,269	5.92	7.51	4.44	6.50–8.00	14.01–15.51	10.94–12.44
Bessemer	5,316	5.49	7.23	4.17	6.50–8.00	13.73–15.23	10.67–12.17
Chattanooga	3,740	5.36	6.42	4.40	6.50–8.00	12.92–14.42	10.90–12.40

Note: It should be emphasized that these figures exclude capital, inventory, and sales expense.

Source: Computed from the Ledger of USCIP&F. Estimates of marginal cost are from Bittlingmayer [(5) p. 225] and the range of iron costs are from *Iron Age* (see text).

11. Since we have been looking at the period from February through April, we will take $6.50 to $8.00 as the range of iron prices in early 1896. We see then that the sum of average direct, indirect, and iron costs amounted to between $12.92 and $15.51 for the southern plants.[65] Note, however, that this neglects capital expense, inventory costs, and—because these figures are based on plant data for the merged firm—selling expense averages about 20 cents per ton. Since each of these probably contains more than the usual proportion of fixed costs, this makes the likely divergence between average total and marginal total costs even greater than the $2 to $3 suggested by the difference between average and marginal direct costs.

The most important conclusion to come from these results, however, is that the southern shops were taking work at distant points in 1896 for a net price less than the sum of direct, indirect, and iron costs. This price seems not to have been as low as our estimate of marginal cost (roughly $10.50 to $12.50), but we should not have expected it to be that low. First of all, if marginal cost *declines* with output (and there are good reasons for thinking that it does up to a point), the lower output rates of 1896 would imply higher marginal costs than in 1906. Second, this work at distant points was lucrative only if it could be taken at prices *above* marginal cost. And finally, the estimates do neglect some marginal expenses that are difficult to isolate, as in the case of the data series on sales expense, indirect cost, and so on. We are left to conclude that $11 to $13 is not an implausible estimate for marginal cost, but that average cost in early 1896, once all costs are taken into account, easily ran to $17, allowing another $2 to $3 per ton above the particular expenses in column 6 of Table 11 to cover capital, inventory, and sales expense.[66]

Contrast this estimate with that of Judge Taft, who concluded that "the cost of producing pipe at Chattanooga, *together with a reasonable profit,* did not exceed $15 a ton. It could have been delivered at Atlanta at $17 to $18 a ton" [*Addyston*, 85 Fed. at 293; emphasis added]. His figures in turn appear to be based on the calculations by the Chattanooga foundry on which Table 11 is based. In short, he argued that if the firms would willingly take orders at $12.57 to $14.40 per ton, then their costs, including a return to capital, were roughly $15, probably less. Yet we see that there are good reasons for suspecting, on the basis of independent evidence— namely, actual cost data from the same plants—that these figures were less than average cost, and perhaps equal only to marginal cost.

Substantially the same conclusion was reached by the business manager of the Chattanooga works, who wrote the following on January 2, 1896:

We find there was sold and shipped into pay territory from January 1, 1895, to date, including the 40,000 tons of old business that did not pay a bonus, about 188,000 tons, and we think a very conservative estimate of shipments into this territory will amount to fully 200,000 this year, more than that, probably overrun 240,000 tons from the fact that Chicago and several other places that annually use large quantities of pipe were not in the market last year, or last season, from the fact that they were out of funds. On the basis given above, if demand should reach 220,000 tons, which would give us our entire 40,000 tons [share of the bonus], provided we did no business, then the association would pay us the average "bonus" which might be from $3.50 to $5.00 on our 40,000. If we cannot secure business in "pay territory" at paying prices, we will be able to dispose of our output in "free territory," and of course make some profit on that. [*Record* at 94]

What this means in terms of the proposed explanation is quite clear. First, 1896 was expected to be a relatively good year with firms operating not too far below full capacity. Since U.S. capacity was roughly 600,000 tons per year in the early 1890s,[67] a predicted 220,000 tons in pay territory to be provided by the defendants represents 37 percent of that total. This amount excludes work that six took outside pay territory. At least Chattanooga, and perhaps others as well, expected to take a good portion of their work in free territory and in work destined for Latin America. Since the six had at most 57 percent of U.S. capacity according to daily melting capacity figures (Table 3), we see that even in 1896 firms expected to operate substantially above 65 percent of full capacity, how much above depending on how much "outside" work they took. Second, even at such fairly high rates of capacity utilization, the Chattanooga works thought that the net prices at which firms were taking work, which we take as upper bounds on marginal cost, were so low that it was more profitable to take work outside pay territory and simply collect its share of the bonus.

B. Some Qualitative Evidence on Costs and Prices

The trade reports of this period can also provide some information about the nature of plant costs. First, it was clear that plants could be shut down and often were. For example, during the first week of July of 1895, perhaps as a result of the July 4th holiday, the Howard-Harrison Pipe Works at Bessemer were shut down for a week and then reopened.[68] Similarly, this firm closed down before the election of 1896. The candidates were William Jennings Bryan and William McKinley, and there was a general slackening of economic activity before the election, attributed in some quarters to an excess of free silver speeches. But once the election was decided in McKinley's favor, business picked up. "At Bessemer the Howard-Har-

rison Pipe Works lighted the fires for resumption of business as soon as
the election was announced, with prospects of immediate business."[69]
These were, as these passages suggest, complete shutdowns; plants did
not vary their output over the whole conceivable range between zero and
"maximum" output, but closed rather than trundle along at one-quarter
speed.

Additional insight concerning the nature of plant costs comes from the
following remarks on the Bessemer plant.

> A visit to the Howard-Harrison Pipe Works, at Bessemer, disclosed
> the fact that they were steadily occupied and hustling for all the
> desirable contracts in sight. It takes a power of work to keep their
> machinery moving, and neither state lines nor the limits of country
> nor distance nor language bars them from getting contracts wherever
> Iron Pipe is needed. They have been lately doing a fine business
> with Mexico, which is reported as very satisfactory in every re-
> spect.[70]

Passages such as these suggest high fixed avoidable costs. These fixed
costs very likely arose from the nature of foundry operations. It is un-
economical to run drying ovens and cupolas at only a fraction of their
designed capacities. At the same time, a substantial portion of their variable cost was quite variable indeed. Workers were laid off for only a few
days before being called back,[71] although it is still possible that some
economies were possible here from "running a full complement of men."

What consequence did these economies of operation have? Over a substantial range of output, marginal cost-pricing will not cover all costs, not
even all short-run costs necessarily. We presented evidence earlier, however, that indicates that prices could drop to this level temporarily. Other
evidence on this subject is available from descriptions of conditions in
the industry. In February of 1892, for example, prices reached a very low
level:

> Excessive competition has reduced prices in this branch of trade
> until it is difficult to see how manufacturers are able to recoup them-
> selves for the mere cost of materials they use and the labor they
> employ.[72]

This article mentions a contract for Minneapolis in which 2,500 tons of
pipe were priced at $22.47, delivered. Supposing that one of the southern
works took it, this contract netted about $17.33 at the shop. This was
only a little more than one year after the census of 1890, when the total

noncapital cost was a little over $20 per ton in all regions [see U.S. Census (55)].

Further evidence of the nature of cost curves can be found in the following description of the industry published in *Iron Age* in early 1896:

> The Pipe trade exhibits the extraordinary condition of a heavy present and prospective tonnage coupled with prices which are unprecedentedly low in some instances. . . . With Pig Iron close to the low notch it will not be long before the most eager shops fill up and an end is put to this cutthroat selling.[73]

Cutthroat selling was apparently not ended, and in June it was reported that eastern shops were again trying to form a pool[74] at the same time that (as we now know) the southern shops were successfully operating one. The southern shops were making bids in the Northeast that left them with $12.15 per gross ton ($13.61 per net ton) at the shop.[75] "Since it is generally estimated that the cost is somewhere between $6 and $6.50 over the cost of Pig Iron, some very cheap metal must be available to Southern melters" [*id.*].

By the next issue, however, it was realized that these bids did not allow the shops to cover full costs and that costs were being covered by other means.

> The only contract closed in this vicinity [New York] is one for 650 tons for Belmont, N.Y. at $19.90 per net ton. It was taken by a Southern shop. It has been noted lately that Western works are making low bids in Eastern territory. The Western works have an understanding in their own territory and are supposed to be eager to increase their tonnage from outside sources.[76]

The main points in these descriptions spanning the years 1892 to 1896 are therefore entirely consistent with the proposed explanation. The cast-iron pipe industry was marked by a type of production in which a large portion of costs was not related to the level at which plants were operated. In addition, average cost rose quite sharply after the point of minimum average cost was reached. This is the implication of the observation above that plants were operating *near* full capacity, yet prices had not stiffened. Repeatedly, also, there is mention that the full costs of production were not being covered.

C. The Puzzling Affidavits

An intriguing feature of the *Transcript of Record* for *Addyston* is that numerous buyers of pipe located in pay territory, 57 in all, submitted affidavits on behalf of the defendants. These adhered, with some variation, to a standard formula:

> I am a citizen of Indiana, and the vice-president of the Indianapolis Water Company, . . . and as such it was my business, in the early part of 1896, to contract for and purchase a large quantity of cast-iron water pipe . . .
>
> Affiant further states that on account of his position as vice-president, he became familiar with the current prices of cast-iron pipe and knew the market value thereof; that the contract price with Addyston Pipe & Steel Company was reasonable and satisfactory to the Indianapolis Water Company, and that there has been no objection raised thereto. [*Record* at 105–106]

Judge Taft, in his opinion, hinted darkly that some conspiracy was at work to produce these affidavits. "A great many affidavits of purchasers of pipe in pay territory, *all drawn by the same hand or from the same model,* are produced, in which the affiants say that, in their opinion, the prices at which pipe has been sold by defendants have been reasonable" [*Addyston,* 85 Fed. at 283]. Certainly, if the agreement was monopolistic and extortionate, the buyers were making either naïve or deliberately false statements. It might be proposed, of course, that these 57 purchasers of pipe were threatened by the six defendants. Perhaps the defendants threatened never to send another shipment of pipe unless such a document was submitted to the court. But what would the consequences have been if testimony concerning such a threat had been presented? Suppose instead that the threat was subtle. Many of those who submitted statements were purchasing agents, city engineers, and others who would not have suffered any appreciable harm if they had declined to perjure themselves. And finally, many affiants were located in states such as Ohio, Indiana, and Illinois where, as we saw, substantial bonuses were paid, but in which buyers had alternative sources, plants located in Ohio, Michigan, and Pennsylvania.

The most fascinating of these affidavits are the two submitted by employees of the city of Atlanta, where the price-fixing agreement was first called to the attention of federal prosecutors. Work in the city had been reserved by the cartel for the Anniston, Alabama, works and in February of 1896 they submitted a bid of $24 per ton of pipe. When an agent from a New Jersey firm submitted a lower bid, suspicion about a price-fixing ring was aroused, and the legal machinery set in motion. It is puzzling, then, that the superintendent of the Atlanta works was among those who submitted an affidavit on behalf of the defendants. Referring to the year's supply of pipe manufactured for the city at Anniston, he said:

> . . . the prices at which the said pipe was furnished were the lowest that could be obtained, and from my knowledge of the manufacture, capital required, and ordinary risks incident to manufacture, I consider said price fair, reasonable and moderate. I know in my official capacity of the charges made during the year 1896 against the Anniston Pipe & Foundry Co . . . pending an investigation of these charges the city withheld the payment of a balance of about $2,700.00, and that after making a thorough investigation, the entire balance due said company was, by resolution of the water board, paid in full, and that since that time the city has continued to purchase what pipe it has required for water-works purposes from said Anniston Pipe & Foundry, at same prices. [*Record* at 166–167]

The superintendent of the Atlanta waterworks also provided other information about the course of events after the high bids were submitted that led to prosecution by the government.

> . . . the bids were deemed by the board too high and were all rejected. Subsequently, in April the board succeeded in making a contract for the year's supply with the Anniston Pipe & Foundry Co. for $22.75 per ton f.o.b. Atlanta. The company, however, filled some orders for $22.50 per ton upon the city's contention that such was the proper price under the conditions respecting these shipments . . .
> . . . The Anniston Pipe & Foundry Company's dealings with the city in furnishing water pipe have been, in my judgment, uniformly fair. [*id.* at 167]

A member of the city water board submitted an affidavit containing substantially the same description of the water board's investigation as well as the effort made by James McClure, an employee of the pipe works' cartel, to persuade the city to agree to turn over 25 percent of any funds recovered from the works in return for evidence he would provide. The water board rejected this course of action, and bought a good deal of pipe from the firm that year. "From the investigation made by me personally while acting as chairman of said [investigative] committee, and from my own knowledge respecting the cost of manufacture and incidents thereto, I consider . . . the prices paid . . . in all cases as honest, fair, reasonable and just" [*id.* at 169].

While I agree that there are reasons why water commissioners, purchasing agents, and others whom I quote here do not always act in their employers' interest, I would not want to push very hard the view that these agents of the people mistook their own welfare for the public welfare in this case, especially in an age when city governments did little else besides provide the city with water. Unfortunately, very few of the buyers of pipe were private firms, and so we have no evidence on the attitude toward such cartels of purchasers for whom, by the usual analysis, the principal-agent problem is less important. In support of my view that these affidavits accurately reflected the views of buyers, and not just their agents, I make two observations. First, in looking at the debate in the 1890s concerning the issues of monopoly and restraint of trade, it is surprising to the modern American observer how many economists, lawyers, and politicians took the view that cartels were partly good and partly bad.[77] This was the view of the reasonable man of affairs of this period. Second, essentially the same view has prevailed for most of the last century in other industrialized countries.

The issues are perhaps best explored with an example. Suppose in the absence of copyright laws I entered into an agreement with other publishers that none of us would print works that any of the others first presents to the public. Would it be odd if during the antitrust litigation that followed, owners of bookstores testified that this was a restraint on competition to which they did not object? Presumably, if I broke this agreement, I could present them with copies of Henry Kissinger's *White House Years* at less cost than the original publishers, but such a breach would not be in the long-run interest of authors, publishers, book dealers, or the public.

The analogy to cast-iron pipe production is straightforward. The full cost of production has to be covered, and under entirely plausible cost and demand conditions, marginal cost-pricing, which was what the court argued for and what most economists today believe to be the proper prescription, will not sustain the operation of the plants. Nor will it lead to plants being operated at the point of minimum average cost, which is what some group composed of plant owners and buyers believes to be in its best interest. In such a case other remedies are required. If some buyers of cast-iron pipe paid more than marginal cost—which they did, regardless of how these events are interpreted—they may still have done so satisfied that this too was the best of all possible worlds.

D. The Costs and Benefits of Different Market Structures

The lack of enthusiasm that buyers showed for punishing cartel members suggests, of course, that they preferred the cartel arrangement to any of the relevant alternatives. They would have liked a competitive solution even more, but for fundamental technological reasons this was not a possibility. Except under special circumstances, there is, as we have seen, no out-and-out competitive equilibrium for industries with these cost conditions.

It must be noted that in most practical examples there are other factors, in addition to the nature of production costs, that stand in the way of competition but that also have the effect of making collusion less of a necessity. Under conditions of flush demand, there are imperfections such as unavoidable location advantage and product differentiation that can be regarded as constituting the basis for "market power." The degree to which particular buyers can be exploited depends, of course, on their opportunities elsewhere. These opportunities need only be feasible; they need not be resorted to very often. Note, however, that even during good times, firms might typically operate with some excess capacity and charge more than marginal cost at current rates because under those circumstances, excess capacity is more valuable than orders taken at a middling price.[78] There is, after all, some positive probability of getting a spot order that would command a high price or of doing a valued customer a favor. Water-pipe breaks are a common occurrence, and it may be cheaper not to keep inventories of all possible types of pipe, but to leave some spare capacity instead. Another way of stating this is to say that the amount of spare capacity depends on the benefits foregone when demand in excess of minimum average cost must be left unsatisfied. As a result, we may very well have situations of good demand accompanied by some excess capacity, but no general need for any sort of collusion among producers because of unavoidable, even beneficial market frictions. Foundries varied in terms of their location advantages, the mix of pipe sizes they commonly produced, and perhaps delivery terms and other aspects of their businesses as well. While these are generally considered to be market imperfections, this is the case only when compared to an abstract ideal. In this instance, and I think in many others, these imperfections actually imparted a measure of stability that would otherwise have been absent. The limits to exploitation were established by competition from less advantageously located producers or from those whose cost of meeting a particular customer's requirements were higher.

All these remarks apply to periods during which demand is fairly good; at other times these market frictions become considerably less important. Firms are, at least in principle, willing to make substantial cuts on prices of particular contracts if it is the only way to get some extra work. Any price greater than marginal cost is better than losing the order. During periods of good demand, equilibrium is preserved because the typical plant can work pretty close to full capacity but at prices that cover costs. During periods of poor demand, however, even the arrangements between a firm and its customers that cover only short-run costs can be undermined by another firm. This situation, we have argued, is unstable.

We now look at the alternatives to unrestrained competition during the relatively poor periods. Although we have seen in this case that cutthroat competition (marginal cost-pricing) can take place, such a situation is not sustainable. One of three things can occur. First, market conditions may change. In that case, the losses in bad times must be made up with gains in good times over the long run. The resulting capacity will generally be suboptimal, however, and with free entry and the possibility of something other than marginal cost-pricing, this would not occur. Moreover, it would be difficult to defend the behavior of plant owners during downturns as being rational because they would be operating below their shut-down point. Second, firms can adopt one of several noncompetitive solutions discussed below. Third, one or more of the firms may be driven to bankruptcy, although this also reflects considerable obstinacy on the part of some market participants. In this last instance the firms may be dismantled, operated by new owners, or acquired and operated by existing firms. Whichever does occur, the resulting solution will also eliminate or mitigate competition, that is, it will inevitably lead to one of first two alternatives. The central point here is that under certain conditions a market must attain a noncompetitive outcome (or suboptimal capacity) either directly or, if it results in bankruptcy, indirectly.[79]

The alternatives to unrestrained competition are (1) cartelization, (2) merger, and (3) tacit collusion. Each of these, at least from a global point of view, has certain advantages, but also attendant costs. The easiest way to address these issues is to separate them into two groups, the private costs and benefits in production of various forms of organization, and the costs and benefits that arise from arrangements with buyers, which is to say the cost of monopoly arising out of inefficiencies in the market. The organizational costs and benefits can be regarded as part of the opportunity cost of the resources devoted to producing a particular quantity, or more generally, a particular path of output. In a sense they are part of the supply curve of ordinary economic analysis, except that this term implies that firms are price takers, which they are not according to the construction of the problem. For ease of exposition assume that all plants produce identical products and that all are located at a single point.

For the genuinely static or deterministic case, it is difficult to distinguish cartelization and merger since the same problem exists whether we are looking at one week, one year, or ten years. The owners decide on the rate of output and any inefficiencies can be removed by side payments. No problems of information or monitoring exist, either among the cartel members or within a plant since the side payments can be made as once-

and-for-all lump sum payments initially. Tacit collusion, on the other hand, is much more likely to involve inefficient allocations of production across firms even in a world of certainty.[80] The most uncomplicated reason for this is that language is a very useful social invention, and a prohibition against its use (as opposed to a voluntary decision not to use it) is likely to raise the costs of any action involving two or more people. There are also good reasons for concluding that various outcomes suggested by game theory, such as the Cournot-Nash solution (to cite one form tacit collusion might take), are inefficient in their allocation of output.[81]

More interesting consequences for the private cost of production occur in a world of uncertainty.[82] Uncertainty makes it necessary for managers to gather information about their markets and the operation of their plants and to act on this information. This problem of coordination of activity in the face of uncertainty can be handled either by the market or within the firm, and as pointed out by Ronald Coase (16), the choice between the two will be governed by the relative costs. For some aspects of a firm's activities, the market provides a better combination of accurate and cheap information, and greater benefits in terms of flexibility and the limited range of issues that must be considered. In other cases, however, the market can become fairly cumbersome and costly. The relevant information may be more costly to assemble and evaluate in a market than within a firm. In other instances the flexibility that markets allow will be sufficiently burdensome to one of the participants to make the net costs lower if this activity is incorporated within a firm and subject to a single authority who takes into account the joint costs. Although the manager's problem becomes more complex, and this system of command generates inefficiencies of its own, the extra costs are more than outweighed because the greater inefficiencies that would result from market arrangements are avoided.

In its simple form, this line of argument explains, for example, why some firms have in-house research and development while others purchase these services, or why some manufacturers purchase components while others produce them. But a closer examination reveals, of course, that coordination by command within a firm and completely unrestricted market arrangements are the extremes of a continuum. In many instances, contracts or informal agreements limit the freedom of parties to a market transaction; similarly, activity within a firm may be partly organized by market incentives. There is available, in fact, a rich variety of arrangements that blend firm and market solutions, as evidenced by the use of long-term contracts, franchise arrangements, and independent profit centers. Ordinarily, these arguments are used to explain the degree of vertical integration, the scope of a firm's product lines, or the degree of autonomy allowed to units producing different products, but they also, of course, are applicable to horizontal arrangements among units producing a single product.

If we admit that the question of firm size can be treated scientifically along these lines, it follows that there was no net gain associated with merger before the cast-iron pipe plants were actively pursued by the antitrust authorities. Rather, the owners of the separate plants preferred to handle collectively only the problems that might arise from independent, unrestricted pricing. The history of the industry also shows that this was likely to occur only occasionally and that at least during the better times, the ordinary frictions would preserve order. Other questions concerning plant operations, such as which sizes of pipe to produce, when to undertake new investment, when to suspend operations, and, most important of all, when to withdraw from the cartel, were still left to the discretion of the owner. This left the owner of each plant free to respond to changes in circumstances, with only his own interests in mind, and without regard to the possible consequences for other firms in the industry. As new situations arose, an independent owner was in many cases able to take action that would result in a better allocation of output or that lowered costs of production but that also harmed others. Now, while it might be suggested that an appropriately detailed cartel agreement could provide for these contingencies, this sort of arrangement is likely to be unwieldy in practice. From a social point of view, the aim of a cartel arrangement should be to preserve independent action in those areas where it results in lowered costs, and to limit independence only where it interferes with production.[83] The reason this cartel arrangement was also preferred by the members was that an efficiently run cartel was in their interests since at least part of the gains accrued to them and because it made entry less likely. Note that if the cartel had been run inefficiently, but with the buyers' interests in mind, the inefficiency still might very well have resulted in entry and the displacement of the cartel. If indeed an attempt had been made to saddle each cartel member with restrictions that would allow a net gain to each and all when circumstances called for a change at one plant, it is unlikely that there would have remained much flexibility or incentive to act on changed circumstances. On the one hand, we have as a possibility independent ownership of the plants. While this always allows unilateral withdrawal, it is also consistent with an array of increasingly complex contracts, which vary in the degree to which they are beneficial in suppressing destructive rivalry and the degree to which they raise costs by making decisions concerning even the day-to-day operation of the plant a subject of the initial agreement or a matter for joint discussion and resolution.

On the other hand, we have the possibility of merger of the firms.

Merger of course has the advantage that there are relatively few sources of disagreement after the initial allocation of stock is made. Each owner's gain now depends solely on the fate of the whole firm. But instead of relying on independent responses to market incentives and the selective use of agreements to guide production and suppress rivalry among the firms, control of the firm must now be more centralized than before. From what does this need for centralization arise? If the actions of each plant did not affect any of the other plants, the different units could be run as independent profit centers. This may be optimal, but there is no necessary advantage to a merger of this sort since any benefit, such as common technical development or internal financing, also has costs. Some firms are run this way, but only if the different activities do not affect each other very much or if competition takes the place of monitoring.[84] But in our case an action at any one plant is likely to have repercussions throughout the firm (without always contributing to its efficiency) so that maximizing the joint return of the whole firm calls for study and the orchestration of the whole firm, and the involvement of many managers in the case of decisions that were previously undertaken unilaterally by perhaps only one person and with only the interests of a single plant in mind.[85] In addition, not only the cost of management, but also the likelihood of certain kinds of mistakes are greater under the consolidated form. So, while the firms certainly had the option of merging earlier than they did, the fact that they did not do so indicates that merger was not without costs, and that only the increasingly unfavorable attitude of the courts tipped the balance in favor of the more tightly organized arrangement.

Although it seems entirely plausible, then, that the cartel arrangement might have allowed cheaper production and was favored by the firms for that reason, the benefits arising from the exploitation of buyers would appear to have been greater under the merged form. This follows from the fact that cheating and unilateral withdrawal from the cartel would be impossible. Once the initial allocation of the spoils was settled at the time of merger, any disagreement concerning the correct prices was most likely to stem from honest differences of opinion. But the fact that merger was not favored seems to indicate that the net profits, after taking into account the effect on production costs, were lower. The interesting implication of this for antitrust policy is that the overall loss from monopoly was probably lower under the cartel arrangement than under the merger that antitrust enforcement appears to have precipitated.

One might propose at this point that the policies concerning merger that have been developed since the decision in *Addyston* will allow a favorable assessment of the whole panoply of antitrust. But consider the effect of the prohibition against mergers that has been developed since the beginning of the century. Because a competitive equilibrium is not possible, independent firms in such an industry will have to resort to secret agreements or to tacit collusion in the short run. Both of these have the drawback that they are much more cumbersome to administer and result in greater inefficiencies than more open forms of price-fixing, which puts them in roughly the same position as merger. On the other side, we can weigh against this objection the likelihood that prices will be lower, since with more cumbersome methods of agreement, exploitation of the buyer will be more difficult. Note, however, that the net effect on welfare will not be clear. In the long run, moreover, the difficulties inherent in this sort of arrangement—in some circumstances, at least—may lead to the abandonment of some independent plants and the construction of new ones by existing firms until the immediate aims of the merger policy are largely defeated.

These remarks underscore the importance of considering the degree to which buyers in a market can be exploited. The most fruitful way to begin a discussion of this issue, I think, is to question the presumption that noncompetitive arrangements, including cartelization, have monopoly gain as their sole purpose. This forces us to recognize the possibility that buyers are not necessarily interested in breaking up price-fixing arrangements, which certainly appears to have been true in the case of *Addyston*. Equally important is the recognition that buyers are not necessarily helpless in the face of a cartel, for which we also have some evidence. If buyers purchase a large fraction of a plant's output, they can plausibly be expected to obtain modification of unfavorable contract terms. The buyers who purchase comparatively small amounts can band together or buy from competing agents (distributors, wholesalers, or jobbers, for example) who bargain on their behalf. Large buyers or associations of small ones can also protect themselves against cartels by vertical integration and long-term contracts. Finally, as the brief history of the soil pipe combination illustrated, entry of new plants places a limit on pricing behavior in an industry.[86]

It should be stressed that these limits on cartel behavior are not arbitrarily restrictive. They cannot be simply what buyers would like them to be. First of all, buyers would not find it in their long-run interest to gang up on the sellers and drive prices down to the marginal cost of existing capacity. Quite simply, capacity would decrease under such a scheme. Second, the appropriate policy will depend on the cost of the alternatives. So, the losses due to the cartel have to be greater than the cost of operating the coalition of buyers. Moreover, there may be other arrangements that avoid the cost of cartels and coalitions altogether. For example, buyers and sellers may agree to long-term contracts under certain conditions. In general, the difficulties associated with the use of markets, in particular assuring that a) buyers do not pay more than the full cost, and b) sellers get reimbursed for their cost, seem to be the best explanation for arrangements other than spot markets, namely, firms, cartels, long-term contracts, vertical restraints, and, if we are prepared to admit a constructive role for government, regulation.

IV. CONCLUSION

The question of whether unrestricted competition is always possible or desirable, although it would seem to lie at the foundation of an analysis of antitrust policy, has been largely ignored by both economists and the courts. A thorough examination of this issue reveals, however, that there are substantial grounds for doubting that competition is always a feasible solution to market allocation. In the typical industrial setting it seems quite clear that the nature of production costs leads to a serious violation of the assumptions of the textbook model. In fact, it is implausible to expect vigorous competition and short-run marginal cost-pricing in these markets, because the cost of production could not be covered under such regimes. As a result, one should expect the emergence of various arrangements that appear anticompetitive, because they allow production to take place. This analysis was supported by a detailed examination of the circumstances surrounding *Addyston Pipe*.

The implications of these results for antitrust policy need to be considered. The current per se restrictions on agreements and the rule-of-reason restriction on merger may indeed be the best that courts with imperfect knowledge can enforce. While there are bound to be social losses from this approach, the difficulty of determining what sort of agreements should be allowed may make it the best feasible strategy. Since other ways of restricting or diverting competition, such as tacit collusion and differentiation of products, still exist, the present policy may be best from a global point of view. But if Congress and the courts have hit upon the correct antitrust policy, it will only have been by chance, and not through an explicit consideration of the issues at stake.

APPENDIX

The core of a game can be thought of as the set returns determined by each player's alternatives. The players can join various coalitions or "clubs," and clubs of various configurations can confer some average level of benefit on their members. For a game with three players, there are three single-member clubs, three clubs of two players, and the club composed of all players. The core of the game is that allocation of benefits is such that no player or group of players can do better by forming one of the other feasible clubs and taking the associated benefits. For example, in the three-player case, the gain to a particular player must be at least as great as that which that player could ensure himself acting alone. The gain must also be as large as the allocation that comes from acting in concert with another player, where the other player is also assured at least his stand-alone gains.

Proceeding to the general formal case, imagine a game with n players denoted by A_1, A_2, . . . , A_n. Each player can assure himself of a return $a_i \geq 0$ and two or more players can assure themselves as a group of at least as large a return as they can obtain if split up into nonintersecting subgroups. This situation is represented by the von Neumann-Morgenstern characteristic function where $V(A_i) = a_i$ is the security value of player A_i and for which it is true that $V(A_i, A_j) \geq V(A_i) + V(A_j)$ for all $i \neq j$. More generally, for any two subsets of players S_1 and S_2 such that $S_1 \cap S_2 = \emptyset$ we have $V(S_1, S_2) \geq V(S_1) + V(S_2)$.

Denote the returns we propose for any player A_i by x_i. Then for any coalition S contained in N, it must be the case that

$$\sum_S x_i \geq V(S), \tag{A.1}$$

that is, the proposed returns to members of the coalition must sum to an amount greater than the amount it can assure itself. It must also be true, however, for the all-player coalition, denoted by N, that

$$\sum_N x_i \leq V(N), \tag{A.2}$$

i.e., the proposed returns cannot exceed what the coalition of all agents can assure itself.

Denote a proposed solution by x. Such a vector is said to be in the core if it satisfies Eqs. (A.1) and (A.2). The core itself consists of all possible vectors satisfying these conditions. It may happen, however, that no proposed vector can provide every coalition with more than it can assure itself without at the same time breaking the resource constraint. If that is the case it is said that the core is empty.

Consider the simple game with three players described above. Each player can assure himself of one dollar, any group of two can assure itself a return of three dollars, and the group as a whole can have four dollars. One may think of this as a case in which there are first increasing and then decreasing returns to scale. (It is equivalent to the case described in Section II.A.) Formally,

$$v(A_1) = V(A_2) = V(A_3) = 1$$

$$V(A_1, A_2) = V(A_1, A_3) = V(A_2, A_3) = 3$$

$$V(A_1, A_2, A_3) = 4$$

Is there a set of returns, x_1, x_2, and x_3, that can satisfy the following inequalities?

$$x_1 \geq 1 \qquad x_2 \geq 1 \qquad x_3 \geq 1 \qquad (A.3)$$

(the amount the players can assure themselves alone),

$$x_1 + x_2 \geq 3 \qquad x_1 + x_3 \geq 3 \qquad x_2 + x_3 \geq 3 \qquad (A.4)$$

(the amount any two can assure themselves jointly), and

$$x_1 + x_3 + x_3 \leq 4 \qquad (A.5)$$

(the feasibility constraint).

Note that Eq. (A.4) implies

$$x_1 + x_2 + x_3 \geq 4.5.$$

But this contradicts the feasibility constraint in this case, so that the core is empty. It may be noted in passing that this example illustrates in a simple fashion the problem frequently encountered in economic applications, namely, the power of coalitions of intermediate size to demand a higher average return than is available for the coalition of all players.

An example of market exchange analyzed by Telser [(49), pp. 19–31] should help to illustrate the usefulness of this approach and its relation to what is usually meant by competition. Imagine a market with n buyers and m sellers, each willing to exchange one unit of the good but having different limit prices. Buyers will not pay more than a given price, and sellers will not accept less than a given price. Let these limit prices be represented by $b_1 \leq b_2 \leq \ldots \leq b_n$ for the buyers and $a_1 \leq a_2 \leq \ldots \leq a_m$ for the potential sellers. The number of inequalities that have to be satisfied are numerous, representing the returns that all possible coalitions could assure themselves. In fact, if there are 11 buyers and sellers, there are $2^{n+m} - 1$ or 2,047 constraints. It is sufficient, however, if we focus on what each participant can assure himself and on what all possible pairs of buyers and sellers can assure themselves.

Individual sellers can always keep their units of the good so that we have $V(A_i) = a_i$ for $i = 1, \ldots, m$. Potential buyers, on the other hand, do not have any units of the good, so that the best they can do by themselves is $V(B_j) = 0$ for $j = 1, \ldots, n$. Together with the pairwise security values $V(A_i, B_j) = \max(a_i, b_j)$ for all i and j, which indicates that these coalitions can always award a unit of the good to the participant valuing it the most; these determine the minimum necessary returns to buyers and sellers. Let x_i denote the return to seller i and y_j the return to buyer j. Then the inequalities $x_i \geq V(A_i) = a_i$, $y_j \geq V(B_j) = 0$ and $x_i + y_j \geq V(A_i, B_j) = \max(a_i, b_j)$ together with the feasibility constraint defined for all i and j

$$\sum x_i + \sum y_j \leq V(N)$$

determine the core allocations. $V(N)$ has the interpretation of the maximum return possible to the participants in the market, and we see that returns are maximized if we transfer units of the good from the potential sellers who value them least and to buyers who value them most until we reach the seller who values the good more than the most eager unsatisfied buyer. If we let these transactions be voluntary, the exact price charged per unit can be indeterminate over a range, but it falls between bounds whose lower limit is established by the least eager seller who does trade or the most eager buyer who does not, whichever is higher, and whose upper limit is established by the least eager buyer who does trade or the most eager seller who does not, whichever is lower. It can be seen that as the number of players increases, and under reasonable assumptions about the distribution of limit prices, this interval is forced to a single point. In such a case the imputations or returns in the core are those that emerge from a traditional supply and demand analysis. In other situations, however, it may no longer be true that there is a set of market clearing prices. An important exception occurs if there are fixed costs in production.

The difficulties in the case of fixed costs in production are best illuminated with a series of examples. Consider the following situation. An industry consists of two plants, one with a capacity of four units and the other with a capacity of six units. The small plant incurs "fixed avoidable" (or "semivariable") costs of $12 if it is in operation, but no costs if it is temporarily shut down. The large plant incurs fixed avoidable costs of $15 if it is operated. The plants do not incur ordinary fixed costs. This assumption does not vitiate the main points of the analysis. It amounts to saying that sunk costs are sunk. One could also include marginal costs in this example, but this is not necessary since it is always possible to regard demand net of marginal costs.[1]

Denote the plants as A_1 and A_2 and let a_1 and a_2 be the security value of each plant. Adopt the convention that the normal or reference state of the world means that there is no output. It follows that the security values for the two plants can be expressed as

$$V(A_1) = a_1 = 12$$

$$V(A_2) = a_2 = 15$$

since a plant can always choose not to operate and keep either 12 or 15. Let $b = 5$ be the limit price of the m identical buyers $B_1, B_2, \ldots, B_m$.

Their security value can be expressed as $V(B_j) = 0$ for all $j = 1, \ldots,$ m since the worst buyers can do is not to fly. On this convention, the gain to plants is their revenue, which must be greater than their security value, and the gain to buyers is their net gain, which is the excess of their valuation of the flight over its cost. This must exceed zero. Formally, $x_1 \geq V(A_1) = 12$ and $x_2 \geq V(A_2) = 15$, and the minimum acceptable gain to each buyer is $y_j > V(B_j) = 0$.

Suppose that there are ten buyers. What are the core constraints? First, for the buyers we have the ten constraints

$$y_j > 0 \qquad j = 1, \ldots, 10, \tag{A.6}$$

and for the plant owners we have the two constraints

$$x_1 \geq 12 \text{ and } x_2 \geq 15. \tag{A.7}$$

The maximum gain (the feasibility constraint) is given by

$$x_1 + x_2 + 10y \leq 50 \tag{A.8}$$

where for economy of notation we let $\sum y_i$ for all $i = 1, \ldots, 10$ be expressed simply as $10y$. This can be interpreted as the gain available from allocating the two plants to the ten buyers. Another partition of buyers and sellers into two coalitions results in

$$x_1 + 4y \geq 20$$
$$x_2 + 6y \geq 30 \tag{A.9}$$

and these constraints, together with Eq. (A.8) imply that both Eqs. (A.8) and (A.9) hold with equality. Other partitions are possible, but all would provide their members with lower returns.

Since $x_1 + 4y = 20$ and $x_2 + 6y = 30$ and since also $x_1 \geq 12$ and $x_2 \geq 15$, we have $y < 2$ and the nonbinding constraint $y < 2.5$. By earlier results we can also say that $0 < y < 2$. The interpretation of these constraints is that the net gain of buyers must be less than 2 and the price per unit of output must be 3 or more. In more traditional terms, the price must cover the cost of the marginal plant, and consumer surplus is the difference between the buyers' valuation and the price. The difference here is that the price must be greater than 3 but less than 5.

Consider now what happens if there are only eight buyers. The optimal solution still calls for both plants to be operating since the total valuation of eight buyers (40) exceeds the total cost of both plants (27). The core constraints for the stand alone (or "singleton") coalitions are

$$y_j > 0 \qquad j = 1, \ldots, 8$$
$$x_1 \geq 12 \text{ and } x_2 \geq 15.$$

The feasibility constraint is given by

$$x_1 + x_2 + 8y \leq 40$$

and this implies that $0 < y < \frac{8}{13}$.

There are now a variety of other constraints, however. One partition calls for both A_1 and A_2 to produce 4 units;

$$x_1 + 4y \geq 20 \text{ and } x_2 + 4y \geq 20$$

and another calls for 3 and 5, respectively:

$$x_1 + 3y \geq 15 \text{ and } x_2 + 5y \geq 25.$$

These last two pairs imply a contradiction since $x_1 + 4y \geq 20$ and $x_2 + 5y \geq 25$ together imply $x_1 + x_2 + 9y \geq 45$ and this, together with $0 < y < \frac{8}{13}$, implies $x_1 + x_2 + 8y \geq 44\frac{5}{13}$. This last inequality violates the feasibility constraint.

This is one situation for which no competitive equilibrium exists, and the problem here is slack capacity. Similar difficulties exist for other rates of demand. So, for example, if there are seven buyers, the optimal solution calls for A_2 to be in operation and only six buyers to be satisfied. The satisfaction of the extra buyer is not worth the cost of the extra plant. However, the market clearing price necessary to achieve the allocation of six units to seven buyers is 5, which would induce the idle plant, A_1, to offer a price of, say, 4, and undermine A_2. Obviously, if there are only six buyers, A_2 can scoop the market and offer a price between its average cost of 2.5 and the average cost of 3 of A_1. The same arguments apply in the case of five buyers. In conclusion, independent operation of the plants and profit maximization do not lead to a stable equilibrium for seven, eight, or nine buyers.

More general results indicate that these difficulties exist for a broad class of cost conditions. Consider the analysis due to Sharkey [(43), pp. 42–48]. Suppose that there are m buyers, $B_1, \ldots, B_m$, with limit prices $b_1 \geq b_2 \geq \ldots \geq b_m$ for one unit of the good, and n sellers (or plants), $A_1, \ldots, A_n$, with capacity costs $h_1, \ldots, h_n$ and capacities $q_1, \ldots, q_n$. Again, consider the limit prices to be net of marginal costs. Then the following theorem holds:

If in the optimal assignment of buyers to sellers, there are $s \geq 2$ active sellers $A_1, \ldots, A_s$ and $b_{K_s} < max_{j=1,\ldots,s} \{h_j/q_j\}$ where $K_s = \sum_i^s q_j$, then the core is empty.

In words, this theorem states that if, for a given set of plants and a given number of buyers, it turns out that more than two sellers should be operating and that the limit price of the least eager customer whom it is optimal to serve is less than the average cost of the least efficient operating plant, then there is no competitive solution. This can be thought of as the case of downward sloping demand in which, because of slack capacity under the optimal configuration of plants, there is competition for the marginal buyer who is only willing to pay an amount less than the minimum average cost of the marginal plant. In cases where the marginal buyer is willing to pay more than the minimum average cost of the most efficient nonactive plant under the optimal assignment, the following theorem applies:

> *If in the optimal assignment of buyers to sellers, there are $s < m$ active sellers $A_1, \ldots, A_s$ and $b_{K_s} + 1$ represents the first inactive buyer (where $K_s = \sum_1^s q_j$), then if $b_{K_{s+1}} > min_{j=s+1,\ldots,m} [max(h_j/q_j, h_j/K_s)]$ the core is empty.*

This theorem says that there is no competitive equilibrium in the case where the optimal assignment calls for some buyers to be inactive (not buying) although they are willing to pay more than the minimum average cost of the low-cost inactive plant.

Some of the implications of these two theorems are worth noting. First, it is always possible to define dummy buyers with limit prices equal to zero so that the first theorem can be applied, that is, we can always define a limit price for the buyer who exhausts the optimal capacity. Second, the special case where h_j/q_j is a constant corresponds to the situation where all plants have the same minimum average cost, and, what is more, this case will imply that the core is empty in all cases where the number of sellers under the optimal arrangement is more than 2 but less than the number that exhausts capacity, except for those rare instances where $b_{K_s} \geq h_j/q_j \geq b_{K_{s+1}}$. Under more general cost conditions other exceptions occur, but these essentially rely on the existence of higher cost firms to create (locally) fixed industry capacity. Low-cost plants supply the output and prices are bid up to where active firms cover costs but high-cost inactive firms cannot undermine the arrangement.

The issues raised by this analysis are not new, although Sharkey and Telser [(50), especially ch. 2] have advanced the discussion considerably. The antecedents to this analysis are discussed in notes 5, 7, and 8. A more extensive history of thought on this issue would probably be fairly interesting. The technical discussion could also be carried to several other issues. I will confine my comments, however, to several objections that have been raised when the insights of this theory are applied to actual industries.

There are essentially two major objections. First, it is argued, the core is not an appropriate equilibrium concept because the idea of groups of buyers and plant owners actually forming coalitions is far-fetched. True, the theory is not descriptively valid in that sense, but it does serve the purpose of illuminating alternatives, or bounds on outcomes. There is no doubt that it is closely related to the theory of competitive equilibrium that constitutes the heart of virtually every intermediate economics textbook. The various coalitions are perhaps only threats, but in any event they are threats that buyers and sellers could take advantage of. Granted, the operation of a market can be costly in many cases, but institutions arise to reduce these costs, with the result, in the case of organized exchanges, for example, that the results predicted by the theory emerge in an obvious way, despite the fact that the "assumptions" are violated.

The second objection is that the analysis ignores transportation costs and product differentiation. In many instances, and the Associated Pipe Works cartel is one of these, transportation costs are not important because the plants are located close together because of some site advantage. Demand can be considered net of transportation costs. Granted, if the plants were some sufficiently large enough distance apart, then they would be local monopolies. In the case at hand, and many others as well, not very much insulation of this sort exists.

Similar remarks apply to product differentiation. Obviously, no two plants make exactly the same product, just as two plants cannot be located on the exact same spot. For a large variety of products, however, there is no possibility of deviating from generally accepted technical norms and inspection by an engineer or other qualified agent is inexpensive.

NOTE TO APPENDIX

1. This sort of example is explored in Telser [(50), pp. 41–87] where the "plants" are airplanes, the capacity is the number of seats on an airplane, and the "buyers" are passengers who each demand one seat. Clearly the hypothesized cost conditions capture an important aspect of airplane costs. The crew's wages, fuel costs, and airport fees depend largely on whether a plane flies, and not on the number of passengers.

ACKNOWLEDGMENTS

I would like especially to acknowledge the advice and encouragement of Lester Telser, my thesis chairman. Donald Dewey, Richard Posner, Sherwin Rosen, David Sappington, and members of the University of Chicago's Seminar in Applied Price Theory provided helpful comments. Financial support for this work came from the Liberty Fund, the Winchester Foundation, and the Charles R. Walgreen Foundation, and United States Pipe and Foundry provided data from its turn-of-the-century cast-iron pipe plants. Tables 1 and 2 are reprinted from Bittlingmayer [(5), pp. 219–221] by permission of the University of Chicago Press.

NOTES

1. *United States v. Addyston Pipe and Steel Co.*, 85 Fed. 271 (6th Cir. 1898), *modified*, 175 U.S. 211 (1899).

2. The first case to reach the Supreme Court under the Sherman Antitrust Act of 1890 was that of the Sugar Trust. See *United States v. E. C. Knight*, 156 U.S. 1 (1895). It was decided in favor of the defendants and has been largely ignored since. But, see Zerbe (61). One case involving a labor dispute followed. Two inconsequential cases involving livestock exchanges reached the Court in 1898. The two significant antitrust cases to reach the Supreme Court before *Addyston* were *United States v. Trans Missouri Freight Ass'n.*, 166 U.S. 290 (1897); and *United States v. Joint Traffic Ass'n.*, 171 U.S. 505 (1898). Interestingly, a merger wave of unequaled proportions started during these years. For discussions of early antitrust enforcement see Thorelli (52), pp. 432–499; Letwin (29); Posner (38), pp. 23–27; and Bork (8), pp. 15–41.

3. Among them a one-time president of the American Economic Association. See Fetter (18). See also the references at note 17.

4. The best known of these is Clark (13) and (15). For another instance in which a balanced view was taken, see Burns (10). Many prominent economists opposed the passage of the Sherman Act and regarded the trusts favorably. See Letwin (29), pp. 71–77.

5. That it could was questioned by Alfred Marshall, who contended that the price producers receive is nearly always above the "prime" or marginal cost of production so that general expenses may be covered.

> In a trade which uses very expensive plant, the prime cost of goods is but a small part of their total cost; and an order at much less than their normal price may leave a large surplus above their prime cost. But if producers accept such orders in their anxiety to prevent their plant from being idle, they glut the market and tend to prevent prices from reviving. In fact, however, they seldom pursue this policy constantly and without moderation . . . [G]eneral opinion is not altogether hostile to that code of trade morality which condemns the action of anyone who "spoils the market" by being too ready to accept a price that does little more than cover the prime cost of his goods, and allows but little on account of his general expenses. [Marshall (30), pp. 311–312; see also Book V *passim*.]

6. One reason for this may have been the comparative ease with which the competitive model could be refined. Hicks (23) and Samuelson (41) are prominent examples. Although Hicks claimed that his dynamic analysis of pricing in Chapter 4 is based on Marshall's Book V, he deliberately ignored the more difficult questions raised by Marshall. Earlier, in his chapter on the equilibrium of the firm, he explained why:

> A competitive firm that operates at a point where average cost exceeds marginal cost must sell at a loss. While we could assume that such firms continue in existence because they face less than perfectly elastic demand curves, that would constitute monopoly. It has to be recognized that a general abandonment of the assumption of perfect competition, a universal adoption of the assumption of monopoly, must have very destructive consequences for economic theory. [Hicks (23), p. 83]

Economic analysis could only be saved from such consequences, according to Hicks, if it can be assumed that the markets in which most firms operate "do not differ very greatly from competitive markets. . . . At least, this get-away seems well worth trying" (pp. 84–85). In a footnote to this passage he justifies the assumption of perfect competition as "an immensely simplifying approximation to the facts."

7. The formal analysis of industries with U-shaped average cost curves dates back to Viner (58). Viner himself seems to have recognized that convexities pose problems for equilibrium (p. 212). In fact, it came to be widely recognized in the 1930s that "the prerequisites of competition . . . prove to be very difficult of attainment" [Burns (11), p. 3]. One early work explicitly devoted to the issue raised here was that of Cady (12). This was a wartime reproduction of typescript and does not appear to have been widely circulated. Farrell (17) is a widely cited analysis of the conditions necessary for competition. Telser (50) has made a detailed study of equilibrium in the familiar market model using the theory of the core. This issue has been largely ignored in the education of economists, however. Varian [(56), pp. 62–63] is, so far as I know, the one book of recent vintage directed at advanced undergraduates or beginning graduate students that indicates even briefly the nature of supply in industries with only a few firms. The typical textbook discussion of the oligopoly problem is carried out without reference to the nature of costs and unmindful of whether competition is possible.

8. Aumann (2) uses the core to explore the conditions under which competitive equilibria exist (1964). More recently, Telser (50) has applied core theory to questions of industry equilibrium and several other topics. The core is defined as the set of returns to all players or participants in a market with the property that no participant or group can do better by acting autonomously. In many cases, however, the core does not exist, and, by implication, no competitive equilibrium exists. The concept is generally credited to Gillies (19), but it has antecedents in the economic literature in work by Edgeworth and Böhm-Bawerk.

9. I presented the formal version originally in Bittlingmayer [(4), pp. 16–17]. A similar example, illustrating the same technical issues, appears in Elizabeth Bailey's foreword to Baumol, Panzar, and Willig (3), pp. xiv–xv] and is attributed to G. Faulhaber.

10. Alfred Marshall appears to have grasped the difficulty here. See his somewhat strained discussion in Marshall (30) at Ch. XII of Book V on *Equilibrium of Normal Demand and Supply, Continued, with Reference to the Law of Increasing Return.* "Abstract reasonings as to the effects of the economies in production, which an individual firm gets from an increase of its output are apt to be misleading, not only in detail, but even in their general effect. This is nearly the same as saying that in such case the conditions governing supply should be represented in their totality." (p. 380) I would interpret these remarks to mean that firms in an industry will not compete unchecked and bring price down to marginal cost, and that economies will not result in one firm or plant. Although his discussion following vacillates between economies of scale and learning economies, he returns again to those economies "which may be expected to arise naturally out of adaptations of existing ideas." He then comments: "The theory of stable equilibrium of normal demand and supply helps indeed to give definiteness to our ideas; and in its elementary stages it does not diverge from the actual facts of life, . . . But when pushed to its more remote and intricate logical consequences, it slips away from the conditions of real life." (pp. 381–382)

11. For a more formal and complete analysis of these issues and the difficulties involved see Telser (50), chs. 2 and 3, and W. W. Sharkey (43).

12. The following discussion of cast-iron pipe production is based on information from several sources: Moore (32), Noble (35), Sharp (44), Stimpson and Gray (48), *Transcript of Record of the Supreme Court of the United States* (53), and U.S. Census Office (55). For a more extensive treatment of these topics see Bittlingmayer (5).

13. The existence of economies is well established by, for example, Walters (59), Johnston (25), Moore (31), and Norman (36). For classic statements on the reasons for economies see Clark (14), Robinson (40). A good presentation of the reasons for economies in railroading appears in Jones (26).

14. Note that higher pig-iron cost per ton for smaller plants, if true, would be the result of the same forces that led them to have higher average inventory costs. A small plant could,

of course, always order quantities as large as those ordered by bigger plants, although less frequently.

15.   Short-term yields on corporate bonds were 3.50 percent in 1905 and rose to 4.75 percent in 1906. See U.S. Bureau of the Census [(54), Series X487–X491, p. 1004]. The total value of properties, it should be noted, is open to the charge that it is an inflated measure, since it would incorporate (in the purchase prices of the plants added in 1899) the expected monopoly gains. This would bias our estimate of capital costs upward. But lower capital costs make the objection in the text harder to sustain.

16.   This was the theme of Clark (13) and (15). Examples of recent theoretical work on this issue are Gould (21) and Sheshinski and Dréze (45).

17.   Representative early treatments include Burns (10), pp. 149–150; Jones (27), pp. 12–13, 395–398; Seager and Gulich (42), pp. 93–94; Stevens (46), pp. 205–209; and Ripley (39), pp. 78–96. These are typically excerpts from the Court of Appeals or Supreme Court opinion, or they are brief summaries and analyses based on these opinions. The first extensive analysis of the case came sixty years later in Whitney (60), p. 3ff. Phillips [(37), pp. 99–118] provides some new information on the case and some interesting observations.

18.   Several empirical studies support the view that collusion is more likely in depressed industries. See Asch and Seneca (1) and Hay and Kelly (22).

19.   P. D. Wanner, "Address to the Foundryman's Association," *Iron Age*, April 13, 1899, p. 8.

20.   This reluctance on the part of the firm in New Jersey may very well be accounted for by the fact that it was well situated for the export trade, which was probably more stable than regional demand.

21.   *Iron Age*, February 25, 1892, p. 353.

22.   *Id.*, December 22, 1892, p. 1235.

23.   *Id.*, January 12, 1892, p. 83.

24.   It would be desirable to know more about the internal bidding arrangement. For example, how was the price (gross of the bonus) arrived at? Unfortunately, there is very little evidence beyond the paragraph quoted above.

25.   An additional change proposed and carried out at the December 1895 meeting was that "upon all inquiries for prices from 'reserved cities' for pipe required during the year 1896" prices and bonuses would be fixed at regular meetings. It was also proposed that the association's headquarters be moved to Chicago because so much of its work was for that city. This topic was the subject of some disagreement among the members. See *Record* at 92–93 and 95–97.

26.   This is supported by the discussion of Table 11, below.

27.   The freight rate appears in *Record* at 76. Although larger orders usually had lower prices per ton, price differentials for lot size were usually smaller than this.

28.   *Iron Age*, March 12, 1896, p. 663.

29.   *Id.*, June 4, 1896, p. 1324.

30.   See the petition for contempt filed January 28, 1897, and related documents in *Record* at 261–274.

31.   *Engineering-News Record*, February 18, 1897.

32.   *Engineering-News*, February 9, 1899. This is not the same periodical as in note 31 above.

33.   *Iron Age*, December 12, 1895, p. 1231.

34.   *Id.*, January 23, 1896, p. 262. Other industries that had pooling arrangements at the turn of the century include the manufacturers of steel rails, steel billets, wire nails, meat products. See Jones (27).

35.   Why didn't pipe producers integrate vertically into pig iron to protect themselves against the pig-iron producers' cartel? One could just as well ask why some pig-iron pro-

ducers didn't set up pipe plants. Indeed, why are monopolies, and the associated triangles of welfare loss, not generally eliminated through vertical integration? One answer is that these are more expensive alternatives, which suggests the possibility that improvements in efficiency partly underlie monopoly and cartel forms of market organization. In the case at hand, there are at least three reasons for separate ownership of pig-iron and pipe plants. First, an integrated operation would have also to incur the expense of idle pig-iron capacity or find some way of selling surplus. Put differently, specialized pig-iron producers have a portfolio of markets. Second, it is by no means clear that the optimal mix of pig-iron and pipe plant sizes calls for a large enough overlap to permit a match up of comparably sized pig-iron and pipe plants into vertically integrated operations, nor, what is more important, that the (variable) demand for pipe and for pig iron will be related over time in exactly such a way that would call for all the matched pairs to be operating simultaneously. (Other arrangements, such as two pipe plants integrated with one pig-iron plant are also possible, but the general problem remains the same.) Finally, since iron had to be remelted anyway to make strong enough pipe, that is, molten iron from the blast furnace could not be poured directly into pipe molds, additional transportation costs for fuel, as well as for drying the sand molds, were necessary. Consequently, the ideal location for pipe plants may not have been close to the pig-iron plants.

36. *Iron Age,* November 7, 1895, p. 956, and December 12, 1895, p. 1231.

37. *Id.,* January 23, 1896, p. 263.

38. *Id.,* February 6, 1896, p. 379.

39. *Id.,* February 13, 1896, at 432. This journal often went to considerable lengths to conceal the identities of the parties to a transaction.

40. *Id.,* January 2, 1896, p. 71.

41. *United States v. Addyston Pipe and Steel Co.,* 85 Fed. 271 (6th Cir. 1898).

42. *United States v. Addyston Pipe and Steel Co.,* 175 U.S. 211 (1899).

43. *Iron Age,* June 2, 1896, p. 28.

44. *Id.,* February 2, 1899, p. 35.

45. *Id.,* February 9, 1899.

46. See Table 3 and Figure 2 for the capacities and locations of the specialized producers at this time.

47. *Iron Age,* March 28, 1899, p. 33. Note that this suggests that the contractors, who were steady customers of the pipe producers, had long-term arrangements for their supplies of pipe.

48. *Id.,* April 13, 1899, p. 8.

49. *Id.,* May 25, 1899, p. 38.

50. *Id.,* November 8, 1899.

51. *Id.,* January 11, 1900, p. 30.

52. *Id.,* April 26, 1900, p. 29, and June 14, 1900, p. 38.

53. *Id.,* August 9, 1900.

54. *Id.,* December 13, 1900, p. 47.

55. The mergers in the cast-iron pressure and cast-iron soil pipe industries were only two of several hundred that occurred in manufacturing in the years 1898 to 1902, and that encompassed nearly one-half of U.S. manufacturing capacity. A seemingly sensible explanation for this merger wave is the adverse antitrust decisions in *Trans-Missouri* (1897), *Joint Traffic* (1898) and *Addyston* (1898 and 1899). Stigler [(47), p. 102], Thorelli [(52), p. 258] and Nelson [(34), p. 135] dispute this explanation. However, Bittlingmayer (6) presents evidence on the increased antitrust agitation in this period at the state and federal level (ten states passed antitrust laws in early 1897) and also provides several examples, including the formation of United Shoe and the extensive railroad consolidations of the 1898–1902 period, in which the threat of antitrust policy seems to have played an important role.

56. *Commercial and Financial Chronicle*, January 28, 1899, p. 185. This reference also appears in Phillips (37), p. 115.

57. *Iron Age,* June 9, 1898, p. 28.

58. Summaries of these and many other similar careers can be found in Moore (32).

59. See the discussion above in Section II.C, especially the quote from the Chattanooga firm.

60. The sources are the same as for Figure 4.

61. See Bittlingmayer (5). This also contains a more detailed treatment of costs in the cast-iron pipe industry. Comparisons of margins over time based on contract data appear in Bittlingmayer (4), pp. 87–89. For trade reports consistent with the view that competition sometimes forced prices to unremunerative levels, see Section III.B below.

62. *Iron Age,* November 16, 1905, p. 1304.

63. See *Moody's Analysis of Investments*, Part II, Public Utilities and Industrials, p. 1297 (1915); *The Manual of Statistics: Stock Exchange Handbook 1915,* p. 835; *Gibson's Manual, 1909,* p. 333.

64. By "classical monopoly gains" I mean the gains that come from price above marginal cost when marginal cost-pricing *will* sustain the industry. In the case here, however, a regime of constant unit prices and the survival of individual plants (with something like the optimal industry configuration of plants and output) *requires* price above marginal cost. Although firms here do seek to raise prices above marginal cost and, naturally, maximize profits, one can at least imagine various constraints (vertical integration, long-term contracts, buyer coalitions, etc.) that can keep prices close to the notional optimum.

65. Note that including the $9.75 figure for January would have resulted in a range with a greater upper limit.

66. See the calculations in Section I.C for support on this figure. Six years earlier, in 1890, total industry capital amounted to $14.2 million (book value), the industry used 573,226 tons of pig iron, and the average commercial paper rate was 6.91 percent. This implies a capital cost of $1.71 per ton.

67. The industry used 573,226 tons of pig iron in 1890. See U.S. Census Office (55), p. 489.

68. *Iron Age,* July 9, 1895, p. 78.

69. *Id.,* November 12, 1896, p. 923.

70. *Id.,* March 19, 1896, p. 714.

71. *Id.,* April 2, 1896, p. 826.

72. *Id.,* February 25, 1896, p. 353.

73. *Iron Age,* February 27, 1896, p. 547.

74. *Id.,* June 4, 1896, p. 1374.

75. Compare this to the averages of $13.28 and $13.55 in Tables 9 and 10.

76. *Iron Age,* June 25, 1896.

77. Letwin [(29), pp. 71–85] and Bullock's (9) survey of literature on the trusts provide some idea of the mix of opinion.

78. See Gould (21). Note also that this implies that it is not unreasonable to find two firms at different locations operating at different marginal costs even though one has an apparent advantage in filling orders because its marginal costs are lower.

79. For some related observations, see Phillips (37), pp. 116–118.

80. There is some question, in fact, whether the concept of collusion is tractable in this case. Telser (51) presents an analysis of the conditions under which self-enforcing agreements can occur.

81. The simplest case in which this is true is that of the mineral water duopolists analyzed by Cournot, modified, however, to cover the case in which the two sellers have unequal marginal costs.

82. Coase [(16), p. 392] observes that "it seems improbable that a firm would emerge without the existence of uncertainty."

83. The explanation offered here in defense of restrictions on competition may resolve a long-standing paradox: If it is true that the unifying theme of the common law is economic efficiency, what explains the common law's apparent laxness concerning combinations in restraint of trade? The English common law governing this area is summarized as follows in Letwin [(28) pp. 381–382]:

> [C]ombinations of merchants to fix prices of goods, share out a market, or otherwise limit competition, were governed by no general statutes, particularly after the laws against forestalling were repealed, and therefore remained under the jurisdiction of common law. In a few instances, such combinations were indicted as criminal conspiracies at common law. But after the beginning of the nineteenth century, the common law came to regard an agreement between competitors to combine an analogous to a contract in restraint of trade, and *judged such agreements by whether they left the parties reasonably free to act as they desired*. All along, less attention was paid to whether the agreement seriously interfered with competition. [Emphasis added, footnotes omitted.]

Indeed, this emphasis on the freedom of those who enter into an agreement in restraint of trade led to the view, in *Mogul Steamship Co. v. McGregor,* Ct. Cust. App. 25 (1892), that "the agreement was unlawful in the sense that the courts would not enforce it, but that it was not '*contrary to law.*' It would become an illegal conspiracy at common law only if it sought an unlawful end or used unlawful means." [*id.* at 383, footnote omitted.] Furthermore, it is clear that the justices deciding this case thought that sanctioning self-enforcing agreements served public policy. Judge Taft, in his opinion in *Addyston,* offered the slightly different view that "[c]ontracts that were in unreasonable restraint of trade at common law . . . were simply void and were not enforced by the courts" and cited *Mogul Steamship* [*Addyston,* 85 Fed. 271 (1898), at 279]. By claiming that "unreasonable" restraints of trade were unenforceable and by ignoring the arguments in favor of such self-enforcing agreements, Taft was able to defend his view that "[t]he effect of the act of 1890 is to render such [unreasonable] contracts unlawful in an affirmative or positive sense" [*id.*]. For a more extensive refutation of Taft's claim that the Sherman Act was grounded in the common law see Bork (7).

84. The important point in this discussion is that the form of the organization is determined by the net costs. For example, the complete independence of the divisions of General Motors would be destructive to the firm as a whole, and, I argue, to consumer welfare. The purpose of the constraints on pricing, body types, use of common components, and so on is to prevent interdivision price wars, duplication of effort on general engineering, and other competitive wastes. On the other hand, the islands of freedom and competition in styling and other dimensions of effort that are hard to evaluate serve as substitutes for monitoring. In the cast-iron pipe industry the situation is similar, but the benefits of restriction were confined to a narrower range. It should be emphasized that the industry as a whole benefited from an efficient organization. This goal was served first and foremost by making the monitoring costs and associated losses as small as possible. This is, of course, the classic source of diseconomies in a large organization. Independent plants have an incentive to control these costs, although there are other benefits, such as competition in the discovery of new technology and competition for experienced personnel that place experienced people in the best possible slots. Indeed, the one crucial area in which competition and independent ownership carried more harm than good was in the matter of the price of the finished good. It is in this area that the firms agreed to limit competition.

85. It might be objected that if the purpose of the merger in this case was to escape the antitrust laws, the various plants could have undertaken a sham merger and so preserve the benefits that come from independent operation. But it must be recognized that collusion of the sort that occurred in this industry would still have been necessary. Moreover, there would certainly have been times when the owners would have been in conflict with each other. The courts, if they originally had declared such collusion to be illegal, would not have been fooled into thinking it was lawful by a ruse merger that left intact the previous rights and responsibilities. This much was clear even in 1896, for example, when mergers and incorporations were routinely struck down if the purpose was to shield some action that was otherwise illegal and against the public interest. The *Addyston* defendants could only substitute for their looser collusive arrangement a recognized form of consolidation, which, although it increased the costs of operating the separate plants, provided the substance of a consolidated operation. The courts could not invalidate this arrangement as easily because the presumption had been that more complete integration resulted in cost savings that the courts were in a poor position to evaluate.

86. It should be noted that completely free entry may be troublesome because it may not be possible to find price and output combinations that serve the consumer interest and that cover all costs while still providing defense against destabilizing entry [Baumol, Panzar, and Willig (3), ch. 9]. It is interesting to note in this connection that international shipping cartels often have restricted membership and impose sanctions against shippers who transport goods outside the cartel. American ships, although partially exempt from the antitrust laws, may not participate in such cartels. See Gordon (20), p. 92, p. 101. *Mogul Steamship,* discussed in note 83, and commonly cited as evidence of the favorable attitude of the common law toward combinations in restraint of trade, dealt with a shipping cartel that not only fixed prices, but also conducted price wars with rival steamship lines and imposed sanctions on those who shipped with outside lines.

REFERENCES

1.   Asch, P., and Seneca, J. J. (February 1976) "Is Collusion Profitable?" *Review of Economics and Statistics,* Vol. 58: 1–27.
2.   Aumann, R. (1964) "Existence of Competitive Equilibria in Markets with a Continuum of Traders," *Econometrica,* Vol. 34: 1–17.
3.   Baumol, W. J., Panzar, J. C., and Willig, P. D. (1982) *Contestable Markets and the Theory of Industry Structure,* New York, Harcourt, Brace, Jovanovich.
4.   Bittlingmayer, George. (1981) *Competition and the Nature of Costs: The Cast Iron Pipe Industry, 1890–1910, and the Case of Addyston Pipe,* Ph.D. dissertation, University of Chicago.
5.   ———. (October 1982) "Decreasing Average Cost and Competition: A New Look at the Addyston Pipe Case," *Journal of Law and Economics,* Vol. 25: 201–229.
6.   ———. (1982) "Did Antitrust Policy Create the Trusts?" Unpublished Working Paper, University of Michigan.
7.   Bork, Robert. (October 1966) "Legislative Intent and the Policy of the Sherman Act," *Journal of Law and Economics,* Vol. 9: 7–48.
8.   ———. (1978) *The Antitrust Paradox: A Policy at War with Itself,* New York, Basic Books.
9.   Bullock, Charles J. (February 1901) "Trust Literature: A Survey and Criticism," *Quarterly Journal of Economics,* Vol. 15: 167–216.
10. Burns, A. R. (1936) *The Decline of Competition,* New York, McGraw-Hill.
11. ———. (June 1937) "The Antitrust Laws and the Regulation of Competition," *Law and Contemporary Problems,* Vol. 4: 301–320.

12. Cady, George Johnson. (1942) *Entrepreneural [sic] Costs and Price: A Reconsideration of Competitive and Monopolistic Market Theory*, Evanston, published by author.
13. Clark, John Maurice. (1923) *Studies in the Economics of Overhead Costs*, Chicago, The University of Chicago Press.
14. ———. (1939) *The Social Control of Business*, New York, McGraw-Hill.
15. ———. (June 1940) "Toward a Concept of Workable Competition," *American Economic Review*, Vol. 30: 24–256.
16. Coase, Ronald. (Nov. 1937) "The Nature of the Firm," *Economica*, Vol. 4: 386–405.
17. Farrell, M. J. (1959) "The Convexity Assumption in the Theory of Competitive Markets," *Journal of Political Economy*, Vol. 67: 377–391.
18. Fetter, Frank. (1931) *The Masquerade of Monopoly*, New York, Harcourt, Brace.
19. Gillies, D. B. (1959) "Solutions to the General Non-Zero-Sum Games," in A. W. Tucker and R. D. Luce, eds., *Contributions to the Theory of Games, IV*, Princeton, Princeton University Press.
20. Gordon, J. S. (1969) "Shipping Regulation and the Federal Maritime Commission," *University of Chicago Law Review*, Vol. 37: 90–158.
21. Gould, J. P. (January 1978) "Inventories and Stochastic Demand: Equilibrium Models of the Firm and Industry," *Journal of Business*, Vol. 51: 1–42.
22. Hay, G. A., and Kelly, D. (April 1974) "An Empirical Survey of Price Fixing Conspiracies," *Journal of Law and Economics*, Vol. 17: 13–38.
23. Hicks, John. (1939) *Value and Capital*, Oxford, Clarendon Press.
24. Hirschl, A. (1896) *Combination, Consolidation and Succession of Corporations*, Chicago, Callaghan and Co.
25. Johnston, J. (1960) *Statistical Cost Analysis*, New York, McGraw-Hill.
26. Jones, Eliot. (1924) *The Principles of Railway Transportation*, New York, Macmillan.
27. ———. (1924) *The Trust Problem in the United States*, New York, Macmillan.
28. Letwin, William. (Spring 1954) "The English Common Law Concerning Monopolies," *University of Chicago Law Review*, Vol. 21: 355–385.
29. ———. (1965) *Law and Economic Policy in America*, New York, Random House.
30. Marshall, Alfred. (1949) *Principles of Economics*, 8th ed. (reset and reprinted), London, Macmillan.
31. Moore, Frederick T. (1959) "Economies of Scale: Some Statistical Evidence," *Quarterly Journal of Economics*, Vol. 73: 232–245.
32. Moore, W. D. (1939) *Development of the Cast Iron Pressure Pipe Industry in the Southern States, 1800–1938*, Newcomen Address.
33. National Industrial Conference Board. (1929) *Mergers in Industry*, New York.
34. Nelson, R. L. (1959) *Merger Movements in American Industry, 1895–1956*, Princeton, Princeton University Press.
35. Noble, H. J. (1940) *History of the Cast Iron Pipe Industry in the United States of America*, Newcomen Address.
36. Norman, G. (1979) "Economies of Scale in the Cement Industry," *Journal of Industrial Economics*, Vol. 47: 317.
37. Phillips, Almarin. (1962) *Market Structure, Organization and Performance*, Cambridge, Harvard University Press.
38. Posner, Richard A. (1976) *Antitrust Law: An Economic Perspective*, Chicago, The University of Chicago Press.
39. Ripley, W. Z. (1916) *Trusts, Pools and Corporations*, New York, Ginn.
40. Robinson, E. A. G. (1931) *The Structure of Competitive Industry*, London, Nisbet.
41. Samuelson, Paul. (1947) *Foundations of Economic Analysis*, Cambridge, Harvard University Press.
42. Seager, H. R., and Gulich, C. A. (1924) *Trust and Corporation Problems*, New York, Harper.

43. Sharkey, William W. (1973) *A Study of Markets Involving Increasing Returns and Uncertain Demand*, Ph.D. dissertation, University of Chicago.
44. Sharp, John. (1900) *Modern Foundry Practice*, New York, Spon & Chamberlin.
45. Sheshinski, E., and Dréze, J. H. (December 1976) "Demand Fluctuations, Capacity Utilization and Costs," *American Economic Review*, Vol. 66: 731–742.
46. Stevens, W. S., ed. (1914) *Industrial Combinations and Trusts*, New York, Macmillan.
47. Stigler, George J. (1968) "Monopoly and Oligopoly by Merger," in *The Organization of Industry*, Homewood, Irwin.
48. Stimpson, W. C., and Gray, B. L. (1944) *Foundry Work*, American Technical Society.
49. Telser, Lester G. (1972) *Competition, Collusion and Game Theory*, Chicago and New York, Aldine-Atherton.
50. ———. (1978) *Economic Theory and the Core*, Chicago, University of Chicago Press.
51. ———. (January 1980) "A Theory of Self-Enforcing Agreements," *Journal of Business*, Vol. 53: 27–44.
52. Thorelli, Hans. (1955) *The Federal Antitrust Policy: Origination of an American Tradition*, Baltimore, Johns Hopkins University Press.
53. *Transcript of Record of the Supreme Court of the United States*. (1899) "Addyston Pipe and Steel et al. vs. the United States," No. 51, October Term 1899.
54. U.S. Bureau of the Census. (1975) *Historical Statistics of the United States: Colonial Times to 1970*, Washington, D.C.
55. U.S. Census Office, Department of the Interior. (1892) "Cast Iron Pipe Industry," *Report on Manufacturing Industries of the United States: 1890, Part III, Selected Industries*, 487–490.
56. Varian, Hal. (1978) *Microeconomic Analysis*, New York, Norton.
57. Vickrey, W. (March 1961) "Counterspeculation, Auctions, and Competitive Sealed Tenders," *Journal of Finance*, Vol. 16: 8–37.
58. Viner, Jacob. (1952) "Cost Curves and Supply Curves," reprinted in G. J. Stigler and K. Boulding, eds., *Readings in Price Theory*, Chicago, Irwin.
59. Walters, A. A. (January–April 1963) "Production and Cost Functions," *Econometrica*, Vol. 31: 1–66.
60. Whitney, Simon N. (1958) *Antitrust Policies: American Experience in Twenty Industries*, New York, Twentieth Century Fund.
61. Zerbe, Richard O. (October 1969) "The American Sugar Refining Company, 1887–1914: The Story of a Monopoly," *Journal of Law and Economics*, Vol. 12: 339–376.

Berkey Photo, Inc. v. Eastman Kodak Co.: A SEARCH FOR AN EXPLANATION OF KODAK'S DOMINANCE OF THE AMATEUR PHOTOGRAPHIC EQUIPMENT INDUSTRY

James W. Meehan, Jr.

The Eastman Kodak Company has dominated the amateur photographic industry for some three-quarters of a century. This paper explores three possible explanations for Kodak's dominance. (1) The company has habitually used predatory and exclusionary behavior to acquire and to maintain its position (the argument used by Berkey Photo in its antitrust suit against Kodak). (2) Kodak acquired "first-mover" advantages by being the first to market a photographic system that could be used successfully by amateurs; and once having acquired these advantages, Kodak has used them to control industry standards so as to prevent its rivals from breaking its stranglehold on the market. (3) Kodak is simply superior to its rivals in producing and selling photographic products. The evidence does not seem to substantiate Berkey's claim that Kodak's dominance of the amateur photographic market is explained by predatory and exclusionary conduct. Kodak's dominance may owe in part to "first-mover" advantages associated with brand loyalty, but the data do not indicate that Kodak manipulated industry standards to

Research in Law and Economics, Volume 5, pages 131–165.
Copyright © 1983 by JAI Press Inc.
All rights of reproduction in any form reserved.
ISBN: 0-89232-419-8

discourage rivals from competing. Indeed, a credible conclusion is that Kodak may well be superior to its rivals. In the absence of more convincing proof that Kodak's dominance results from strategic behavior, prudent policy makers will wait for market forces to erode Kodak's market share rather than use antitrust laws to attack the company.

I. INTRODUCTION

The amateur photographic industry[1] had its beginning in 1888 when George Eastman introduced the revolutionary "roll film" system that greatly simplified the process of photography, making it accessible to the novice for the first time.[2] Shortly thereafter, Eastman sought to consolidate his company's position in the newly created amateur market through a series of horizontal acquisitions. From 1890 to 1905, the Eastman Kodak Co. (hereinafter referred to simply as Kodak) purchased some twenty rival companies, thus permitting George Eastman to gain control of all of the competing roll film patents and to acquire a dominant position in such markets as roll film, dry plates, photographic paper, and cameras.[3] To the present day Kodak's dominance has persisted; its share of the number of units sold during a period from the early 1950s until the mid-1970s averaged 68 percent in the amateur still camera market, 86 percent in the film market, and 89 percent in the color print paper market.[4] Moreover, Kodak controlled over 95 percent of the photofinishing market for color film until 1954 when it signed a consent decree with the Department of Justice,[5] a decision that led to the entry into this market of over 600 independent photofinishers. Since that time Kodak's share of the market has fallen to about 10 percent in 1976.[6]

In this paper I will attempt to determine some of the reasons that explain Kodak's ability to dominate the amateur photographic markets for almost a century. Three explanations have already been offered or hinted at by one or the other of the parties in *Berkey v. Kodak*. The main thrust of the plaintiff's case is that Kodak's dominance is explained by its use of predatory and exclusionary behavior. Another possible explanation, which Berkey only insinuated and consequently never fully developed, is that Kodak had acquired "first-mover" advantages in the amateur market; and once having acquired them, it was able to maintain its advantage by controlling industry standards in such a manner as to make it virtually impossible for rivals to break its stranglehold on the market. The final explanation, offered by the defendants, is that Kodak's dominance is explained by its absolute superiority in producing and selling amateur photographic products.

The analysis will first examine Kodak's questionable behavior to determine if it has an anticompetitive effect (i.e., is it output restricting?)

and if that behavior can be remedied by antitrust policy. The alternative explanation, that such behavior improves productive efficiency,[7] will also be explored; but since it is difficult to prove a direct causal link between firm behavior and improvements in productive efficiency, this analysis will have to rule out the anticompetitive explanation before concluding that the questionable conduct is either neutral or truly more efficient.[8] If, on the other hand, anticompetitive effects cannot be completely ruled out, we must decide whether some antitrust relief is desirable, or whether a more prudent policy would be to leave Kodak's conduct unchallenged and to wait for the market to erode the company's dominance.

Following this plan, I will examine Berkey's allegation that Kodak's conduct is predatory and exclusionary, and explore some recent literature which provides a framework for determining whether or not Kodak's dominance can be explained by first-mover advantages and the market's failure to erode those advantages over time. If these explanations can be ruled out, it will be appropriate to conclude that the courts would be well advised to leave the market to its own devices.

Part II will provide an outline of the major issues in *Berkey v. Kodak*. Part III will use microtheory to analyze Berkey's claim that Kodak's conduct is predatory and exclusionary, and it will also inquire into some of Kodak's explanations that are consistent with productive efficiency. Part IV will examine the possibility that Kodak's dominance can be explained by first-mover advantages. Finally, Part V will suggest some conclusions and recommendations for public policy.

II. THE MAJOR ISSUES IN *BERKEY V. KODAK*

The argument that Kodak's dominance is the result of predatory and exclusionary conduct was fully articulated in *Berkey v. Kodak*. In 1973, Berkey Photo, a large independent photofinisher and manufacturer of amateur cameras,[9] filed an antitrust suit, charging Kodak with illegally monopolizing the amateur photographic market in violation of Section 2 of the Sherman Act and engaging in a conspiracy with flash cube manufacturers in violation of Section 1.[10] Berkey's case was based on claims that Kodak illegally acquired its dominance in the amateur market near the turn of the century[11] and had maintained it by adopting such exclusionary practices as marketing products as a complete system and refusing to sell products in formats other than its own.[12] According to Berkey, these practices, and in particular the practice of systems selling,[13] permitted Kodak to lever its monopoly position in a number of related markets.

Since the key to this argument is the use of systems selling, the photographic systems at issue in the case must be described before proceeding to a detailed explanation of the leverage argument. Berkey alleged that the practice of systems selling began in 1963 when Kodak introduced the "126 photographic system,"[14] which included a new camera (called the Instamatic), a new color print film (called Kodacolor X), a new chemical process for photofinishing (a series of chemical baths controlled for time and temperature, called C-22), and a completely new set of photofinishing equipment. The new system had the advantage of being considerably easier for the amateur photographer to operate; the most important innovation in the system was that the film was prespooled into a plastic cartridge so designed that it could be easily "dropped" into the back of the camera, thereby eliminating the need for manual loading.[15] In 1972 Kodak next introduced the new 110 "Pocket Instamatic" system. This system included a camera, which is significantly smaller than the Instamatic, and a new, smaller film cartridge designed especially for the 110 camera. Instead of repackaging its existing color print film, Kodacolor X, in the smaller cartridge, Kodak chose to introduce the new system with an entirely new color print film called Kodacolor II.[16] The new film was initially packaged exclusively for the 110 format, and it also required a new chemical process (called C-41), new processing equipment, and a new color print paper.

The remainder of this section will examine Berkey's claim that systems selling is the means by which Kodak is able to maintain its dominance in four segments of the amateur photographic market.

A. Cameras

Berkey claimed that Kodak's dominance of the camera market can be explained by its ability to lever its monopoly power from film into cameras. Berkey used two arguments to support its claim. One, rivals have been denied the opportunity to compete with Kodak by selling innovative camera formats that differ substantially from those being sold by Kodak because the latter refuses to sell film in formats other than that for which it sells a compatible camera.[17] And since Kodak sells approximately 90 percent of all color film sold in the United States, competing camera manufacturers will probably not attempt to sell cameras that are incompatible with Kodak film. Therefore, rivals have little choice but to sell a camera that is an imitation of Kodak cameras.[18]

The second argument is that by physically tying the sale of the 110 Pocket Instamatic camera to the sale of a new film, Kodacolor II, and advertising it as a "remarkable new film" that produces "big sharp pictures," Kodak was able to increase its sale of cameras at the expense of its rivals.[19] Presumably consumers purchased the 110 camera because they wanted to use the new film. And since Kodak sold Kodacolor II only in the 110 format for a period of eighteen months after its introduction, the consumer who wanted to use the new film had no choice but to buy the new 110 camera from Kodak, at least until such time as rivals were able to produce their own versions of the camera.

To support its claim that the policy of introducing new products as a system was a strategic tool that enabled Kodak to lever its monopoly position from film into cameras, Berkey sought to demonstrate that Kodacolor X was capable of producing high quality prints in the 110 format and that Kodacolor II was inferior to Kodacolor X in many respects. As evidence, Berkey cited the testimony of the manager of Kodak's Film Emulsion Division who indicated that Kodacolor X would produce acceptable pictures in the 110 format.[20] Berkey also pointed out that Kodacolor II did not retain its "speed" after it sat on the shelf for periods longer than three to six months, and the film had difficulty retaining a latent image if it were not developed soon after exposure.[21]

B. Photofinishing

Although Berkey did not contend that Kodak had a monopoly in photofinishing, it did argue that Kodak's dominance in the film market enabled that company to maintain control over the photofinishing market. At the heart of this claim is the fact that the sale of film and the photofinishing process were physically tied together for a period of a few weeks after the introduction of the 110 system. Even though the new Kodacolor II film necessitated a new chemical process (C-41),[22] Kodak did not disclose this requirement to independent photofinishers until after the new system was introduced. Consequently, if consumers purchased the new system, they had no alternative but to have their film processed by Kodak until other independents had time to adopt the new C-41 process.[23]

Berkey also alleged that Kodak employed at least four other practices to lever its monopoly power into photofinishing to the disadvantage of the independents. First, Kodak did not predisclose to rival equipment manufacturers that the new film required new photofinishing equipment; hence, independent photofinishers had to buy new equipment from Kodak, equipment which was sold to them at excessive prices. Second, Kodak supplied the independents with less efficient processing equipment.[24] Third, Kodak refused to supply the independents with chemicals in bulk or to disclose the chemical formula for the C-41 process; therefore, independents were forced to buy the chemicals in premixed kits from Kodak at almost twice the price of the bulk chemicals that Kodak used in its own processing plants. And finally, Kodak frustrated the efforts of independent photofinishers to control the quality of their processed film by failing to disclose the existence of two different populations of Kodacolor II film with different color characteristics.[25]

C. Color Paper

As was the case in a number of other amateur markets, Kodak acquired a dominant position in the photographic paper market through a series of acquisitions at the turn of the century.[26] The company was able to maintain that dominance until 1954 because it processed over 95 percent of the color film sold in the United States,[27] and it refused to use color print paper produced by any other manufacturers. Berkey contended that Kodak has been able to maintain its dominance since 1954 because it physically ties the sale of color print paper to the sale of film. Here Berkey's argument repeated the earlier logic of the alleged tie-in between film and photofinishing. The introduction of Kodacolor II required the use of a new color paper to produce a finished print, and since Kodak did not predisclose the specifications of the new paper to rival manufacturers, Kodak was the only paper manufacturer in a position to take advantage of the sales generated by Kodacolor II film. Berkey also claimed that Kodak had purposely kept independent photofinishers small and fragmented so that they would be more likely to buy color paper from Kodak, the leading supplier.[28] Furthermore, Berkey alleged that Kodak make it difficult for other color paper manufacturers to compete because it aggressively promoted its paper and refused to supply paper without the Kodak trademark printed on the back.[29]

D. Film

A 1915 antitrust case was cited by Berkey to show that Kodak illegally acquired its monopoly position in film.[30] And, in a reversal of its previous claims, Berkey contended that Kodak leveraged its monopoly from cameras into film by physically tying the sale of film to cameras. In this version of Berkey's argument, consumers who wanted to avail themselves of the new Pocket Instamatic camera had to purchase their film from Kodak until such time as rival manufacturers geared up to produce their own film in 110 cartridges approximately two years after Kodak introduced the system in March of 1972.[31] Berkey also asserted that the length of the physical tie-in was extended by Kodak's failure to predisclose the technical specifications of the 110 system and by the fact that the 110 system was introduced with a new film (Kodacolor II) and a new chemical process (C-41). The basis for the latter claim is that had the 110 system been introduced with the existing color print film, Kodacolor X, Kodak's rivals in the film market would have been able more rapidly to introduce their own film in a 110 cartridge. Instead of completely redesigning their film to be compatible with Kodak's new C-41 chemistry, rival companies could have simply cut their existing C-22 film down to fit the 110 cartridge. With the change in film chemistry, however, Berkey contended that Kodak's rivals had to redesign their film to be compatible with C-41 because they would have found it difficult to sell their film when independent processors rapidly phased out their C-22 processing lines and changed over to the C-41 process. In support of this contention, Berkey referred to the fact that GAF, the only manufacturer to sell a 110 film compatible with C-22 chemistry, dropped out of the market in 1977.[32]

III. AN ANALYSIS OF BERKEY'S CLAIM THAT KODAK'S DOMINANCE CAN BE EXPLAINED BY EXCLUSIONARY BEHAVIOR

As the previous description indicates, Berkey contended that the key to Kodak's continued dominance of the amateur market was its ability to lever its monopoly power among the various markets by physically tying the sale of photographic products. Since Berkey simply asserted the leverage argument instead of demonstrating why it is profitable for Kodak to attempt to lever monopoly,[33] this claim needs to be examined. A number of alternative explanations for the physical tie-in also need to be explored.

A. Leverage

The essence of the leverage argument is that two monopolies are better than one, but economic theory teaches that such will not be the case when two or more complementary products or services are used in fixed proportions [Bowman (6), Burstein (8, 9)]. In the fixed proportions case, the relevant demand curve for suppliers is the joint demand for the complementary products; therefore, a firm holding a monopoly in one of the products can fully exploit that power by charging the monopoly price for that product. If the firm attempts to extend its monopoly power into other markets, it will find that its monopoly profits in the first market will be reduced by a dollar for every dollar its profits are increased in the other market.[34] The only exception to this rule would be a case in which the firm's control over the market for two or more products makes entry more difficult.[35]

Most of Berkey's argument that Kodak attempted to lever its monopoly power pertained to products that are used in fixed proportions; that is, film and photofinishing, and color print paper and color film. Each roll of exposed film must be processed with a series of chemical baths that are controlled for time and temperature, and each roll of film of similar type (black and white, color print, and color slide) employs exactly the same process. Therefore, it seems unlikely that Kodak was trying to use its monopoly in the film market to gain a monopoly advantage in the photofinishing market. It is also unlikely that Kodak would want intentionally to injure those independent photofinishers who process approximately 88 percent of Kodak's color film.[36] Moreover, if the independents charged higher prices to cover the higher costs associated with the inefficient equipment and supplies sold to them by Kodak at monopoly prices, the demand for Kodak's film would fall. Color print paper and color film are also used in fixed proportions; a fixed amount of paper is used to print a picture from each color negative. Therefore, it also does not appear that Kodak was attempting to lever its monopoly power from the film market into the color paper market.[37]

One might argue that cameras and film are not used in fixed proportions because consumers may find it possible to substitute cameras for film by buying a more expensive amateur camera and then taking fewer exposures to produce a picture of a given quality. However, there are severe limits to the extent to which an amateur photographer can substitute a more sophisticated camera for film. A more expensive 110 camera will allow the consumer some freedom in focusing the lens and varying the shutter speed, but the improvement in the quality of the final picture that the amateur consumer acquires with the more expensive 110 camera is not very great.[38]

B. Barriers to Entry

Still another explanation for the physical tie-in is that it may be used as a strategic mechanism to raise the barriers to entry. Williamson (45) suggests that Kodak's pre-1954 practice of tying the sale of color film and photoprocessing is a good illustration of the means by which a tie-in can raise the barriers to entry.[39] As a consequence of the pre-1954 tie-in between color film and photoprocessing, Kodak developed 96 percent of the total color film processed in the United States;[40] likewise, Kodak refused to process the color film manufactured by any of its rivals. Therefore, if a firm wanted to enter the film market, it faced the option of entering both markets simultaneously or first entering the film market and then coordinating its entry with that of independents into the photofinishing market. The first option would raise the barriers to entry if there were imperfections in the capital market that increase the cost of capital to the potential entrant by an amount greater than the cost to the established firms.[41] The second option would also impose a cost on the potential entrant, one which Kodak did not incur, if there were substantial transaction costs for coordinating joint entry by independent firms.[42]

Whatever the merits of this argument with regard to the tie-in that Kodak employed between film and photofinishing[43] prior to 1954, it is a less valid explanation for a physical tie-in because it is not as binding as the more formal tie-in. If a firm wants to enter one of the amateur photographic market today, it can do so by simply producing a product that is technically compatible with the complementary products in the system. For example, a firm can enter the film industry without entering either the camera or the photofinishing market as long as its film is compatible with the existing camera formats and the photofinishing chemistry used to process Kodak film.[44,45]

C. Goodwill and Other Efficiency Explanations

A final explanation for the physical tie-in of amateur photographic products is that it may simply be the means by which Kodak can most efficiently market its products and protect its goodwill. The amateur photographic system is technically complex, and very few amateur photographers know how to determine the cause of a failure within the system; that is, they may know that the picture is unacceptable to them, but they are unable to pinpoint the exact cause of the failure.[46] If consumers purchase each component from a different manufacturer and wrongly assign the responsibility for a failure within the system, they may impose a substantial loss on an innocent manufacturer by depreciating its goodwill. The failure of consumers to be able to assign appropriate responsbility for an unacceptable picture will, in turn, provide the manufacturer of the separate components within the system with an incentive to "free ride" on one another's goodwill; and if the market failure is serious enough, consumers may not get the quality of photography they are willing to pay for. The market failure can be eliminated, however, if a manufacturer integrates into the production of all of the products and services within the system and ties the sale of any one component to the rest.[47] A tie-in arrangement assures that the manufacturer of any of the products or services that cause a failure within the system is assigned the liability for that failure, thus insuring that consumers will receive the quality and reliability they are willing to pay for.

The goodwill argument for tying the sale of amateur photographic products is weaker today than it was earlier in the industry's history. The 126 and 110 cartridge-loading cameras have practically eliminated most of the problems that consumers formerly encountered in loading and unloading their cameras. Furthermore, a large number of independent photofinishers have demonstrated that they have the ability and knowledge necessary to produce quality color photoprocessing. It is still possible, on the other hand, to make the case that a temporary tie-in is needed in order to protect Kodak's goodwill during that crucial period soon after a new amateur photographic system is introduced.

Although conclusive proof is lacking, the goodwill explanation is consistent with the facts surrounding the physical tie-in of the products and services included in the 110 system. Early in the development stage of the new system, Kodak concluded that Kodacolor X, its existing color print film, would not produce a high quality print if it were used in the smaller 110 format. Kodak decided to introduce its new system simultaneously with the introduction of Kodacolor II, a film that is capable of being enlarged without producing speckled or pebbly prints.[48] In an effort to meet its deadline for announcing the new system, Kodak rushed the Kodacolor II film into production, and as a result, the company encountered a number of problems with the film: its shelf-life was shorter than expected, and the exposed film lost some of its latent image if too much time elapsed between the time when the film was exposed and when it was processed.[49] Kodak believed that these defects would be more serious if the film were used in the existing camera formats than they would be in the new camera format. Past experience at Kodak indicated that films used in new camera formats are sold very quickly, and are returned for processing shortly thereafter.[50] Consequently, in order to protect its goodwill, Kodak may well have decided to produce the Kodacolor II for the 110 system, then limit its sale to that format until the film could be improved.[51]

Kodak's short-term physical tie-in of Kodacolor II film to photofinishing may also be explained as an attempt to protect goodwill. When a new product, especially one as technically complex as film, is introduced into the mass market, minor quality-control problems normally exist until the bugs can be worked out of the system.[52] Since Kodacolor II required a new chemical process (C-41) and new photofinishing equipment, and since the new film had been processed only under laboratory conditions before its introduction, it is only reasonable to expect that Kodak would have wanted to monitor the photofinishing of the new film during the introductory period in order to ensure that consumers received quality prints.[53] To minimize these problems at the photofinishing stage Kodak faced two alternatives: it could have predisclosed the new film and chemical process to over six hundred independent photofinishers and then monitored their performance during the break-in period, or it could have found some means (e.g., a physical tie-in between film and photofinishing) to ensure that all of the new film was returned to Kodak for processing during this period. The former alternative would not have been very attractive; predisclosure of the new film and the new chemical process to a large number of independent photofinishers would have substantially increased the risk of prematurely disclosing the details of the new 110 system to rival camera and film manufacturers.[54] Although the trial at the District Court did not produce any firm evidence on this point, predisclosure would have undoubtedly entailed higher monitoring costs. Had Kodak chosen to predisclose its film, it would have had to provide extensive training to independent photofinishers in a very short period of time, it would have had to monitor the performance of a large number of photofinishers during the break-in period, and it would also have had to stand ready to provide technical assistance to the independents during this period.[55] The cost to Kodak was probably lower when it channeled the film back through its own photofinishing plants because only eight plants needed to be monitored, and Kodak's personnel already possessed an intimate knowledge of the new film's technical peculiarities.[56]

IV. MARKET FAILURE CONSIDERATIONS

The analysis in the previous section suggests that it is unlikely that Kodak's continued dominance of the amateur photographic equipment industry can be explained by exclusionary conduct. Williamson (44) has argued that even if single firm dominance cannot be explained by exclusionary practices, it does not necessarily follow that dominant firms should be immune from antitrust liability. He notes that single firm dominance should be subject to remedial action if three conditions exist: (1) dominance cannot be explained by contemporaneous absolute superiority of the leading firm; (2) evidence shows that the dominant firm's monopoly will probably not be eroded by market forces in a reasonable period of time; and (3) an effective remedy can be fashioned.[57] Williamson's argument will be summarized, then employed to determine if it sheds any light on our understanding of Kodak's dominance of the amateur photographic industry[58]

Williamson has contended that a firm's continual dominance of an industry may not be explained by current managerial superiority over its rivals. He recognizes three possibilities: (1) a firm may acquire a dominant position at an early point in its history because of the acumen of its original managers, and the dominance will persist to the present even though its current managers are no more competent than those of its rivals; (2) a firm's dominance may be explained by the particular ineptitude of its rivals, rather than by absolute managerial superiority (called "default failure"); and (3) single firm dominance may be the result of historical accident or the laws of chance (called "chance event failure").[59] If markets are working perfectly, such single firm dominance will not continue for very long. If a firm exploits its power, smaller rivals will expand and new entry will occur. Williamson, however, suggests that the market may not perform its self-policing function in a timely fashion because there may be advantages to being first in the market, advantages that inhibit the growth of late entrants and deter new entry.[60] Williamson (44), p. 1520, describes those potential advantages this way:

> . . . the potential entrant into a mature industry must not only raise capital sufficient to finance plant and equipment at an efficient scale

but must, in addition, have resources sufficient to cover the start-up costs which, in a mature industry, may be considerable. Unlike entry at an early stage in an industry's development, where differential experience and reputation effects, are perforce, negligible, costs differences between established firms and new entrants at a mature stage are to be anticipated precisely because these may be said to favor those firms which, for whatever reason, were there early.[61]

Therefore, Williamson concluded that antitrust action may be appropriate in the absence of exclusionary practices if dominance cannot be explained by contemporaneous absolute superiority and if the market fails to perform its self-policing function.[62] Determining the desirability of antitrust action in a particular case requires an examination of the means by which dominance has been achieved and maintained.

A number of elements played an important role in Kodak's development as the dominant firm in the amateur photographic market. As indicated above,[63] George Eastman sought to gain complete control of the new roll film system and embarked on a campaign to acquire all of the competing patents of any significance; he also initiated a series of horizontal mergers that provided Kodak with a number of valuable patents and the opportunity to consolidate its market position in other key industries such as film and dry plates, photographic papers, and cameras. History also provides some evidence of default failure; several of Eastman's rivals lacked the foresight to develop the potential improvements that they had made in various photographic products and processes.[64] Much of Kodak's early success, however, can be explained by the indisputable technical an1 entrepreneurial genius of George Eastman.[65] Therefore, although the reasons for Kodak's early dominance of the amateur photographic market are varied, an impartial observer[66] would have to grant that Kodak's management, and in particular George Eastman, possessed the characteristics of absolute superiority. On the other hand, it is also possible to argue that Kodak's dominant position would not have become as firmly entrenched had it not been for a series of horizontal acquisitions that the company made near the turn of the century.

The Williamson model, however, does not require that the early causes of dominance be untangled. The critical issue is whether or not remedial action would "wastefully" disrupt an existing management team that is absolutely superior. Accordingly, it is necessary to determine whether Kodak's current management possesses the characteristics of absolute superiority or whether first-mover advantages explain the company's continued dominance. Kodak's recent record in the innovation and marketing of new products suggests that its management continues to be superior.

Williamson, nevertheless, cautions against drawing any conclusions about management superiority on the basis of observations of ex post outcomes because superiority in the development of new products could just as convincingly be explained by the failure of rivals to take advantage of the opportunities that have presented themselves (default failure) as it could by the dominant firm's absolute managerial superiority.[67]

Perhaps the most appropriate way to distinguish absolute from relative superiority is to examine the ex ante decision-making processes of both Kodak and its rivals in order to ascertain how each responded to available opportunities [see the discussion in Williamson (44), p. 1526]. However, the record in *Berkey v. Kodak* does not contain sufficient documentation of ex ante decision-making, especially for Kodak's rivals, for analysts to make a certain judgment about Kodak's absolute superiority.[68] As an alternative, the proposition that Kodak's dominance can be explained by first-mover advantages that allow it to control the market for technical change, and thereby to frustrate rivals from competing by introducing new products, will be explored.[69] If the analysis supports this conclusion, a case can be made for remedial action. If, on the other hand, there is no evidence that Kodak took advantage of its dominant position to manipulate the market for technical change, the need for remedial action is more questionable.

Recently, Richard Schmalensee has developed a model that may shed some light on Kodak's continued dominance of the amateur photographic market.[70] His model demonstrates that when purchasing products that have the characteristics of "experience goods,"[71] consumers tend to become very loyal to the first brand marketed, remaining loyal even if later entrants produce goods which possess the same characteristics, perform as well, and sell at slightly lower prices than the first brand. Such loyalty derives from the perception that it is always more costly for consumers to experiment with a new brand than it is for them to continue to purchase an established brand. Once they are satisfied with the brand they have been purchasing, they will receive some consumer surplus (the difference between the value they place on the good and the price they pay for it); and if they experiment with a new brand, they will lose that surplus during the trial period. Before the introduction of the first brand, however, no consumer surplus exists, and therefore if the early entrants can gain a sufficient lead on potential rivals they can acquire some lasting advantages because the cost to the consumers of trying the first brand is less than it is for the brands of succeeding entrants [see Schmalensee (36), esp. pp. 24–30].

The model also demonstrates that the first-mover advantages are stronger the smaller the price differential between the new and the established brand, the greater the subjective probability that a product will not work, the greater the cost to the consumer if the product fails to work, the less frequently the consumer employs alternative sources of information (e.g., word of mouth or sources such as *Consumer Reports*), and the more risk-adverse consumers are. Each of these points will be explained in turn.[72]

1.   Since consumers who are satisfied with the existing brand receive a surplus equal to the value they place on the consumption minus the price they must pay for that brand, the new brand will have to sell at a substantially lower price than the established brand in order to induce consumers to sacrifice this surplus;[73] the smaller the price differential, the more difficult it will be for the new entrant to erode the dominance of the established brand.

2.   When consumers are using a product which has a high subjective probability of failing, they will be reluctant to switch brands once they have found one that satisfies them.[74]

3.   Product failure may impose a cost on consumers (e.g., defective bleach may ruin articles of clothing), and if these costs are significant, satisfied consumers will switch to a new brand only if they are offered a substantial premium for doing so.

4.   If consumers find it more costly to acquire information about a new brand by search than by experience, they will also be less likely to try a new brand because they must sacrifice some consumer surplus during the trial period.

5.   If consumers are risk-adverse, they will be even more reluctant to switch brands once they find a satisfactory one.

In Schmalensee's model the brand loyalty acquired by early entrants occurs in the absence of advertising or any other brand-name capital investments. More recent analyses by Klein and Leffler (27) and by Leffler (28) demonstrate that informative advertising may reinforce first-mover effects and make it even more difficult for later entrants to compete. In markets where it is costly for consumers to acquire information about the various products they are purchasing, firms have an incentive to invest in firm-specific capital, such as advertising, because it provides consumers with indirect information about the reliability of the brands being advertised. An investment in a nonsalvageable asset is a signal to consumers that a firm has a significant stake in producing products that are satisfactory to the consumer. And, if advertising leads to an increase in consumer experience with the products of the early entrants, advertising will increase the first-mover effects and make subsequent entry more difficult [Leffler (28), p. 65].[75] In other words, the interaction of three factors creates the barriers to new entry: the cost that the consumers encounter in acquiring information about the quantity and performance of some of the products they consume, the effort on the part of consumers to minimize these costs and the risks inherent in incorrect decisions, and the investment in firm-specific assets such as advertising by the early entrants [Demsetz (16), p. 50].

Two empirical studies by the Federal Trade Commission [FTC (20, 21)] have provided some confirmation of the first-mover advantages. Ronald Bond and David Lean [FTC (20), p. 77], examining prescription drug markets, found that "[t]he advantage to firms from being first to offer a new type of drug is considerable, and physician's long-term preference for the first brands appear to insulate firms from competition and even more effectively than do patents." In a second study by the FTC (21), Ira Whitten examined seven separate segments within the cigarette industry,[76] and concluded that "[i]n six of the seven submarkets . . . under study, the first firm to offer, promote, and widely distribute a brand for which there was a favorable market trend received a substantial and often times enduring sales advantage" (p. 47). Both of these studies also suggest that late entrants can most successfully erode first-mover advantages by offering a new product which is sufficiently different from the existing brands so that at least some subset of consumers considers the new product to be more compatible with their needs.[77] Bond and Lean found that late entrants into two prescription drug markets only dislodged first-movers when the new brands offered a significant therapeutic gain over existing drugs.[78] And although Whitten did not directly analyze this question, the performance of the cigarette market is consistent with Bond and Lean's conclusion: the leading cigarette manufacturers were dislodged from their positions only when one of the smaller firms was the first to introduce a brand in a new market segment (e.g., low-tar filters) that was growing in importance within the overall cigarette market.[79]

First-mover advantages associated with the Schmalensee model provide a plausible starting point for developing an understanding of Kodak's dominance of the amateur market. The component products and services of the amateur photography market have a number of characteristics in common with the kind of industries that the model suggests may be dominated by the first firm to enter. Cameras, film, and photographic processing are still technically complex, and they interact with one another in a very complex way; for that reason most amateurs lack the experience necessary to evaluate performance characteristics and the quality of alternative photographic products and services before purchase.[80] Furthermore, since these products and services are low-priced, and since amateurs only rarely spend a large percentage of their yearly budgets on photography, consumers have little real incentive to acquire systematic information about photographic products before purchase.[81] Finally, the cost to the consumer of a new brand's failure to perform satisfactorily can be quite large. Amateur photographers frequently take pictures of an important event in their lives (e.g., an anniversary or a vacation to some far-off spot), and if the pictures are unacceptable because of a failure of one of the components of the photographic system, the opportunity to record that event is lost forever.

The existence of the strong brand preference that consumers have for Kodak's products is consistent with the arguments that Kodak's dominance of the amateur photographic market is explained by first-mover advantages.[82] Brand loyalty was not a major issue in the *Berkey v. Kodak* case, but the fact that Kodak was consistently able to set the prices of its products above those of its competitors and to maintain those premiums over time suggests that consumers have very strong preferences for products that carry the Kodak brand name.[83] Furthermore, it would be only a slight exaggeration to claim that Kodak invented the use of trademarks to convey information about the quality and reliability of its products. From the very beginning, the name of Kodak has been synonymous with amateur photography in the eyes of the consumer.

While the first-mover model is a useful starting point for understanding Kodak's dominance of the amateur photographic industry, it does not provide a complete explanation. As noted above, Schmalensee implies that late entrants can most effectively compete by introducing new products that offer consumers significant improvements over those offered by the dominant firm; and this strategy would also seem to be most likely to succeed in those markets in which opportunities for new product introduction are greatest.[84] And although measuring these opportunities is difficult, the fact that a significant number of product improvements have occurred throughout the history of amateur photography suggests the existence of a base of technological opportunities that would be sufficiently large for Kodak's rivals to exploit if they so desired. Therefore, the question remains: why haven't Kodak's rivals taken advantage of these opportunities?

In its brief before the Court of Appeals, Berkey hinted at a possible explanation: Kodak has used its dominant position to control the market for significant new product innovations, thereby foreclosing competition from rivals by offering important new product advantages on their own.[85] Berkey's argument with respect to the film market is that each type of film (color, print, slide,[86] and black and white) requires a unique chemical process, and if an independent photofinisher wishes to process a particular type of film, he must use a separate processing line for each.[87] Since Kodak manufactures over 85 percent of all of the film sold in the United States, almost all of these photofinishers have installed processing lines that are compatible with Kodak's films.[88] Therefore, if a rival wants to compete with Kodak by introducing a new and improved film, it must ensure that the film is compatible with existing Kodak film. Were the film not compatible with the Kodak film chemistry, it would have to be processed separately from the Kodak film. Since rival film manufacturers have only a relatively small share of total film sales, independent photofinishers are reluctant to install a new processing line for non-Kodak film because they fear that a sufficient volume of business will not be generated in order to exploit the economies of scale associated with the new line. This reluctance implies that a rival film manufacturer would have to choose one of the following two strategies if it wanted to introduce a new and improved film: (1) it could enter the photofinishing market itself by building its own network of photofinishing plants;[89] or (2) it could convince a number of independents to set up a separate processing line to develop its film. No matter which alternative it chooses, a rival will face higher costs when introducing a new noncompatible film than Kodak will[90] because Kodak's market share guarantees that independent photofinishers will have a sufficient volume of business to fully exploit the economies of scale associated with a new processing line.[91] The implication of Berkey's reasoning is that existing and potential rivals face an artificial barrier to competition because Kodak's market dominance forces its rivals to imitate Kodak's innovations rather than introduce film products that offer significant improvements over Kodak's existing film.[92,93] Furthermore, the barrier to competition will be greater the more important are economies of scale in processing the film and the more extensive is the network of photofinishing plants which are needed to ensure consumer acceptance.

Berkey also implied that Kodak's control of the industry's technical standards foreclosed rival camera manufacturers from introducing new products that would erode Kodak's power in that market.[94] Berkey claimed that a new camera format frequently requires that a new film be specifically designed for it; and if the new film employs a different chemistry than the one demanded by the existing Kodak films,[95] the new format will face all of the problems of consumer acceptance that were described above.[96] In addition, Berkey also contended that other camera manufacturers were inhibited from competing with Kodak in the introduction of new products because Kodak refused to sell its film for camera formats other than its own.[97]

Manufacturers of color print paper face some of the same problems because the paper must also be technically compatible with the chemical process required by the film; and since Kodak manufactures most of the film processed by independent processors, rival paper manufacturers must produce paper that is compatible with Kodak's.[98] If another manufacturer offers for sale new color paper that is not compatible with Kodak's existing process, it must persuade a film manufacturer to introduce a new film that is suitable for use with the new paper. This feat would be difficult to accomplish because the film manufacturer would find it hard to induce independent photofinishers to process its film.

To determine the extent to which rivals are foreclosed from introducing a new film that is incompatible with Kodak's requires that estimates be made of the importance of product-specific economies of scale associated with the new film.[99] An estimate of the size of the photofinishing network required to assure consumer acceptance of the film and the capital cost of building the desired network of photofinishing plants of minimum efficient size are also required. I have used a number of sources to provide these estimates: the *Financial Planning Manual* prepared by Eastman Kodak Co. (18) to aid prospective photofinishers in their decision to enter the market; an extensive review of trade publications; and interviews with the executives of six independent photofinishers and independent consultants to the industry.

Data from the *Financial Planning Manual* (18), p. 32, indicate that the per unit cost of processing color print (C-41) film falls from approximately $2.71 to $2.22 a roll when the volume of film processed increases from 62,500 to 250,000 rolls per year.[100] Interviews also revealed that per unit costs would continue to decline if volume were increased to about one million rolls per year, but costs would fall only slightly at still larger volumes.[101] If one million rolls per year is assumed to be the minimum efficient size of the processing line required for a new film,[102] a photofinisher would have to acquire approximately 0.4 percent of the total amount of the color print film processed in the United States to exploit fully the product-specific economy of scale.[103] However, the photofinishing market is a regional market, and any estimate has to be adjusted to account for that fact. If it is assumed that the United States is divided into ten regional markets,[104] and that each market has an equal share of the total volume of film processed nationwide, a plant of minimum efficient size would have to acquire approximately 4 percent of the average regional market in order to exploit product-specific economies.[105] To ensure that a new film will be accepted by consumers, photofinishers should establish a network of film-processing plants geographically spaced in such a way that consumers can have their film processed quickly and conveniently; for that reason, manufacturers of a new film will assuredly want to begin with at least ten plants, one in each regional market.[106] Although there is no firm estimate of the cost of building a network of ten plants of minimum efficient scale, fragmentary estimates suggest that such a network can be built for approximately $15 million.[107]

On the basis of the analysis in this section, it is difficult to conclude that Kodak used its dominant position in the film market strategically to manipulate the industry's technical standards in such a way as to exclude rival film manufacturers from competing against Kodak by introducing new products. A minimum efficient scale of plant that requires an entrant to capture 4 percent of the relevant market and a capital cost of $15 million dollars are obstacles that should not prove insurmountable to such large integrated film manufacturers as Fuji, Konishiroku, Agfa-Gevaert, or 3M.[108] Since exclusionary conduct has already been ruled out as a possible explanation for Kodak's dominance, the most satisfactory explanation is that Kodak enjoyed some first-mover advantages, and it is simply more efficient in developing, producing, and marketing new products.[109]

Proving that Kodak is more efficient than its rivals is difficult,[110] but significant learning curve effects are conceivably involved in the development and marketing of complex photographic systems. Therefore Kodak would surely have an advantage over rivals if such benefits do exist because it has been a leader in developing new products for almost a century.[111]

Kodak may also have an advantage over some of its rivals because it is integrated across all of the amateur markets; and since photographic products are technically interrelated in many complex ways, it is reasonable to assume that significant transaction economies are generated by developing and producing intrafirm photographic products rather than coordinating the development between firms.[112] Kodak's high degree of integration has also helped the company to facilitate the physical tie-in that existed in the 126 and 110 systems, a move which, as indicated above,[113] may have enabled Kodak to protect its goodwill more effectively.

V. CONCLUSION

Because it is difficult to prove conclusively that productive efficiency explains single firm dominance,[114] antitrust analysis must proceed by examining the alternatives to see if they can be ruled out before concluding that efficiency is the answer. The problem with this approach is that we must be certain that *all* the competing alternatives have been ruled out before we can conclude for efficiency. The analysis in Part III of this paper did not substantiate the claim that Kodak has maintained its dominance by using a physical tie-in to lever its monopoly from one segment of the market into another. In fact, Kodak's physical tie-in could well have been used to enable the company to protect the goodwill embodied in its brand name. In Part IV the possibility that Kodak's dominance may be explained by first-mover advantages associated with brand loyalty was examined; and although this explanation cannot be completely ruled out, the evidence indicates that Kodak did not strategically exclude rivals from competing by offering consumers significant product improvements that have the best chance of eroding Kodak's dominance.

Even if Kodak's dominance can be completely explained by brand loyalty attributed to first-mover advantages, we are hard pressed to conclude that any relief destructive of those advantages would be socially desirable. Such relief may possibly improve static allocative efficiency by reducing the prices and expanding the output of existing products, but it would significantly weaken the incentive of firms to compete by being the first to enter new markets with new products [Demsetz (16), p. 57]. The trade-off between static allocative efficiency and the more dynamic aspect of efficiency is not an easy one to make. As Demsetz (p. 56) has pointed out:

> The valuation process must necessarily be one that is rich in intuition and faith, and poor in discernible measurements. A person possessing a deep faith in the strength and beneficent effect of competitive imitation will value the implied tradeoffs differently than a person possessing an equally deep faith in the process of "creative destruction." There exist neither cost-benefit analyses nor market-given prices by which to weigh benefits and costs in most of these tradeoffs. If the concept of barriers to entry is to be policy useful, it must be able to distinguish these cases and attach value weights to them. The entire problem of desirable and undesirable "frictions" in economic systems has resisted analysis when it has not been simply ignored.

Attaching value weights in the instant case makes us mindful that evidence (admittedly inconclusive, but still substantial) points to Kodak's superiority over its rivals. Therefore, in the absence of a more convincing case that Kodak's dominance can be explained by strategic behavior, prudent policy makers would be well advised to wait for market forces to erode Kodak's dominance. This conclusion is especially true in light of the length of time it takes to litigate a complicated monopoly case, and in light of the newly emerging technical developments that may eventually lead to increased competition within the amateur market.[115]

ACKNOWLEDGMENTS

This paper is supported in part by a grant from the Mellon Foundation through Colby College and a Social Science Grant from Colby College. An earlier version of this paper was presented at the Western Economic Association Meetings in San Francisco, July 2–6, 1981, and at the Industrial Organization Workshop at the Federal Trade Commission.

Peter Ashton, Arnold Baker, Charles Bassett, Mark Gildersleve, Robert Larner, H. Michael Mann, Richard Schmalensee, Edward Snyder, Richard O. Zerbe, Jr., and two anonymous referees provided helpful comments on earlier drafts of this paper. I would also like to thank Ian Robinson, Richard Thatcher, and the executives of six film processors for providing me with helpful information about the film-processing market; and I am grateful to Barry I. Brett of Parker, Chapin, Flattau, and Klimpl for his generous help.

NOTES

1. The amateur photographic equipment industry was defined in *Berkey v. Kodak* to include: the amateur conventional still camera market, which is comprised almost completely of the Pocket Instamatic (110) and Instamatic (126) cameras; conventional film, which includes color print film, color slide film, color movie film, and black and white film; photofinishing services (i.e., the processing of exposed film) and photofinishing equipment (film splicers, film and paper processors, printers, and chemicals); and color print paper, which is a specially treated paper that accepts an image from color film. *Berkey Photo, Inc. v. Eastman Kodak Co.*, 457 F. Supp. 404 (S.D.N.Y. 1978), *rev'd and remanded*, 603 F.2d 263 (2d Cir. 1979), *cert. denied*, 444 U.S. 1093 (1980). For a description of the market definition used above, see 603 F.2d at 268–274.

2. The roll film system included a flexible film that was spooled onto a roll, a roll holder that fit into the back of the camera, and a box camera (called a "Kodak") that required the photographer simply to press a button.

Prior to the introduction of the roll film system, photographers had to know a great deal about practical chemistry and photo-optics; they had to be capable of preparing photosensitive materials, operating a camera that required a number of different settings, developing the exposed negative, and making a positive print. For a more complete description of the roll film system and the historical development of the amateur market see Jenkins (25).

3. For an excellent description of the mergers and the role that they played in Eastman's successful effort to consolidate Kodak's position in these various markets see Jenkins (24), ch. 9.

4. These averages were derived from Addendum A to the defendant's brief before the Court of Appeals for the Second Circuit. Brief for Defendant at Addendum A, *Berkey Photo, Inc. v. Eastman Kodak Co.*, 603 F.2d 263 (2d Cir. 1970).

5. Before 1954 Kodak sold all of its color film at a price that included a charge for the processing of the film; therefore, consumers had to have their film processed by Kodak's Color Print and Processing Laboratories (CP&P) unless they wanted to pay an additional charge to have the film processed by a non-Kodak photofinisher. In 1954 Kodak signed a consent decree which required the company to sell color film and film processing separately, and it was also required to provide independent processors with technical information and sell its processing equipment, chemicals, and color paper to independents at reasonable prices. *United States v. Eastman Kodak Co.*, 1957 Trade Cases (CCH) ¶67,920; 1961 Trade Cases (CCH) ¶70,000.

6. Brief for Defendant at Addendum A.

7. Bork (4) defines productive efficiency broadly to include ". . . any activity by a business firm that creates wealth."

8. The use of economic theory in antitrust analysis is most powerful when it is used to demonstrate the ways in which firm behavior is competitive. In many cases the theory will provide very clear indications of the market conditions that are necessary for that behavior to have an adverse effect on allocative efficiency. Theory can also be used to

demonstrate how firm behavior is consistent with improvements in productive efficiency, but it can rarely spell out the market conditions in which that outcome will unambiguously occur. Therefore, antitrust analysts best proceed by determining if the questionable behavior, for example, a tie-in, has an adverse effect on allocative efficiency, and if it doesn't, then they can safely conclude that the net effect of the practice is either neutral or it improves efficiency [Bork (4), pp. 22–123].

9.   Berkey sold its Keystone camera operations in 1978. 603 F.2d at 267.

10.   15 U.S.C. 1 and 2 (1976). Berkey charged that Kodak had engaged in an illegal conspiracy with two flash manufacturers (Sylvania and General Electric) to withhold new flash devices (the Magicube manufactured by Sylvania and the Flipflash manufactured by GE) from the market until such time as Kodak was prepared to introduce a camera capable of using the new devices. Kodak argued that it was a joint participant in the development of both of the new flash devices, and therefore it was legitimate to withhold information on these devices until such time as it was ready to market a camera that could use them. The jury ruled in favor of Berkey on this charge, and the verdict was upheld by the Court of Appeals. 457 F. Supp. 404; 603 F.2d at 299–305.

11.   Berkey's claim was based upon a 1915 antitrust case [*United States v. Eastman Kodak Co. et al.,* 226 F.62 (W.D.N.Y. 1915), *appeal dismissed,* 225 U.S. 578 (1921)], in which Kodak was found guilty of monopolizing the manufacture and sale of cameras, photographic plates, photographic paper, and film by means of a series of over twenty acquisitions that took place around the turn of the century and a variety of other exclusionary behavior (e.g., vertical price-fixing and territorial restrictions).

Although the horizontal acquisitions may explain how Kodak initially acquired a dominant position in a number of segments of the amateur market, they do not explain how Kodak was able to maintain its market position for over three-quarters of a century.

12.   Kodak does sell film for the 35mm format even though it has not manufactured a 35mm camera since 1970. However, this fact does not alter the thrust of Berkey's claim because 35mm cameras were considered to be in a separate market at the time of the trial.

All 35mm cameras are excluded from the amateur market because they are much more complicated to operate than either the 126 or 110 cameras, and they are substantially more expensive; consequently, they are sold to a different group of customers (advanced hobbyist and professionals) from those buying amateur cameras. Some would argue that the 35mm and amateur cameras are becoming competitors in the past few years because the electronic revolution has made the 35mm camera easier to operate. Furthermore, the shift to a more automated production process has narrowed the price differential between 35mm and amateur cameras.

13.   Systems selling, or a physical tie-in as it is sometimes called, has been defined as ". . . a new product system consisting of two or more new complementary goods that are physically compatible with each other but physically incompatible, at least temporarily, with other existing goods" [Note (30)].

The term "physical tie-in," which first appeared in Comment (13) implies that a seller who designs two or more products as a system can tie the sale of one of the products to the sale of another because each must be used in conjunction with the other. Physical tie-ins differ from the more traditional contractual tie-ins in three ways:

First, they differ in the nature of the tie. The tie in a physical tie-in results from physical incompatibility with competing products. With traditional tying arrangements, however, there need be no physical relation between the tied products. . . .

Second, physical tie-ins and traditional tying arrangements differ in who determines their duration. The time period of a tying arrangement is defined by the initial parties and is potentially permanent, while a physical tie-in lasts only as long as it takes a competitor to develop a compatible product. Finally, because of their duration, the reasons for creating traditional tying arrangements and physical tie-ins differ. [Note (30), pp. 772–773]

14.   Brief for Plaintiff at 19, *Berkey Photo, Inc. v. Eastman Kodak Co.*, 603 F.2d 263 (2d Cir. 1979). Actually, the first camera, the "Kodak," was introduced as a system. See Jenkins (25), pp. 12–18.

15.   The 126 system had other advantages as well. Kodak's new Instamatic camera used a small fixed-aperture plastic lens that was less expensive to produce and easier to use than the finely ground lenses that could be adjusted to changing light conditions. The small fixed-aperture lens, however, required a higher speed (i.e., more light-sensitive) film because the smaller aperture lens exposed the film to less light. Since the Instamatic was designed to use film rated at ASA 64, which was the speed of its existing black and white film, Kodak had to increase the speed of its color print film from ASA 32 to ASA 64. See Sheehan (39), p. 156.

16.   Kodak claimed that it was necessary to introduce a new film with the new format because the smaller camera decreased the area of exposed film; therefore, the negative had to be blown up to produce an acceptable print in size. Kodak believed that if the existing Kodacolor X film were used in the smaller format, it would produce prints that were pebbly in appearance; consequently, a finer grained film had to be produced, one that would not encounter this problem when it was blown up. 603 F.2d at 277.

17.   Kodak does sell film for the 35mm camera (see note 12, *supra*), but it has refused to sell film, either under its own label or in bulk, for the miniature cartridge-loading cameras manufactured by such firms as Minox, Minolta, and Mamiya. These cameras have been on the market since the 1930s when Minox introduced its "spy camera," but they have never become a significant factor in the amateur camera market. Berkey argued that these cameras never had a chance of commercial success because Kodak, the dominant film manufacturer, did not supply its film in a format compatible with these cameras. 603 F.2d at 284.

18.   Based on this argument Berkey contended that Kodak had a duty to predisclose its new systems in sufficient time for rivals to introduce a new camera simultaneously with Kodak because, without predisclosure, Kodak would always be in a position to lever its monopoly from film into cameras. 603 F.2d at 279.

19.   Berkey confined its arguments to the 110 Pocket Instamatic system because the District Court instructed the jury to exclude pre-1969 conduct from its deliberations.

20.   However, two Kodak scientists testified to the effect that improvements in the Kodacolor X film would be "most welcome." See 603 F.2d at 286.

21.   *Id.* and in particular n.33.

22.   The C-41 process reduced the number of steps used in developing film from nine to six; it reduced the processing time to one-half that required by the C-22 process; and it reduced the pollution associated with processing. Brief for Defendant at 51 n.23.

23.   603 F.2d at 290.

24.   Berkey claimed that the independents had to buy equipment that processed film at 2 feet per minute when Kodak was using equipment that processed film at 26.5 feet per minute. Brief for Plaintiff at 47–48.

25.   603 F.2d at 290. When different populations of film exist, adjustments must be made in the various stages of the developing process to maintain a consistent quality of print.

26.   See the discussion between notes 2 and 3, *supra*, and the appropriate citations.

27.   See the discussion between notes 4 and 6, *supra*.

28.   Presumably, smaller photofinishers would be more likely to buy paper from the dominant firm than would larger ones.

29.   603 F.2d at 293–294.

30.   226 F. 62. Berkey also attempted to demonstrate that Kodak's film monopoly could not be explained by superior performance, arguing that: (1) Kodak's color film technology was acquired from two amateur inventors, Leopold Mannes and Leo Godowsky, and not derived from the fruits of its own research efforts; (2) Kodak made only two new product improvements (Kodacolor X and Kodacolor II) in color film technology in the twenty years preceding the trial (the Court of Appeals found that Kodak made additional improvements in Kodacolor in 1945, 1949, and 1955; see 603 F.2d at 270 n.7); (3) other film manufacturers had also made improvements in color film technology; and (4) other film manufacturers also produced color film that was of a quality equal to, or superior to, Kodak's. Brief for Plaintiff at 31–33.

31.   Fuji, 3M, and Konishiroku introduced films that were compatible with the C-41 chemistry in the latter part of 1974 and 1975; and GAF introduced a film that was compatible with C-22 chemistry in a 110 cartridge in 1973. Brief for Plaintiff at 36.

32.   Brief for Plaintiff at 36–37.

33.   The jury in *Berkey v. Kodak* (457 F. Supp. 404) accepted most of the plaintiff's arguments and found that the physical tie-in did violate Section 2. The Court of Appeals (603 F.2d 263) reversed these findings on the grounds that the physical tie-in was not a product of Kodak's monopoly power but a result of Kodak's integration into various product markets. The Court of Appeals also remanded certain parts of the jury verdict for further hearing. For a discussion of the lower court opinion, see Comment (14), and for a discussion of the Court of Appeals decision, see Comment (15).

34.   If some substitutability exists between two products, it may be profitable for the firm to tie the sale of the two products and set their price simultaneously. If, for example, a firm has a monopoly in the production of A but not B, which is a substitute for A, and it attempts to exploit its monopoly in A, it will not be able to earn the full monopoly profit in A because consumers will substitute B for A as the price of A is increased toward the monopoly level. To prevent the erosion of monopoly profit, the firm would have to tie the sale of B to A and set the price of both A and B proportionately above their respective marginal costs. For a more detailed discussion, see Bowman (6) and Burstein (8 and 9).

35.   See the discussion between notes 38 and 45, *infra*.

36.   Kodak produced 283 million rolls of color film in 1975 and it processed 35 million rolls in its own plants. Since Kodak processes only its own film, it processed approximately 12 percent of the Kodak film; the remaining 88 percent was processed by independent photofinishers. Data used are from Brief for Defendant at Addendum A, tables 7 and 10.

37.   Data introduced at the trial indicate that Kodak earned a very high rate of return on investments in both the film and color paper markets; the average rate of return on investment from 1964 to 1975 was 66.07 percent in the film market and 59.75 percent in the color paper market. At first glance, this evidence would seem to be inconsistent with the argument that Kodak did not lever its film monopoly into the color paper market and earn monopoly profit in both markets. Two reasons, however, lead one to believe that the evidence is not inconsistent with the above analysis. One, the trial record did not produce an explanation of how the data were compiled, a gap which leaves a number of questions unanswered. Without more detailed information on the method used to allocate common costs, it seems unwarranted to put too much weight on the rate of return earned in specific markets. Two, even if the data provide a good indication of the economic rate of return in each market, they do not disprove the argument that a monopolist who ties the sale of complementary products used in fixed proportions can only earn one monopoly profit. The firm can choose to earn the entire profit in one or the other of its markets, or it can distribute its profits among the markets, but it cannot earn more than one monopoly profit.

38.   To improve the quality of the picture significantly would require the consumer to shift to a 35mm camera, which, at the time of the trial, was defined as being in a separate market. See note 1, *supra*.

39. Williamson (45) uses the film and photofinishing tie-in as an illustration of his argument, but he presents no evidence to support the importance of the tie-in as a barrier to entry into the film industry. See note 5, *supra,* for a description of the pre-1954 tie-in.

40. Brief for Defendant at Addendum A, Table 9.

41. Professors Bork and Bowman have argued that if it is profitable to enter one stage of production, it should be profitable to enter each stage in the vertical chain; therefore, entry should occur at both stages and the capital market should supply the resources necessary to enter both stages. Professor Williamson, on the other hand, argues that imperfections in the capital market do exist, and they are usually greater when the simultaneous entry into more than one market is required. The reason is that potential entrants have to convince lenders that they have the skills and knowledge to make a profit; and it is usually more difficult to so convince lenders when the firm is planning to enter more than one market, especially when the markets require different skills and experience. To compensate for this imperfect information, lenders will charge a higher interest rate to potential entrants than they do to established firms who have built up a successful record.

Williamson has also pointed out that the effects of this barrier to entry will not be too severe unless the industry is highly concentrated and the amount of foreclosure created by the tie-in is very high.

For more details on the debate among Bork, Bowman, and Williamson, see Bork (3), Bowman (7), and Williamson (45), pp. 655–659, particularly n.30.

42. Williamson (45) points out that a potential entrant may face higher transaction costs of coordinating joint entry because "[l]ack of common information among [film] producers and processors with respect to market opportunities, investment intentions, or interfirm performance qualifications . . . can impede effective coordination" (p. 657).

43. Since the tie-in employed by Kodak had foreclosed approximately 96 percent of the photofinishing market prior to 1954, entry into the film market would have required the potential entrant to set up a network of photofinishers to handle its film. The capital cost barrier to entry into both stages would be greater when the number of photofinishing plants needed to provide adequate market coverage is large, when the volume of photofinishing sales needed to produce at minimum optimal scale is large, and when the cost of constructing an optimal size photofinishing plant is significant.

Although there is no systematic evidence on the importance of these factors in 1954, there is some reason to believe that they were not important. One source estimated the cost of building a photofinishing plant of optimal scale to be $250,000 in the mid-1950's [*Business Week* (10)]. If it is assumed that ten processing plants are needed to provide national coverage for the new entrant (see the discussion at note 104, *infra*), the cost of entering the photofinishing market would be $2.5 million, an amount that Bain considered only moderately important in his 1956 book [Bain (1), p. 159]. Furthermore, the skills and knowledge required to process film are directly related to those required to produce film, and, therefore, a potential entrant into the film market would not face any additional capital cost barriers because it had to enter both markets simultaneously.

44. Kodak still refuses to process the film of rivals. Its share of the processing market, however, is now less than 10 percent, and over 600 independent photofinishers can now process the film of any potential entrant. At the same time, most of the film sold in the country is compatible with Kodak's film chemistry because almost all of the independent photofinishers use Kodak compatible chemistry to process their film. They do so because Kodak sells almost 90 percent of all color film sold, and, therefore, if a firm wants to be assured of a large enough volume to exploit economies in photofinishing, its equipment and chemistry must be compatible with Kodak film. The importance of this issue will be discussed further below. See the discussion between notes 85 and 92, *infra.*

45. Another possible explanation for the physical tie-in is that it can provide a convenient mechanism to facilitate price discrimination among Kodak's customers. Kodak prob-

ably had an incentive to discriminate in price among the buyers of the 110 camera if each buyer placed a different value on the use of the camera and that value varied with the individual's intensity of use of the camera. However, the price discrimination explanation of the physical tie-in between film and cameras is not as convincing as it might be because a physical tie-in is an imperfect mechanism to use in metering the consumers' intensity of use. Once a rival manufacturer produces a film that is compatible with the Kodak system, Kodak will find it difficult to appropriate the additional profits that price discrimination generates because consumers will be free to substitute the film of rival manufacturers who have an incentive to beat Kodak's prices. Still, it is impossible completely to rule out price discrimination as an explanation for the physical tie-in. The temporary nature of the physical tie-in may have been minimized by the strong loyalty that consumers have for Kodak film; and the fact that Kodak's share of the film market averaged 86 percent between 1952–1975 suggests that Kodak may not have been concerned about its rivals' ability to erode film sales.

The metering argument is not a valid explanation for the physical tie-in between film and photofinishing because these products are used in the same proportion by all consumers.

46.   Failure may occur in any of the three components of the system: the camera, the film, or the photofinishing process. Of course, problems may occur because of mistakes made by the photographer, but these problems have been minimized in the amateur market by the introduction of the Instamatic camera which only requires the consumer to drop in the cartridge, frame the picture, and push the button.

47.   It is not necessary for a firm to produce each of the components; it could simply contract to have components produced to its specifications. However, if the transaction costs among the various stages of production are significant, there will be strong incentives to completely integrate into the production of each of these components. See Williamson (43) and Klein, Crawford, and Alchian (26).

48.   603 F.2d at 277–278.

49.   *Id.* at 286, in particular n.33.

50.   Brief for Defendant at Addendum B.

51.   The issues of whether or not Kodacolor X would produce an acceptable print in the 110 format and the quality of the new Kodacolor II film were the subject of an extensive debate during the trial. As Judge Kaufman recognized, these controversies could only be resolved in the marketplace. For a discussion of the evidence introduced on these issues, see 603 F.2d at 277–278 and 286–288.

Kodak would probably not risk its reputation by introducing a new photographic system that would produce pictures of poor quality. After all, Kodak did not remove the 126 format (including Kodacolor X film) from the market at the time that it introduced the 110 format; if the pictures produced from the 110 format were unacceptable, consumers could always choose to purchase the 126 format sold by either Kodak or its rivals.

52.   Extensive pretesting in a laboratory can minimize (but not completely eliminate) these problems because production and marketing on a large scale introduce factors that do not exist in the laboratory. These problems will be especially true for products, such as film, which require extensive postsale service (photofinishing).

53.   In addition to monitoring quality at the photofinishing stage, Kodak may also have wanted to ensure that it received a timely flow of information on any problems with the new film so that the defects could also be quickly corrected.

54.   This argument was emphasized by Kodak in defense of its decision not to predisclose the new chemical process to independent photofinishers. Brief for Defendant at 37.

55.   Some of these costs were eventually incurred when the independents adopted the new C-41 process. For example, Kodak had to provide the technical specifications for the new process and it also provided training and technical assistance to its chemical and photofinishing equipment customers. However, these costs would have been much greater had

Kodak chosen the predisclosure alternative because the company would have had to provide the specifications not only to its customers but to almost all of the independents if it wanted to maintain the integrity of its new products during the break-in period.

56.   Some of Kodak's other behavior is also consistent with the goodwill explanation. Berkey's allegation that Kodak's refusal to make film available in formats other than its own facilitated Kodak's leverage of its monopoly from film into cameras (see the discussion at notes 17 and 18, *supra*) can also be explained as an attempt by Kodak to protect its reputation as a manufacturer of high quality products. Kodak's refusal to supply film for the cartridge loading "spy" cameras produced by Minox, Minolta, and Mamiya is consistent with this explanation. Prior to the introduction of Kodacolor II in 1973, Kodak believed that its existing film (Kodacolor prior to 1963 and Kodacolor X after 1963) would not produce an acceptable print when used in a small camera format (see discussion in note 16); therefore, Kodak conceivably did not make its existing film available in these formats because it did not want to risk its reputation for producing high quality film.

57.   Whether single firm dominance should be the subject of remedial action in the absence of exclusionary behavior is a subject of much debate, and it will be taken up in more detail in the conclusion of the paper.

58.   The following discussion is based on Williamson's article (44) and it will only be cited when a direct quotation is used.

59.   The courts have created an immunity to the antitrust laws for single firm dominance that has been acquired by managerial acumen or historical accident. *United States v. Grinell Corp.*, 384 U.S. 563 (1969).

60.   For a discussion of the symmetry between barriers to entry and barriers to the expansion of existing firms within an industry, see Caves and Porter (12).

61.   In a footnote to the quoted paragraph (not cited), Williamson recognizes that there may be some advantages to late entry because an opportunity is provided to imitate the successes and avoid the failures of the early entrants; but he believes that on balance these advantages are offset by the disadvantages of late entry.

First-mover advantages are reinforced if the dominant firm finds it profitable to engage in strategic behavior that inhibits the growth of rivals and potential rivals. See Schmalensee (35), Dixit (17), and Spence (40, 41). Some examples of the advantages of being first can be found in two Federal Trade Commission studies (20, 21).

62.   The assumption, of course, is that effective relief can be fashioned; that is, relief that will restore competition without destroying a firm's incentives to be efficient. Williamson argues that relief in such cases would not destroy incentives if the antitrust remedy were imposed after a reasonable period of time. See Williamson (44), pp. 1522–1525.

63.   See the discussion between notes 2 and 3 and the references cited therein, *supra*.

64.   See Jenkins' [(24), pp. 129–130] account of Hannibal Goodwin's failure to pursue his application for a patent on a celluloid film as an example of the ineptitude of some of Eastman's rivals.

65.   Not only did George Eastman make a number of technical improvements in the development of celluloid film, the roll film camera, and the film manufacturing process, but he also made a significant contribution in other aspects of the photography business. Eastman initiated a number of imaginative marketing schemes; he was one of the pioneers of advertising; and he was effective in raising large amounts of capital [Jenkins (24), particularly chs. 4–11].

66.   Berkey argued that Kodak's early dominance of the industry could be completely explained by acquisitions made at the turn of the century and illegal conduct (e.g., vertical price-fixing and territorial restraints). See Brief for Plaintiff at 18, 31, and 40.

67.   Berkey challenged the claim that Kodak is absolutely superior. As evidence, Berkey cited the fact that the technology necessary for the development was based upon the work of two independent inventors, Leopold Mannes and Leo Godowsky; Berkey also noted that

other film manufacturers also made significant contributions to the development of color photography. See note 30, *supra*.

While it is true that Mannes and Godowsky, two professional musicians, had developed the basic elements of color photography in their bathrooms, it was Dr. C. E. Kenneth Mees, vice-president in charge of research at Kodak, who recognized the importance of their work and brought them to Rochester. In addition to supplying the financial backing and the facilities for their work, Kodak provided a significant amount of additional technical help for later developments of color photography. See Wechsberg (42). Moreover, it was Kodak that developed the small finer grained 110 film, and it was Kodak that first introduced a commercially successful cartridge-load camera (126) and the pocket-sized version of this camera (110).

68.   Berkey claimed that there was evidence to demonstrate that Kodak's rivals were as capable as Kodak of producing high quality products (note 31, *supra*), and more recently it was Fuji who first introduced the new high-speed (ASA 400) film [see Elia (19)].

69.   Although "market failure" was not a major issue in the case, Berkey's brief did hint at this explanation. Berkey not only contended that Kodak's power resulted from a series of illegal acquisitions and conduct (Brief for Plaintiff at 18, 31, and 40), but Berkey also suggested that Kodak was in a position to manipulate industry standards to its own advantage because Kodak dominated the market (Brief for Plaintiff at 13).

70.   The earliest version of this model can be found in Schmalensee (36); further extensions of the model can be found in Schmalensee (37) and (38).

71.   Consumers can only make a judgment about whether an "experience good" will perform satisfactorily after they have consumed it. These goods are contrasted with "search goods," which have qualities that can be evaluated by the consumer prior to search. This distinction was first made by Philip Nelson (29).

Schmalensee's model does not apply to "search goods" because consumers can make a determination of whether these goods will perform satisfactorily prior to purchase; therefore, there will be little or no risk in purchasing a late entering brand once the consumer determines that it will perform as satisfactorily as the existing brand.

72.   The discussion following is based on Schmalensee (37), pp. 18–33, and (38).

73.   The assumption is that the new brand is an imitation of the existing brand; that is, the consumers perceive the new brand to have the same characteristics as the existing brand, and they do not believe that it will perform any better.

74.   This is true in Schmalensee's model even if both the existing brand and the new one have the same ex ante probability of failure.

75.   It is also worth noting that advertising and other types of firm specific investments by a late-entrant may help them reduce the advantages of the first-mover [Leffler (28), pp. 65, and Demsetz (16), p. 50].

76.   The seven submarkets are: regular cigarettes, 70mm nonfilters; king size; 85mm nonfilters; plain filters; menthol filters; charcoal filters; low tar filters; and high filtration filters. Federal Trade Commission (21), p. 9.

77.   Schmalensee (37), pp. 22, 27, makes the same point.

78.   For example, Bond and Lean [FTC (20), p. 29] found that in the market for oral diuretics (drugs which reduce fluids within the body), those "[b]rands offering important or modest therapeutic gains on average accounted for about five percent of 1971 oral diuretic sales while brands that offered little or no gain on average each accounted for less than one percent of 1971 . . . sales." Their findings [(20), pp. 54–56] for antianginal drugs also support this claim.

79.   Whitten maintained that a firm's first-mover advantage did not carry over into new submarkets unless it was the first firm to market a brand in the new submarket. Therefore, as new submarkets became more important the leading firm in that submarket started to

make substantial inroads into the dominant firm's position within the overall cigarette market. See Federal Trade Commission (21).

80. Complexity not only reduces the ability of consumers to acquire and process information, but it also increases the probability of a product failure; this is particularly true of complementary products that are used in a system. As noted above (see discussion at note 74), if consumers estimate the probability of product failure to be significant they will probably stay with a brand with which they are satisfied.

81. Of course, this argument is not quite so apt in the market for 35mm cameras. These expensive cameras have been, at least until recently, much more complicated to operate. Moreover, sophisticated consumers in this market are more likely to carry out a search before purchase. Much more consumer information is available to the users of 35mm cameras (for example, photographic magazines specifically devoted to providing information) than to users of amateur equipment, thus supporting the conclusion that search is more important for the former market than it is for the latter. However, recent trends (such as 35mm cameras that are easier to operate) suggest that distinctions between these two markets may be blurring.

82. Strong brand loyalty is also consistent with the hypothesis that Kodak has produced products superior to those offered by its competitors. While it is difficult to sort out the conflicting explanations by Kodak's strong brand loyalty, some evidence was introduced at the trial supporting the contention that the products of Kodak's rivals were at least as good as Kodak's.

Kodak's brief before the Court of Appeals (Brief for Defendant at 41-43 and in particular n.21) argued that Berkey's 110 camera failed to sell because it was an inferior product, but it was also argued that other competitors in the camera market did not face the same problems. As evidence, Kodak cited the fact that by 1976 (four years after the 110 was introduced) its rivals had captured 50 percent of the 110 camera market. Kodak also cited the testimony of retailers who were touting the products of other manufacturers because they were cheap and had a number of desirable qualities. Berkey also referred to Kodak documents showing that Kodak tested its rivals' films and found them to be of consistently high quality. Brief for Plaintiff at 32-33. Finally, interviews with six independent processors and experts in the industry confirmed the desirability of non-Kodak photographic products.

83. 603 F.2d at 270 and Brief for Plaintiff at 18, 31, and 40.

84. Product improvements can be made in one of two ways. One, rivals can introduce new products that have the same characteristics as the old products but provide them in different proportions; for example, the major advantage of the 110 system over the previous systems is that it is more convenient for consumers to use. Or two, they can create a new product that emphasizes characteristics unavailable in previous products; such as Polaroid's entry with an instant print system that emphasized, for the first time, the immediate availability of a finished photographic print. The latter example is also proof that the best way to compete with a dominant firm in consumer markets is to introduce products that are substantially different from existing products.

85. Brief for Plaintiff at 13-14 and 36-37.

86. Two types of slide film are in use, each requiring a unique developing process: Kodachrome-type film, and Ektachrome-type film.

87. Each roll of color print film (approximately 75 percent of all film sold in the United States) that comes into a photofinishing plant is spliced together and wound upon a spool. The spool is then placed in a film processor that continuously moves the film through a series of chemical baths controlled for time and temperature; after the negative is processed, it is placed in a printer that continuously transfers a print from the negative onto a strip of color print paper that is then spooled and placed in a paper processor that moves the printed paper through a final series of controlled baths. Ultimately, the completed prints are cut

and packaged together with the negatives for return to the consumer. The processing of black and white film is similar, but the processing of slides and movie film is different because no prints are involved.

88.   To my knowledge only two film manufacturers—Dynacolor, which was later acquired by 3M Company, and Agfa-Gevaert—have produced a color print film that is not compatible with Kodak film; the only color print film that Agfa currently sells in the United States is designed to be used solely with the Rapid system, which is sold principally in Europe and is not compatible with C-41 chemistry.

89.   Two of the most important characteristics of a film, from the consumer's point of view, are the speed and convenience with which it can be processed. To provide a film with these two characteristics, a manufacturer must ensure that there are sufficient numbers of photofinishers, geographically spread throughout the market, who are prepared to process its film.

90.   See the discussion at notes 39 to 42, *supra*.

91.   Berkey argued that the introduction of Kodacolor II, which employed a new chemical process (C-41), supports this claim. After the introduction of Kodacolor II, photofinishers rapidly switched their plants over to the new C-41 process, a change which, in turn, forced other film manufacturers to introduce their new 110-size film in the C-41 chemistry instead of the C-22 chemistry that they had previously been using. Berkey claimed that Kodak's rivals had to change their chemistry; consequently, rivals' introduction of a 110 film was delayed for up to two years. GAF, which introduced a C-22 film in the 110 size, found that it could no longer compete with Kodak and left the market. Brief for Plaintiff at 36-37.

The issue of whether or not Kodak's rivals were forced to change the chemical process of their 110 film for the C-22 to C-41 process is debatable; they might have made the change because they felt it was necessary so that their film could produce high quality prints in the smaller 110 format. Kodak continued to produce film (in other formats) that used the C-22 process, and several photofinishers continued to process C-22 film for a number of years after the C-41 film was introduced in 1972. Brief for Defendant, *supra* note 4, at 41. Furthermore, if Kodak's new Kodacolor II film was inferior to the C-22 film, as Berkey alleged (see discussion between notes 19 and 21, *supra*), Kodak's rivals could have made serious inroads into Kodak's film sales by producing a superior 110 size film that could be processed in C-22 chemistry.

92.   It is difficult to prove conclusively that a rival's film which simply imitates Kodak's existing film is less likely to erode Kodak's first-mover advantages, but there is some reason to favor this hypothesis. A new film that is compatible with Kodak's existing film should be easier for Kodak to imitate; thus, Kodak could minimize the effect of the new product on its market share by being a fast-second in the market [see Baldwin and Childs (2)]. In October 1976 Fuji introduced an ASA 400 color film that was at once four times as fast as any existing color film and compatible with Kodak's existing chemistry. Kodak followed suit in a matter of months [Elia (19)], thereby preventing Fuji's film from making any serious inroads on its market share.

93.   Kodak has introduced most of the major advancements in color film. It produced the first commercially popular color movie and slide film in 1935; in 1942 it originated the first amateur color print film (Kodacolor); and it inaugurated an improved color print film (Kodacolor X) with the 126 format in 1963. Kodacolor X was twice as fast (ASA 64 as compared to ASA 32) as existing film, and it required a new chemical process (C-22). In 1972 Kodak introduced another new film (Kodacolor II), only one-third the size of a 126 negative. This new film had a finer grain which allowed it to be blown up to produce a print comparable to those produced from the 126 negative. Brief for Defendant at 21-23. To my knowledge, Fuji's introduction of the 400 ASA color film is the only example of a rival introducing an improved film before Kodak.

94. Brief for Plaintiff, *supra* note 14, at 13-14.

95. A significantly improved camera may not necessarily require a film that uses a new chemical process, but this has been the case in the past. The 126 format was introduced with a new film and new chemical process, as was the 110 format.

96. These difficulties will occur whether the camera manufacturer produces its own film or not. If it does not manufacture its own film, the manufacturer will face additional problems in coordinating the joint development of a new camera and a new film; and, as Judge Kaufman pointed out [603 F.2d at 276], there may be significant transaction economies when these type of activities are carried out within the same firm. Since some of Kodak's most significant competitors (Fuji, Konishiroku, and Agfa-Gevaert) manufacture both cameras and film, this problem would not be a significant obstacle to their introduction of a new camera format.

97. This inhibition should not pose any problem for those camera manufacturers that also manufacture their own film, such as Fuji, Konishiroku, and Agfa-Gevaert.

98. Brief for Plaintiff at 13-14.

99. Product-specific economies are those associated with the processing of a particular kind of film (e.g., C-41 color print film); plant-specific economies are those associated with the total output of a processing plant (including all of the various kinds of film it processes); and multiplant economies are those associated with the operation of a number of plants by a single firm. For a more complete discussion of these categories and the explanation of them see Scherer (34).

Product-specific economies are emphasized for two reasons. One, a film manufacturer desiring to introduce a non-Kodak compatible film can do so by inducing the network of independent photofinishers to introduce a separate processing line to handle its film instead of building its own network of photofinishing plants. And two, interviews of the executives of six independent processors revealed that plant-specific economies are very modest while multiplant economies are nonexistent. In fact, a large number of small photofinishers (250,000 to 500,000 rolls per year) only process C-41 color print film, and most of the larger photofinishers process only two types of film (C-41 color print film and slide film that is compatible with Ektachrome film). Most of the photofinishers farm out their black and white, Kodachrome, and Ektachrome-compatible films to one of the very few photofinishers capable of processing them (e.g., only one independent photofinisher in New England is capable of processing Kodachrome film).

100. Estimates are made for color print film because it accounts for over 75 percent of all film sold. The per unit cost figures are based upon the cost of labor and materials, depreciation of equipment, employee benefits, and miscellaneous burdens (utilities, advertising, etc.). Based on information acquired in the interviews, I assumed that a processing line operates 250 days per year and that a roll of film contains 20 prints.

101. Most product-specific economies occur because larger volumes allow the use of film processors, printers, and color paper processors that are capable of higher volume operations. Some economies of specialization also occur at large volume (up to some one million rolls per year) because a photofinisher can dedicate separate negative film processors and printers to films of a certain size (for example, one film processor can be set up to handle 110 C-41 film, while another can be set up to handle 135 and 126 C-41 film).

102. The relevant question is: what is the minimum efficient size of a processing line needed to process the improved film? A new film that is incompatible with existing film may increase the size of a minimum efficient plant, or it may decrease it. Past changes in film have led to a number of improvements in the processing of film; the most significant shift was from the old "dip and dunk" method to "continuous film processors" (Brief for Defendant at 20) which had the effect of increasing the size of a minimum efficient plant. It is difficult to guess what effects the new disk film will have on the minimum efficient size of a processing line, but evidence suggests that the next advances may reduce it. Trade

sources indicate that the next amateur photographic system will use a film disk instead of a roll film. The new disk film will lead to a further reduction in the size of the camera and produce sharper prints, and it will probably be developed in a batch process, which, in turn, suggests that the minimum efficient size of a processing line may be reduced. For more information on the new format and Kodak's plans for introducing it, see *Photographic Trade News* (31).

The introduction of this new amateur system was announced by Kodak on February 3, 1982. See Hughey (23), p. 52.

103.   This figure is derived by dividing one million rolls by 284 million rolls, an estimate of the number of rolls of color print film processed in 1976.

No direct evidence was provided in *Berkey v. Kodak* on the number of rolls of color print film processed in the United States. However, the 284 million rolls of color print film were estimated as follows: 370 million rolls of color film (print, slide, and movie) were sold and the same amount was processed in the United States in 1976; 284 million of these rolls were color print film. Since almost all color print film sold in that year was C-41 film, this figure (284 million rolls) was assumed to be the total number of C-41 film processed in 1976. Data are drawn from Brief for Defendant at Addendum A, tables 7–9.

104.   Direct evidence is lacking on this specific point, but we can reasonably assume that a network of ten plants would provide a firm with sufficient coverage of the national market. At least three of the largest photofinishers (Kodak, Fotomat, and Berkey) are capable of achieving national coverage with eight to twelve plants [Robinson (33), p. 47]. Additional information derived from interviews supports this conclusion.

105.   This estimate is consistent with information obtained about the New England market. One source estimated that the total number of rolls of C-41 processed in this market was about 25 million; and if the estimate of minimum efficient scale (one million rolls per year) is divided by 25 million rolls, the percentage of the New England market needed to exploit the product-specific economies is also 4 percent.

106.   If a firm wants to emphasize 24-hour service, it may need a larger number of plants: Fox-Stanley, which advertises 24-hour service, operates thirty plants in one (the Southwestern) section of the United States [see Robinson's estimates (33), p. 47]. Although 24-hour service is becoming more popular, survey data for 1979 shows that some 54 percent of consumers wait about one week before picking up their film, and 21 percent wait three days. When asked what time span they felt was reasonable for returning processed film, 55 percent indicated one week and 24 percent said three days [*Photo-Marketing* (32), p. 20].

If photoprocessing by mail becomes more important than it is today (in 1977 it accounted for approximately 20 percent of all film photofinishing transactions), a firm may be able to provide national coverage with fewer than ten photofinishing plants. Trade sources indicate that the new film disk, which will be the next film innovation, should make photofinishing by mail more attractive [see *Photographic Trade News* (31), p. 17].

107.   Eastman Kodak Co. (18), pp. 31–36, estimates that the cost of building a plant capable of processing 250 thousand rolls of C-41 film per year is $381,455. To produce a million rolls a year a processing firm would not simply expand its existing operation by a factor of four. Instead, a photofinisher would probably use faster processing equipment and printers costing considerably less than four times the expenditures for the equipment used to process 250 thousand rolls of film per year. Therefore, if $381,455 is multiplied by four, an estimate of the capital cost of a one million-roll per year plant is $1,525,820. The total cost of a ten-plant network is found by multiplying this figure by ten.

The $381,455 figure includes the cost of equipment needed to process C-41 film, the cost of enlargement equipment, and building cost.

108.   Fuji, Konishiroku, and Agfa-Gevaert also produce cameras and color print paper; consequently, they should be able to compete with Kodak on an equal footing if the new

film requires a new camera format and a new color print paper, as well as a new chemical process.

109. Default failure cannot be completely ruled out as an explanation without more detailed information about Kodak and its rivals, but no evidence in the trial record suggests that Kodak's rivals were inept. Furthermore, a search of public sources revealed no such evidence. Firms such as Fuji, Konishiroku, and Agfa-Gevaert, which have a reputation for producing quality films and have been successful in their own home markets, are almost certainly not inept.

110. At about the time Kodak introduced its 126 Instamatic (cartridge-load) camera, a number of European manufacturers also introduced a fast-loading camera of their own called the Rapid. The Rapid camera used a film canister similar to that used in 35mm cameras except that it featured a protruding leader of film that was automatically fed onto the take-up spool. The primary advantage of this system over the Instamatic was supposed to be that the operator had more control over the distance of the film from the lens, a feature which would result in consistently higher quality pictures. See *Business Week* (11). The fact that consumers preferred the Instamatic to the Rapid system supports the argument that Kodak is more efficient than its rivals, but the fact that Kodak failed to acquire rights to manufacture the Polaroid Camera when it was offered to Kodak demonstrates the even Kodak makes mistakes. See *Fortune* (22).

111. These efficiencies may be attributed to Kodak's first-mover advantages. When a new generation of products is an evolutionary descendant of previous generations and when technological change is rapid, rivals may have difficulty catching up with Kodak because the latter is further down its learning curve. Kodak may have an additional first-mover advantage if consumers are more likely to accept Kodak's new photographic products because of its past successes.

112. No direct evidence was introduced at the trial on the amount of the cost savings, but the president of Kodak did testify to his belief that Kodak's processing division provided the film manufacturing division with valuable information which helped in evaluating and determining product specifications for new products [Brief for Defendant at 61]. Although the point was debated by Berkey, the fact that the new color print films introduced with the 126 (Kodacolor X) and 110 (Kodacolor II) cameras had some very desirable properties that were important for their success (see notes 15 and 16, *supra*) is consistent with the existence of transaction economies associated with integration.

113. See the discussion between notes 45 and 56, *supra*.

114. See the discussion at note 7, *supra*.

115. Two particular developments merit notice: (1) the improvements made on the 35mm system the past few years and a reduction in the price have increased the substitutability between them and the amateur (126 and 110) systems (see note 11, *supra*); and (2) recent announcements, by Sony, that the photographic systems of the future will use electronic tape instead of the traditional film suggests that electronic firms may soon be competing with the more traditional photographic firms. See *Boston Globe* (5), p. 46.

REFERENCES

1. Bain J. (1956) *Barriers to New Competition*, Cambridge, Harvard University Press.
2. Baldwin, W., and Childs, G. (July 1969) "The Fast Second and Rivalry in Research and Development," *Southern Economic Journal*, Vol. 36: 18–24.
3. Bork, R. (1969) "Vertical Integration and Competitive Process," pp. 139–149 in J. F. Weston and S. Peltzman, eds., *Public Policy toward Mergers*, Pacific Palisades, Calif., Goodyear Publishing Co.

4. ———. (1978) *The Antitrust Paradox: A Policy at War with Itself,* New York, Basic Books.

5. *Boston Globe.* (October 29, 1981) "Kodak Delays Filmless Camera," p. 46.

6. Bowman, W., Jr. (1957) "Tying Arrangements and the Leverage Problem." *Yale Law Journal,* Vol. 68: 19–35.

7. ———. (1973) *Patent and Antitrust Law: A Legal and Economic Appraisal,* Chicago, University of Chicago Press.

8. Burstein, M. (February 1960) "The Economics of Tie-In Sales," *Review of Economics and Statistics,* Vol. 42: 68–73.

9. ———. (March/April 1960) "A Theory of Full-line Forcing," *Northwestern University Law Review,* Vol. 55: 62–95.

10. *Business Week.* (July 30, 1955), pp. 50–56.

11. ———. (February 13, 1965) "New Fast-Load Cameras Focus on U.S. Market," p. 122.

12. Caves, R., and Porter, M. (May 1977) "From Entry Barriers to Mobility Barriers," *Quarterly Journal of Economics,* Vol. 91: 241–261.

13. Comment. (1975) "Physical Tie-Ins as an Antitrust Violation," *Illinois Law Journal,* Vol. 1975: 224–237.

14. ———. (1979) "Berkey Photo, Inc. v. Eastman Kodak Co.: The Predisclosure Requirement—A New Remedy for Predatory Marketing of Product Innovations," *Rutgers-Camden Law Journal,* Vol. 10: 395–429.

15. ———. (Dec. 1979) "Antitrust Scrutiny of Monopolists' Innovations: Berkey Photo, Inc. v. Eastman Kodak Co.," *Harvard Law Journal,* Vol. 93: 408–418.

16. Demsetz, H. (March 1982) "Barriers to Entry," *American Economic Review,* Vol. 72: 47–57.

17. Dixit, A. (March 1980) "The Role of Investment in Entry Deterrence," *Economic Journal,* Vol. 90: 95–106.

18. Eastman Kodak Co. (1978) *Financial Planning for the Prospective Color Finisher,* Rochester, N.Y., Eastman Kodak.

19. Elia, C. (March 3, 1977) "Fresh Rivalry Is Anticipated between Kodak and Fuji for Mass Market High-Speed Film," *Wall Street Journal,* p. 35.

20. Federal Trade Commission. (1977) *Staff Report on Sales Promotion and Product Differentiation in Two Prescription Drug Markets,* Washington, D.C., Government Printing Office.

21. ———. (1979) *Staff Report on Brand Performance in the Cigarette Industry and the Advantages of Early Entry,* Washington, D.C., Government Printing Office.

22. *Fortune.* (July 1954) "Eastman Kodak Enlarged," p. 15.

23. Hughey, A. (February 4, 1982) "Kodak Unveils Its Line of 'Disk' Cameras: Analyst Enthusiastic, Inventors Cautious," *Wall Street Journal,* p. 52.

24. Jenkins, R. (1975) *Images and Enterprise Technology and the American Photographic Industry, 1839–1925,* Baltimore, Johns Hopkins University Press.

25. ———. (January 1975) "Technology and the Market: George Eastman and the Origins of Mass Amateur Photography," *Technology and Culture,* Vol. 16: 1–19.

26. Klein, B., Crawford, R., and Alchian, A. (October 1978) "Vertical Integration, Appropriable Rents, and the Competitive Contracting Process," *Journal of Law and Economics,* Vol. 21: 297–326.

27. ——— and Leffler, K. (August 1981) "The Role of Market Forces in Assuring Contractual Performance," *Journal of Political Economy,* Vol. 89: 615–641.

28. Leffler, K. (April 1981) "Persuasion or Information? The Economics of Prescription Drug Advertising," *Journal of Law and Economics,* Vol. 24: 45–74.

29. Nelson, P. (March 1970) "Information and Consumer Behavior," *Journal of Political Economy,* Vol. 78: 311–329.

30. Note. (March 1980) "An Economic and Legal Analysis of Physical Tie-Ins," *Yale Law Journal,* Vol. 89: 769–800.

31. *Photographic Trade News.* (1981) "Forecast 81," p. 17.

32. *Photo-Marketing.* (December 1979) "Overnight Delivery: Is It Worth It?" p. 20.

33. Robinson, I. (October 1979) "Photo-finishing Outlook," *Photo-Marketing,* p. 47.

34. Scherer, F. (1980) *Industrial Market Structure and Economic Performance,* 2nd ed., Chicago, Rand McNally.

35. Schmalensee, R. (Autumn 1978) "Entry Deterrence in the Ready-to-eat Breakfast Cereal Industry," *Bell Journal of Economics,* Vol. 9: 305–327.

36. ———. (April 1979) "On the Use of Economic Models in Antitrust: The Realemon Case," *University of Pennsylvania Law Review,* Vol. 127: 485–504.

37. ———. (1980) "The New Industrial Organization and the Economic Analysis of Modern Markets," Massachusetts Institute of Technology Working Paper, WP#113-80, Cambridge, Mass.

38. ———. (June 1982) "Product Differentiation Advantages of Pioneering Brands," *American Economic Review,* Vol. 72: 349–365.

39. Sheehan, R. (May 1965) "Picture-Sunshine and Shadow," *Fortune,* p. 156.

40. Spence, M. (Autumn 1977) "Entry Capacity, Investment and Oligopolistic Pricing," *Bell Journal of Economics,* Vol. 8: 534–544.

41. ———. (Spring 1979) "Investment Strategy and Growth in a New Market," *Bell Journal of Economics,* Vol. 9: 1–19.

42. Wechsberg, J. (November 10, 1956) "Profiles: Whistling in the Darkroom," *New Yorker,* pp. 61–109.

43. Williamson, O. (May 1977) "The Vertical Integration of Production: Market Failure Considerations," *American Economic Review,* Vol. 61: 112–123.

44. ———. (June 1972) "Dominant Firms and the Monopoly Problem: Market Failure Considerations," *Harvard Law Review,* Vol. 85: 1512–1531.

45. ———. (January 1974) "Book Review," *Yale Law Journal,* Vol. 83: 647–661.

A GUIDE TO THE HERFINDAHL INDEX FOR ANTITRUST ATTORNEYS

Paul A. Pautler

With the 1982 Justice Merger Guidelines, the Herfindahl index attained greater importance as a measure of market concentration. This paper illuminates the characteristics, flaws, and uses of the index. We briefly indicate why one might use the Herfindahl index rather than alternative measures, and show how one can evaluate merger outcomes using this index. The paper should give the reader an intuitive understanding of the index as well as a working knowledge.

I. INTRODUCTION

For years economists and antitrust attorneys have believed that the distribution of market shares among competing firms was an important factor in antitrust analysis. It has been argued that this distribution is either an important direct determinant of economic performance or that it at least gives us an indication of the circumstances in which poor performance

Research in Law and Economics, Volume 5, pages 167–190.
Copyright © 1983 by JAI Press Inc.
All rights of reproduction in any form reserved.
ISBN: 0-89232-419-8

is possible. Unfortunately, the market-share distribution for the entire industry is often too cumbersome for use in stating general merger policies. Given that the government would like to have some means of communicating merger-policy intentions to the business community, it would be useful to have a single measure of the firm-share distribution that efficiently summarizes the information contained in the full distribution.

There is no shortage of candidates for the position of leading market-share-distribution summary measure. The best known of the alternatives is the four-firm concentration ratio (CR_4). This measure is calculated by adding the market shares of the top four firms in a given market. Some other relatively familiar alternatives include the two-firm or eight-firm concentration ratios, which use the shares of the top two or eight firms in their calculation. There are also a number of more exotic alternatives; among these is the Herfindahl (H) index.[1]

This paper will discuss this particular index in some detail and familiarize the reader with its definition, characteristics, and flaws in practice. In addition, we will try to briefly indicate why one might want to use the Herfindahl index, rather than its alternatives, in a merger guideline. If we have been successful, the reader should obtain both an intellectual understanding of and a "feel" for the H-index and the changes that occur in the index when a merger occurs. In addition, one might also obtain an idea of which mergers might be subject to review or challenge under the new 1982 Department of Justice Merger Guidelines. Finally, the paper should leave the reader with a vague but discernible uneasiness about using any summary measure of the market-share distribution as a reliable indicator of market power or performance.

II. DEFINITION OF THE HERFINDAHL INDEX

The Herfindahl index[2] is calculated by adding together the squared market shares of the various firms.[3] For example, suppose we have a market with eight firms whose market shares are 25, 22, 18, 10, 8, 7, 6, and 4 percent, respectively. The H-index is found to be 1,698, as shown in Table 1.[4] From the example in Table 1, we can see that large firms have a relatively great impact in the index and as the share of the firm falls, its impact on the H-index falls rapidly, since each component is squared before it becomes part of H. Table 1 also includes a calculation of the cumulative sums of the market shares (column 2). From this column we can see that for this example, the four-firm concentration level, $\sum_{i=1}^{4} s_i$, is 75 percent and eight-firm concentration, $\sum_{i=1}^{8} s_i$, is 100 percent. As we will see in a moment, many different H-index levels are consistent with a 75 percent four-firm concentration level. However, the H-index will usually fall in

Table 1.   Calculation of the H-index from a Hypothetical Market-share
Distribution

Firm Rank	Market Share of Firm i (s_i)	Cumulative Sum of Shares	Squared Shares (s_i^2)
1	25	25	625
2	22	47	484
3	18	65	324
4	10	75	100
5	8	83	64
6	7	90	49
7	6	96	36
8	4	100	16
Totals	$100 = \sum_{i=1}^{8} s_i$		$1,698 = \sum_{i=1}^{8} s_i^2 = H$

Note: s_i is the market share of firm i; H is the Herfindahl index.

the 1,450 to 2,500 range if four-firm concentration is 75 percent and the firm-share distribution is not totally dominated by one firm.

III. CHARACTERISTICS OF THE H-INDEX AND THE HERFINDAHL NUMBERS EQUIVALENT

Before giving any additional examples of H-index calculation from firm share distributions, it might prove useful to indicate some of the characteristics of the H-index. For instance, the H-index approaches a value of zero if the market consists of an infinitely large number of infinitely small firms and approaches 10,000 as we move along the spectrum toward one firm with a 100 percent share.[5] A second characteristic of the H-index is that it can be decomposed to reveal the effects of two different elements—the number of firms and the variability of firm market shares.[6] For any given variation in firm shares, the H-index value is inversely related to the number of firms. That is, as the number of firms increases, the H-index value decreases. Also, for a given number of firms, the H-index value is directly related to the variability in firm shares. That is, as the market shares of the firms become more unequal, the H-index tends to rise. If all firms in a market are of equal size (and thus all firms are of average size), H is simply equal to 10,000 divided by the number of firms in the market.[7]

As an illustration, suppose that in the example in Table 1 all eight firms had equal shares of $12\frac{1}{2}$ percent. In that case, each squared share would equal 157.25, and the H-index would equal 1,250. This is the lowest H-index value consistent with having exactly eight firms. If we had 10 equal-sized firms, each with a 10 percent share, the H-index would equal 1,000. Table 2 gives some additional examples.

The examples in this table follow a pattern that illustrates the characteristic that $H = \dfrac{10,000}{n}$ whenever n equal-sized firms exist in a market. This property of the H-index might allow us to get a slightly better "feel" for what a given H-level tells us. Since $H = 10,000/n$ for equal-sized firms, we might ask the related question: "How many equal-sized firms are consistent with a given H-index when the H-index is calculated from an observed firm-size distribution (which usually includes unequal-sized firms)?" To answer this, we simply use the relationship that assumes equality of firm size: $H = 10,000/n$. Since we know H (which we assume to be calculated from an observed distribution), we simply plug that value into our formula and solve for n, the number of equal-sized firms corresponding to our given H-index value.[8] For our example in Table 1 where H equaled 1,698, the corresponding n value is 5.89. This number of equal-sized firms, consistent with our given industry structure, is often referred to as the Herfindahl Numbers Equivalent, or HNE for short.

One useful (if not quite precise) way of interpreting the Herfindahl Numbers Equivalent is to think of it as a measure of expected market performance. If HNE equals 15, then we might expect the industry to behave as if 15 equal-sized firms existed. That is, we might expect competitive performance.[9] If the HNE is 2, then we might expect performance to be less than perfectly competitive, since the share distribution is equivalent to that of a duopoly.[10] Additional examples of the HNE consistent

Table 2.   The H-index When Firms Are of Equal Size

Number of Equal-sized Firms (n)	Implied Share of Each Firm (s_i)	Herfindahl Index Level ($\sum s_i^2$)
1	100	10,000
2	50	5,000
3	33.33	3,333
4	25	2,500
5	20	2,000
6	16.66	1,666
7	14.29	1,429
8	12.50	1,250
9	11.11	1,111
10	10	1,000

Note: The H-index can be calculated as $\sum_{i=1}^{n} s_i^2$ or $100^2/n + \sum_{i=1}^{n} [s_i - (100/n)]^2$. In the case of the equal-sized firms, $\sum_{i=1}^{n} [s_i - (100/n)]^2$ equals zero, since $s_i = 100/n$ for all i. Thus, H reduces to $10,000/n$ in this special case. In this notation, s_i is the share of the i*th* firm, and 100/n is average firm share.

Table 3. Hypothetical Firm Share Distributions and Associated Summary Statistics of Market Structure

Example Number	Firm Share Distribution											Summary Statistics				
	s_1	s_2	s_3	s_4	s_5	s_6	s_7	s_8	s_9	s_{10}	SOR	CR_4	CR_8	H	HNE	n
1	50	10	10	10	8	8	4	—	—	—	—	80	100	2944	3.40	7
2	50	10	8	7	5	5	5	5	5	—	—	75	95	2838	3.52	9
3	35	20	10	10	8	7	5	5	—	—	—	75	100	1988	5.03	8
4	25	20	15	15	12	10	3	—	—	—	—	75	100	1728	5.78	7
5	19	19	19	18	5	5	3	3	3	3	3	75	91	1502	6.66	11
6	30	15	15	5	5	5	5	5	5	5	5	65	85	1550	6.45	11
7	30	20	5	5	5	5	5	5	5	5	10	60	80	1550	6.45	12
8	35	8	7	5	5	5	5	5	5	4	16[a]	55	75	1550	6.45	16
9	20	10	10	10	10	10	10	10	10	—	—	50	90	1200	8.33	9
10	30	4	3	3	3	3	3	3	3	3	42[b]	40	52	1114	8.97	24

Note: s_i is the market share of the ith firm; SOR is the sum of the market shares of the remaining firms if the number of firms exceeds 10; CR_4 is the four-firm concentration ratio; CR_8 is the eight-firm concentration ratio; H is the Herfindahl index, $\sum_{i=1}^{n} s_i^2$; HNE is the Herfindahl Numbers Equivalent, $10000/H$; and n is the number of firms in the market.

[a] The end of this distribution is 4,3,3,2,2,2.

[b] The end of this distribution consists of 14 firms each of which holds a 3 percent share.

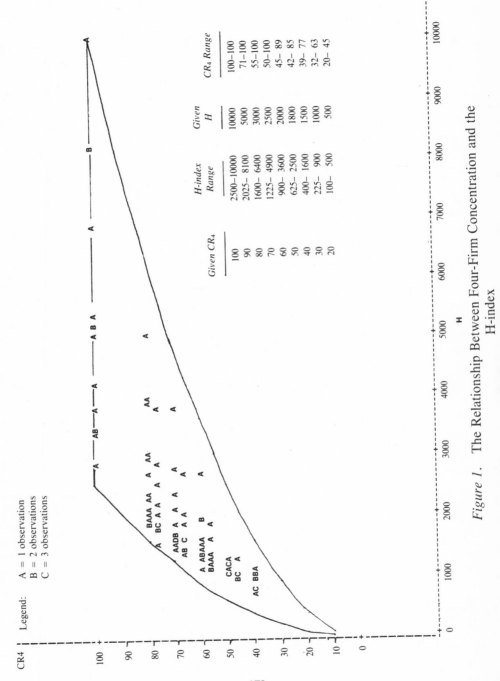

Figure 1. The Relationship Between Four-Firm Concentration and the H-index

172

with various H-index values can be derived just by working backwards in Table 2. Simply divide any assumed H-index level (column 3) into 10,000 to obtain the HNE (column 1).[11]

While the HNE gives one some intuition about the relative ranking of Herfindahl index levels that is lacking from a casual glance at various H-index values, additional experience with using H-index levels themselves can also lead to a "feel" for the information content of the index. Thus, in Table 3, we provide several sample firm-share distributions and calculate some summary measures for those distributions. This table gives 10 different share distributions and the associated values for four-firm concentration, CR_4; eight-firm concentration, CR_8; the Herfindahl index, H; the Herfindahl numbers equivalent, HNE; and the actual number of firms, n.[12] Examples 2 through 5 indicate that a fairly wide range of H-index levels can be consistent with any given four-firm concentration level. In addition, a comparison of examples 6 through 8 in Table 3 indicates that any given H-index level can be consistent with differing CR_4 values. Thus, there is not a one-to-one correspondence between CR_4 and H.

This fact is illustrated graphically in Figure 1 which plots four-firm concentration against the H-index for 100 hypothetical market-share distributions that are listed in the appendix. This figure also depicts the highest and lowest possible H-index values that are consistent with a given four-firm concentration value.[13] As the graph indicates, the H-index range is rather narrow at very low four-firm concentration levels but it rises quickly as higher concentration levels are approached. Indeed, the H-index can range anywhere from 2,500 to 10,000 for a given CR_4 of 100. Looking at the graph in the opposite way, we note that for a given H-index level the greatest CR_4 range occurs when H is approximately 2,500. At this point CR_4 can range from a low of 50 percent to a high of 100 percent. This CR_4 range narrows as we move away (in either direction) from an H level of 2,500.

These examples indicate that while CR_4 and H are positively related, the relationship is imperfect.[14] Given that the two summary statistics measure different things this fact should not be too surprising.

IV. CHANGES IN THE H-INDEX DUE TO MERGERS

Having obtained a feel for the H-index level that corresponds to various firm-share distributions, we can explore the ramifications of a change in the H-index due to a merger. It turns out that the change in the H-index is relatively simple to compute, since we only require the shares of the two merging firms to calculate the change. The postmerger H-index exceeds the premerger H by two times the product of the shares of the merging firms.[15] Thus, the change in the H-index due to a merger can be derived exactly, even if one knows only the shares of the merging firms.

To illustrate this point a number of examples are given in Table 4. In this table, we first calculate pre- and postmerger H-indices from some hypothetical market-share distributions (columns 2 and 5). Next, we subtract the premerger index from the postmerger index to obtain the change in the H-index due to the merger (column 6). As an alternative means of deriving the H-index change we simply use our knowledge of the shares of the merger partners to calculate two times the product of the shares of merger partners directly. This result is shown in column 7. In each example, we find that this column-7 result is identical to that obtained in column 6, which required considerable information and calculation. Thus, the examples indicate that we do not need knowledge of the nonmerging firms' shares to calculate the change in the H-index due to a merger. The merging firms' shares alone provide sufficient information.[16]

A final way to depict the change in the H-index is simply to draw its graph. Since the change is two times the product of the market shares of the merging firms, we can graph the relationship using the market shares of the two merging firms on the two axes of the graph. This is done in Figure 2, where various changes in the H-index (ΔH) are depicted. Each curve shows the market-share pairs that yield a given change in the H-index. As such, they may be called "iso-Herfindahl change curves."

Notice, for instance, that an increase of 200 in the H-index can occur from mergers of firms with shares of 10 and 10, 15 and $6\frac{2}{3}$, 20 and 5, 25 and 4, or any other share combination whose product is 100. Thus, for a given ΔH level, the market share of the ultimate merged entity may be somewhat larger when one firm is relatively small initially. One should also notice that points above and to the right of a given iso-Herfindahl change curve indicate market-share pairs consistent with a larger change in the H-index. Points below and to the left of a given iso-Herfindahl change curve indicate market-share pairs that produce a smaller change in the H-index.

As a reference point in Figure 2, we have also added a dashed line that represents the 1968 Department of Justice (DOJ) Horizontal Merger Guidelines for Less Highly Concentrated Markets ($CR_4 < 75$). These guidelines made share combinations above and to the right of the dashed line subject to probable challenge, while mergers of firms with share pairs below the line were not as likely to be prohibited. One might note that a 75-point change in the H-index is a fairly good approximation of this previous DOJ guideline. The recently issued 1982 DOJ horizontal-guideline levels use of $\Delta H = 100$ as a cutoff for possible (or probable) antitrust challenge, but this criterion would not be used unless the H-index level already exceeded 1,000 after the merger.

Table 4.   Changes in H-index Values Due to Mergers

Example Number	(1) Premerger Firm Share Distribution						(2) Premerger H-index $(\sum_{i=1}^{n} s_i^2)$	(3) Ranking of the Merging Firms (market shares in parentheses)	(4) Postmerger Firm Share Distribution					(5) Postmerger H-index $(\sum_{i=1}^{n-1} s_i'^2)$	(6) Change in the H-index due to the Merger (5) minus (2)	(7) Two Times the Product of the Shares of the Merging Firms $(2s_i s_j)$
	s_1	s_2	s_3	s_4	s_5	s_6			s_1'	s_2'	s_3'	s_4'	s_5'			
1	40	25	20	15	—	—	2850	3 and 4 (20 and 15)	40	35	25	—	—	3450	600	600
2	40	20	15	10	10	5	2450	5 and 6 (10 and 5)	40	20	15	15	10	2550	100	100
3	35	25	15	10	10	5	2300	5 and 6 (10 and 5)	35	25	15	15	10	2400	100	100
4	35	20	18	15	9	3	2264	4 and 5 (15 and 9)	35	24	20	18	3	2534	270	270
5	30	25	15	15	8	7	2088	5 and 6 (8 and 7)	30	25	15	15	15	2200	112	112

Note: s_i is the share of the ith firm prior to the merger; s_i' is the market share of the ith firm after the merger occurs; n is the number of firms in the market prior to the merger.

175

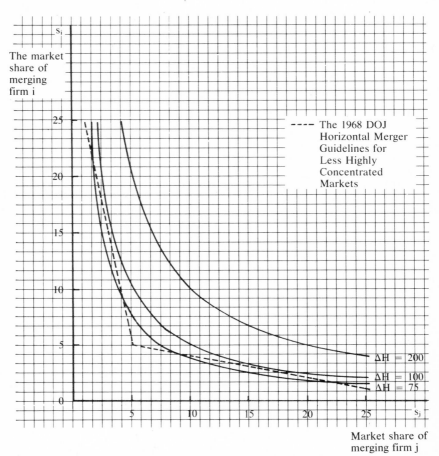

Note: The change in the H-index, ΔH, equals $2s_i s_j$. Thus ΔH = 200 occurs when
the product of the shares, $s_i s_j$, equals 100.

Figure 2.   The Change in the H-index Due to Mergers of Various Size
Firms (and the 1968 DOJ Merger Guidelines)

V. THE H-INDEX AND DATA ACCURACY

Calculation of the H-index ideally requires information on the shares of
all of the firms in a market. This is a somewhat heavier data burden than
is imposed by the four-firm concentration ratio, which only requires
knowledge of the shares of the four highest ranking firms. However, the
H-index can often be approximated fairly accurately even if we do not
possess all of the relevant information or if some of our information is
somewhat inaccurate.

To illustrate the effects of incomplete information, recall that since the shares of the firms are squared in calculating the index, the smaller shares at the end of the firm-share distribution do not have a great deal of weight in the index. These are likely to be the firms for which we will have relatively little information. Thus, even if they are ignored or approximated, we can still gain a fairly accurate idea of the H-index level. For example, suppose we had a true 12-firm share distribution of 20, 15, 15, 10, 8, 7, 5, 5, 5, 4, 4, 2 but only observed shares of 20, 15, 15, 10, 8, 7, 5, ... That is, we know the shares of the seven leading firms (which total 80 percent), but lack information on the distribution of the remaining 20-percent share and on the total number of firms in the market.[17] The H-index for the "true" distribution is 1,174. From our observed shares, we know that H must be at least equal to $20^2 + 15^2 + 15^2 + 10^2 + 8^2 + 7^2 + 5^2 = 1,088$.[18] We can also calculate an upper bound on H by assuming that the remaining 20 percent of the share distribution is held by the smallest possible number of firms. This will give us the largest H-index consistent with the known firm shares. Since the seventh largest firm has a 5 percent market share, the remaining firms can be no larger than 5 percent. Dividing this largest possible firm share into the 20 percent share held by an unknown number of firms indicates that we could have as few as four more firms in the tail of the firm-share distribution. This means that the largest possible H-level is consistent with a full distribution of 20, 15, 15, 10, 8, 7, 5, 5, 5, 5, 5. The H-index level corresponding to this distribution is 1,188. Thus, with knowledge of only seven firm shares, we know that the true H falls in the range 1,088 to 1,188.[19] This brackets the true value, which we already calculated to be 1,174. In many instances, this level of accuracy in calculating H may be more than sufficient for our purposes.

In the previous example, we assumed that n was unknown. However, if we know the first 7 shares and also know that the number of firms in the "true" distribution is 12, we can obtain an even narrower range of estimates for the "true" H-value. Our upper bound on H would be only infinitesimally lower than our previous 1,188, since the added twelfth firm could be infinitesimally small and thus draw a very small share away from any of the other firms in our earlier 11-firm upper-bound distribution.[20] However, the real gain in knowing that only 12 firms exist comes not from lowering the upper bound but from raising our lower-bound estimate for H. Previously, our lower-bound estimate was obtained by assuming that the 20 percent market share not held by the seven leading firms was distributed among an infinitely large number of firms. However, we now know that this 20 percent is held by only 5 firms (12 minus 7). To obtain our new lower bound for H, we must determine the distribution of the 20 percent share among these five firms that minimizes the sum of the squared shares. This will insure the smallest addition to H, given that five firms share the remaining 20 percent.[21] The distribution of 20 percent among five firms that yields the smallest squared shares is 4, 4, 4, 4, 4.[22] This means our new lower-bound distribution, in full, is 20, 15, 15, 10, 8, 7, 5, 4, 4, 4, 4, 4. The H associated with this distribution is 1,168. Thus, the added knowledge that only 12 firms exist in the market, combined with the known shares of the 7 leading firms, allowed us to narrow the range of possible H values from 1,168 to 1,188. This range rather closely brackets the "true" H-value of 1,174 derived from our hypothesized true full distribution of firm market shares.[23] In virtually all cases, this level of accuracy in estimating H would be sufficient for the purposes of merging firm's counsel, arbitrageurs, and the antitrust authorities.

One final related characteristic of the H-index should be mentioned at this point. We have seen from some of the previous examples that an error in estimating the small shares in a firm-share distribution need not cause a large problem in calculating the H-index level. Nor will it cause any problem in calculating the change in the H-index due to a merger (so long as we know the shares of the merger partners themselves). However, an error in allocating market shares to the largest firms can cause relatively large swings in the calculated H-index. Since the shares are squared before being added to the index, an error of 5 percent for a large firm can change the index much more than simply ignoring a small 5 percent firm. Since we live in a world in which our information is often incorrect, and it is often quite costly to obtain complete and accurate information, this could pose a practical problem for use of the H-index. The examples given in Table 5 should make the possible magnitude of this problem more obvious. Each of the examples given in this table compares a "true" distribution of firm shares (column 1) and the "true" summary measures CR_4 and H (columns 2 and 3) with a hypothetical observed distribution (column 4). We assume that we make errors in observing the market-share distribution. These errors will lead to incorrect summary measures of the market-share distribution (columns 5 and 6). A comparison of the correct and incorrect summary measures is given in columns 7 through 10.

The first six examples in Table 5 each use the same "true" distribution, with H = 2,000 and CR_4 = 80. The first four related erroneous distributions allow no more than a 5 percent share error for any one firm's share. As we can see in the first four examples, a shift of share from one firm to another affects the H-index somewhat more than it affects the CR_4 index based on the percentage error in the index from its true value (compare columns 9 and 10).[24]

Examples 5 and 6 in Table 5 give the results of some larger errors in observing the firm-share distribution. In these cases, the divergence of H from its true value is rather pronounced, while the divergence of CR_4

Table 5. Errors in Calculating the H-index When Market Share Data are Erroneous

	(1) True Distribution								(2) True H-index $\sum_{i=1}^{n} s_i^2$	(3) True CR$_4$ $\sum_{i=1}^{4} s_i$	(4) Erroneous Distribution								(5) Erroneous H-index	(6) Erroneous CR$_4$	(7) Absolute Value of True H minus Erroneous H	(8) Absolute Value of True CR$_4$ minus Erroneous CR$_4$	(9) Percent Error in H	(10) Percent Error in CR$_4$
Example Number	s_1	s_2	s_3	s_4	s_5	s_6	s_7	s_8			s_1'	s_2'	s_3'	s_4'	s_5'	s_6'	s_7'	s_8'						
1	30	25	15	10	10	5	5	5 —	2000	80	35	20	15	10	10	5	5 —		2100	80	100	0	5.00	0.00
2	30	25	15	10	10	5	5	5 —	2000	80	35	25	15	10	5	5	5 —		2250	85	250	5	12.50	6.25
3	30	25	15	10	10	5	5	5 —	2000	80	25	20	20	15	10	5	5 —		1800	80	200	0	10.00	0.00
4	30	25	15	10	10	5	5	5 —	2000	80	25	20	15	10	10	10	10 —		1650	70	350	10	17.50	12.50
5	30	25	15	10	10	5	5	5 —	2000	80	40	15	15	10	10	5	5 —		2300	80	300	0	15.00	0.00
6	30	25	15	10	10	5	5	5 —	2000	80	40	35	5	5	5	5	5 —		2950	85	950	5	47.00	6.25
7	25	20	15	10	8	8	7	7	1576	70	30	20	10	10	8	8	7	7	1726	70	150	0	9.52	0.00
8	25	20	15	10	8	8	7	7	1576	70	35	25	10	8	7	5	5	5	2138	78	562	8	35.66	11.43
9	25	20	15	10	8	8	7	7	1576	70	20	20	20	8	8	8	8	8	1520	68	56	2	3.55	2.86

179

from its true value is not very large.[25] A comparison across all of the examples in Table 5 shows that for a given number of firms, errors that tend to reduce market-share variability cause the H-index to be below its "true" value. Conversely, errors that increase share variability tend to push H above its "true" value.[26] This is akin to the lesson we learned in Section III that showed that equality of shares minimized the H-index value for any given number of firms.

VI. SOME FINAL CONSIDERATIONS

Up to this point, we have been mainly concerned with defining the Herfindahl index and illustrating its characteristics. However, we have not focused on two related and potentially important issues. First, we want to know why the H-index would ever be used in a merger guideline. Second, we want to know if the H-index is preferable to using the more familiar four-firm concentration measure. These issues will be very briefly discussed in turn.

The most basic economic rationale for using any measure of market structure in a merger guideline is that the measure bears some systematic relationship to the performance level that is expected to be observed in the market.[27] Thus, the market-structure measure serves as a rough proxy for the performance of the market. A closely related but less hopeful notion is that a particular type of market structure (for example, high concentration) may be a necessary (but not a sufficient) condition for poor economic performance. In this view, the structural summary statistics do not proxy expected economic performance but only give us an indication of those markets in which at least one necessary condition for poor performance is met.[28] Thus, they help us segregate those markets in which poor performance is possible from those in which it is not possible. Since some subset of the economics literature can be used to support either of the two stated rationales for using market-structure measures in a merger guideline, we will not pursue that issue here.[29]

A final issue to be addressed briefly concerns the value of using the Herfindahl index rather than a concentration ratio as our measure of market structure. To some extent, this choice must be based on the practical characteristics of the rival indices rather than on theoretical considerations. Both the H-index and the four-firm concentration measure can be derived from rather standard economic models.[30] Furthermore, it is not clear that one measure has an empirical edge over the other. In fact, some very recent empirical research leads one to wonder whether either measure has a systematic relationship with economic performance.[31] Despite these ambiguities, one might be able to choose between the two indices on the basis of their characteristics. For example, consider the fact that the CR_4 measure is invariant with respect to the distribution of shares among the top four firms. This means that the distributions 60, 5, 5, 5, 5, 5, 5, 5, 5 and 20, 20, 20, 15, 10, 5, 5, 5 each have a CR_4 of 75, yet one might think that the performance of industries would differ when one very large firm exists as opposed to when four relatively equal-sized leading firms exist. The H-index would differentiate between these two situations and assign a much higher value to the first distribution, in which the variance of the firm shares was very large.[32] Thus, if one has a prior belief that market performance worsens when large-firm dominance occurs, then an H-index rather than CR_4 might be the most appropriate choice as a market-structure measure.

Regardless of one's prior beliefs about the "competitiveness" of various firm-share distributions, we can see from the many examples here that no single index is likely to capture perfectly the information contained in the full firm-share distribution. Since a given H-level is consistent with a wide range of different distributions, its meaning is somewhat ambiguous. Use of such an index in a merger guideline will therefore lead to some ambiguity in application. Despite this, a summary measure of share distributions is probably necessary if we are to have usable merger guidelines, and the H-index is at least as good a summary measure as any of the popular alternatives.

APPENDIX A

Additional Hypothetical Firm-Share Distributions and Associated Summary Statistics

Example No.	Firm Market Share Distribution														Summary Statistics				
	S1	S2	S3	S4	S5	S6	S7	S8	S9	S10	S11	S12	S13	SOR	H	HNE	CR4	CR8	N
1	100	0	0	0	0	0	0	0	0	0	0	0	0	0	10000	1.00	100	100	1
2	90	10	0	0	0	0	0	0	0	0	0	0	0	0	8200	1.22	100	100	2
3	90	5	5	0	0	0	0	0	0	0	0	0	0	0	8150	1.23	100	100	3
4	80	20	0	0	0	0	0	0	0	0	0	0	0	0	6800	1.47	100	100	2
5	70	15	15	0	0	0	0	0	0	0	0	0	0	0	5350	1.87	100	100	3
6	70	10	10	10	0	0	0	0	0	0	0	0	0	0	5200	1.92	100	100	4
7	60	40	0	0	0	0	0	0	0	0	0	0	0	0	5200	1.92	100	100	2
8	50	50	0	0	0	0	0	0	0	0	0	0	0	0	5000	2.00	100	100	2
9	70	4	3	3	3	3	3	3	3	3	2	0	0	0	4992	2.00	80	92	11
10	60	20	10	10	0	0	0	0	0	0	0	0	0	0	4200	2.38	100	100	4
11	60	15	3	2	2	2	2	2	2	2	2	2	2	2	3878	2.58	80	88	14
12	60	10	5	5	4	4	4	4	4	0	0	0	0	0	3830	2.61	80	96	9
13	60	8	4	3	3	3	3	3	3	3	3	3	1	0	3762	2.66	75	87	13
14	50	25	25	0	0	0	0	0	0	0	0	0	0	0	3750	2.67	100	100	3
15	60	4	3	3	3	3	3	3	3	3	3	3	3	3	3724	2.69	70	82	14
16	50	20	20	10	0	0	0	0	0	0	0	0	0	0	3400	2.94	100	100	4
17	40	40	10	10	0	0	0	0	0	0	0	0	0	0	3400	2.94	100	100	4
18	50	18	16	16	0	0	0	0	0	0	0	0	0	0	3336	3.00	100	100	4
19	50	20	5	5	4	4	4	4	4	0	0	0	0	0	3030	3.30	80	96	9
20	50	10	10	10	8	8	4	0	0	0	0	0	0	0	2944	3.40	80	100	7
21	50	10	8	7	5	5	5	5	5	0	0	0	0	0	2838	3.52	75	95	9
22	40	20	20	20	0	0	0	0	0	0	0	0	0	0	2800	3.57	100	100	4
23	50	10	6	4	4	4	4	4	4	4	4	2	0	0	2768	3.61	70	86	12
24	50	8	4	3	3	3	3	3	3	3	3	3	3	8	2692	3.71	65	77	16

25	50	4	3	3	3	3	3	3	3	3	13	2652	3.77	60	72	18		
26	40	30	5	5	4	4	4	3	0	0	0	2630	3.80	80	96	9		
27	45	15	5	5	5	5	4	4	0	0	0	2488	4.02	75	95	9		
28	40	8	7	10	10	5	5	2	2	2	12	2350	4.26	80	100	6		
29	40	15	10	10	2	2	0	0	0	0	0	2298	4.35	70	78	19		
30	40	25	3	2	2	2	5	3	1	0	0	2250	4.44	80	100	8		
31	40	15	10	5	5	5	5	5	0	0	0	2178	4.59	75	93	11		
32	40	15	5	5	5	3	3	3	2	0	0	2100	4.76	70	90	10		
33	40	10	5	5	3	3	3	0	0	0	0	2058	4.86	80	92	11		
34	30	10	20	3	0	0	0	5	0	0	0	2000	5.00	80	100	5		
35	35	20	20	20	7	5	5	5	5	0	0	1988	5.03	75	100	8		
36	40	10	10	8	5	5	0	0	0	22	22	1988	5.03	65	85	11		
37	30	8	7	5	2	2	2	2	2	4	4	1950	5.13	80	100	6		
38	40	15	15	10	4	4	4	4	4	0	0	1918	5.21	60	68	24		
39	40	10	3	2	5	0	0	0	0	0	0	1910	5.24	60	76	14		
40	30	20	5	4	5	5	3	0	0	18	18	1850	5.41	80	100	8		
41	30	25	15	5	5	5	5	3	3	0	0	1850	5.41	75	95	9		
42	40	8	10	3	3	5	5	0	0	0	0	1824	5.48	55	67	19		
43	19	19	19	18	7	3	3	0	0	0	0	1804	5.54	76	100	6		
44	25	25	15	5	5	0	0	5	5	0	0	1800	5.56	80	100	8		
45	22	20	16	14	10	5	5	0	0	0	0	1800	5.56	78	100	6		
46	30	25	5	5	7	0	0	0	0	0	0	1800	5.56	70	90	10		
47	35	10	10	10	10	5	5	5	5	0	0	1800	5.62	65	95	9		
48	19	19	18	18	7	0	0	0	0	0	0	1780	5.79	75	100	6		
49	25	20	15	12	10	3	3	0	0	0	0	1728	5.92	75	100	7		
50	20	10	10	8	7	7	6	3	3	0	0	1688	5.94	70	95	9		
51	30	17	17	17	13	5	5	0	0	0	0	1684	6.22	70	100	6		
52	18	15	10	8	7	0	0	3	3	0	0	1608	6.25	71	91	11		
53	21	21	17	8	8	7	7	6	6	0	0	1600	6.25	70	100	8		
54	18	17	15	17	7	6	6	0	0	0	0	1600	6.25	70	100	7		
55	15	15	15	10	10	7	7	4	1	1	0	1600	6.25	67	94	7		
56	25	10	10	10	7	6	6	5	0	0	0	1600	6.25	65	95	11		
57	30	15	10	10	10	5	5	5	0	0	0	1600		65	95	9		

APPENDIX A   (Continued)

Example No.	Firm Market Share Distribution														Summary Statistics				
	S1	S2	S3	S4	S5	S6	S7	S8	S9	S10	S11	S12	S13	SOR	H	HNE	CR4	CR8	N
58	35	8	7	7	7	7	7	4	3	3	3	3	3	3	1600	6.25	57	82	15
59	30	15	15	5	5	5	5	5	5	5	5			0	1550	6.45	65	85	11
60	30	20	5	5	5	5	5	5	5	5	5	5		0	1550	6.45	60	80	12
61	30	10	10	10	8	8	8	8	8					0	1520	6.58	60	92	9
62	19	19	19	18	5	5	3	3	3	3	3			0	1502	6.66	75	91	11
63	20	18	17	15	10	8	7	5						0	1476	6.78	70	100	8
64	15	15	15	15	15	15	10							0	1450	6.90	60	100	7
65	25	20	15	5	4	4	4	4	4	4	4	4	3	0	1412	7.08	65	81	13
66	20	18	17	15	10	3	3	3	3	3	3	2		0	1396	7.16	70	89	12
67	25	15	15	10	8	7	5	5	5	5				0	1388	7.20	65	90	10
68	30	10	10	10	4	4	4	4	4	4	4	4	4	4	1360	7.35	60	76	14
69	20	15	15	15	10	8	8	4	3	2				0	1326	7.54	65	95	10
70	20	20	10	10	8	8	8	8	8					0	1320	7.58	60	92	9
71	30	10	10	5	4	4	4	4	4	4	4	4	4	9	1302	7.68	55	71	16
72	30	12	10	3	3	3	3	3	3	3	3	3	3	18	1288	7.76	55	67	19
73	30	8	7	5	5	5	5	5	5	5	5	5	5	5	1288	7.76	50	70	14
74	20	15	13	12	8	8	8	8	8					0	1258	7.95	60	92	9
75	30	5	5	5	5	5	5	5	5	5	5	5	5	10	1250	8.00	45	65	15
76	25	15	10	5	5	5	5	5	5	5	5	5	5	0	1200	8.33	55	75	13
77	20	10	10	10	10	10	10	10	10					0	1200	8.33	50	90	9
78	25	10	8	7	6	6	6	6	6	5	5	5	5	0	1130	8.85	50	74	13
79	14	12	12	12	10	10	10	10	10					0	1128	8.87	55	90	9
80	20	15	10	10	8	7	7	7	6	5	5			0	1124	8.90	55	84	11
81	30	4	3	3	3	3	3	3	3	3	3	3	3	33	1114	8.98	40	52	24
82	20	20	5	5	5	5	5	5	5	5	5	5	5	5	1100	9.09	50	70	14
83	20	15	13	12	4	4	4	4	4	4	4	4	4	4	1098	9.11	60	76	14
84	15	15	15	10	10	8	7	5	5	5	5			0	1088	9.19	55	85	11

#	S(1)	S(2)	S(3)	S(4)	S(5)	S(6)	S(7)	S(8)	S(9)	S(10)	S(11)	SOR	H	HNE	CR4	CR8	N
85	25	8	7	5	5	5	5	5	5	5	5	10	1016	9.84	45	65	17
86	18	17	10	6	6	6	6	5	5	5	3	3	1000	10.00	51	74	14
87	20	10	10	10	10	5	5	5	5	5	5	0	1000	10.00	50	75	13
88	20	17	6	6	6	6	6	5	4	4	4	7	1000	10.00	49	72	16
89	12	12	12	12	10	10	10	6	6	4	0	0	1000	10.00	48	84	11
90	10	10	10	10	10	10	10	10	0	0	0	0	1000	10.00	40	80	10
91	25	5	5	5	5	5	5	5	5	5	5	15	1000	10.00	45	60	16
92	20	10	8	5	7	7	7	7	4	4	0	0	992	10.08	40	73	12
93	25	6	5	4	4	4	4	4	4	4	4	24	942	10.62	45	56	19
94	15	10	10	10	10	8	5	5	5	5	0	0	938	10.66	40	80	12
95	20	7	7	6	6	6	6	6	6	6	6	0	894	11.19	45	64	14
96	15	15	8	7	6	6	6	6	6	6	6	1	888	11.26	40	69	14
97	20	15	3	2	2	2	2	2	2	2	2	42	758	13.19	40	48	34
98	15	10	10	5	5	5	5	5	5	5	5	15	750	13.33	40	60	16
99	20	7	7	6	3	3	3	3	3	3	3	33	714	14.01	40	52	24
100	15	15	8	2	2	2	2	2	2	2	2	42	638	15.67	40	48	34

Note: S(I) is the market share of the i*th* firm; SOR is the summation of the shares of the firms ranked 14th to last; H is the Herfindahl index, the sum of the squared market shares; HNE is the Herfindahl numbers equivalent (10000/H); CR₄ is the four-firm concentration ratio; CR₈ is the eight-firm concentration ratio; and N is the total number of firms in the market.

185

ACKNOWLEDGMENTS

The opinions expressed are those of the author and do not necessarily reflect the views of the Federal Trade Commission, individual commissioners, or other individual staff members. I would like to thank Daniel Alger, Robert Lande and Walter Vandaele for comments on an earlier draft.

NOTES

1. The Herfindahl index is probably the least esoteric of the exotic alternatives to k-firm concentration ratios. For a discussion of some of these other alternatives see Miller (13); Stigler (18); Kwoka (9); Dansby and Willig (3); and Dickson (4). Two very recent papers which examine aspects of the H-index are Kwoka (9a) and Miller (13a).

2. This index is sometimes referred to as the Herfindahl-Hirschman index to indicate at least dual paternity. See Hirschman (7). The H-index has been given some judicial recognition within the last ten years. In *FTC v. Litton Industries, Inc.*, 82 FTC 904-15 (1973), the initial decision placed considerable emphasis on the desirability of using the H-index relative to using the four-firm concentration ratio to measure market structure in the typewriter industry. However, not all courts have embraced the use of the index, due in part to the paucity of precedent based on it. See *United States v. Black and Decker Manufacturing Co. and McCulloch Corp.*, 1976 Trade Cas. ¶61,033 at note 38. The H-index has also been used or at least recognized as a valid measure of market structure in more recent cases. See *FTC v. Kellogg Company et al.*, Initial Decision, Docket 8883, at findings 170-72, 181; and *Marathon v. Mobil etc., et al.*, 530 F. Supp. 315 at note 15.

3. The H-index formula is

$$(1) \qquad H = \sum_{i=1}^{n} s_i^2 = s_1^2 + s_2^2 + s_3^2 + s_4^2 + \cdots + s_n^2,$$

where n is the total number of firms in the market and s_i indicates the market share of the i*th* firm.

4. One can treat each share as a fraction rather than a whole number. This simply leads to the placement of a decimal point in H but does not change any calculations or characteristics of the H-index. The Department of Justice Antitrust Division seems to prefer to treat shares as whole numbers rather than fractions, and we will follow that convention.

5. If we use decimals rather than whole numbers to designate the shares, then the H-index range is between zero and one.

6. This characteristic can be seen by rewriting the H-index formula as

$$(2) \qquad H = \frac{100^2}{n} + \sum_{i=1}^{n} \left(s_i - \frac{100}{n} \right)^2,$$

where 100/n is the average firm's market share.

In this formula, the first term on the right-hand side gives us the overall effect of the number of firms in the market, while the second term on the right-hand side describes the variability of individual firm shares, s_i, around the average share, 100/n. For those who wish to see that Eqs. (1) and (2) are indeed equivalent, we provide this proof. We start with Eq. (2), expand the squared expression, perform some algebra with the summation sign, and collect terms to obtain Eq. (1).

$$(2) \qquad H = \frac{100^2}{n} + \sum_{i=1}^{n} \left(s_i - \frac{100}{n} \right)^2$$

$$= \frac{100^2}{n} + \sum_{i=1}^{n} \left(s_i^2 - 2s_i \frac{100}{n} + \left(\frac{100}{n} \right)^2 \right)$$

$$= \frac{100^2}{n} + \sum_{i=1}^{n} s_i^2 - 2 \frac{100}{n} \sum_{i=1}^{n} s_i + \sum_{i=1}^{n} \left(\frac{100}{n} \right)^2$$

$$= \sum_{i=1}^{n} s_i^2 + \frac{100^2}{n} - 2 \frac{100^2}{n} + n \frac{100^2}{n^2} .$$

$$(1) \qquad H = \sum_{i=1}^{n} s_i^2 .$$

For an alternative derivation and explanation see Scherer (16), p. 59, n. 45.

7. All of these characteristics are evident from an examination of Eq. (2) in note 6 *supra*. Notice that if variability in market shares, $\sum_{i=1}^{n} [s_i - (100/n)]^2$, is low because all firms are of nearly equal size, the H-index is dominated by the first term on the right-hand side of equation 2, $100^2/n$. This implies that for a given number of firms, the share distribution that minimizes H is the one with no variability in individual shares. In that case there is no variability component to add to the 10,000/n term.

8. You might note that in Table 2 we performed the opposite procedure, since we knew the number of equal-sized firms, n, and used that value to solve for H.

9. The literature relating market structure to economic performance does not allow us to make precise predictions concerning the performance to be expected from a given structure. However, there is no literature that would indicate that a market consisting of 15 equal-sized firms will yield anything other than a competitive outcome in the absence of overt collusive behavior. See Pautler (14).

10. There are, however, some problems with this "intuitive" approach to the Herfindahl Numbers Equivalent. Industries with identical H-indices (and thus the same HNE) might in some instances perform quite differently. Consider, for example, two industries that each have an H of 2000 (HNE = 5), yet one industry has five firms, each with a 20 percent share, and the other industry has many more firms but one dominant firm with a 40 percent share. It is quite conceivable that the appropriate economic model for use in the two cases differs and that the performance actually observed might differ substantially. Thus, the H-index does not necessarily capture all of the information about the market-share distribution that one might want. Further, it clearly does not capture all of the relevant information concerning conduct and performance that one would want to incorporate in a complete analysis of a market.

11. Although only whole-number results are shown in Table 2, it is clear that the HNE can take on any value. For instance, if H equals 700 or 2,100, the corresponding HNE's are 14.29 or 4.76, respectively.

12. An additional 100 examples of differing firm-share distributions and their associated summary statistics are given in the appendix. These added examples give many distributions that yield H-index values close to 1,000 or 1,800. The focus is on these levels because Department of Justice mentions them as being useful cutoff points in their 1982 merger guidelines. See U.S. Department of Justice Merger Guidelines, June 14, 1982, at 16–20.

13. The maximum and minimum values of the H-index for a given CR_4 value may be derived from the following equations: $H_{max} = (CR_4)^2$; $H_{min} = 4 \times (CR_4/4)^2$. The H_{max}

value is obtained by assuming that the largest firm holds all of the top four-firm share and the remaining firms are infinitesimally small. For example, for $CR_4 = 50$ we assume the largest firm has essentially a 50 percent share while all other firms are very small and contribute nothing to the H-value. This assumption maximizes H for any given CR_4 value as long as CR_4 is not below 25. The H_{min} value assumes that the top four firms in the market are of equal size while all remaining firms are infinitesimally small. That is, if $CR_4 = 50$ the top four firms each have a 12.5 percent share and the remaining firms are all very small. These distributions (particularly the H_{max} distribution) are not typical and are only used to obtain boundaries for H and CR_4 pairs. In practice one would probably encounter more observations lying close to the upper boundary line than to the lower boundary line in Figure 1 since widely different firm sizes are not the norm.

14.   This is not to say that the CR_4 and H measures are uncorrelated. For most standard firm-share distributions that one would encounter in practice, the correlation of H and CR_4 will be fairly high. However, even a high correlation does not insure that the two measures contain the same information. See Kwoka (10).

15.   To see this, let us assume that there are four firms in a market and that the market shares of these firms are s_1, s_2, s_3, and s_4, respectively. Prior to the merger the H-index is $H = \sum_{i=1}^{4} s_i^2 = s_1^2 + s_2^2 + s_3^2 + s_4^2$. Now suppose that firms 2 and 3 merge. This leaves us with a new firm-share distribution of s_1', s_2', s_3', where $s_1' = s_1$, $s_2' = s_2 + s_3$, and $s_3' = s_4$. The postmerger H-index is

$$H' = \sum_{i=1}^{3} s_i'^2 = s_1'^2 + s_2'^2 + s_3'^2$$

$$= s_1^2 + (s_2 + s_3)^2 + s_4^2$$

$$= s_1^2 + s_2^2 + 2s_2s_3 + s_3^2 + s_4^2.$$

Notice that H' exceeds H by exactly $2s_2s_3$, or two times the product of the market shares of the merging firms. This result follows directly from the quadratic nature of the H-index.

16.   Note that this cannot necessarily be said for the four-firm concentration measure. Knowledge of the merging firms' shares alone will not tell us how large the change in CR_4 due to the merger will be.

17.   For purposes of this first example only, we suppose that we do not know the total number of firms in the market. Having such knowledge will only improve our approximation, as we will see in the second example in this section.

18.   This forms a lower bound for the H-value of the "true" distribution. It assumes that the remaining 20 percent of the distribution is held by a very large number of very small firms.

19.   The "true" H-value would have been close to the lower bound if the remaining 20 percent were distributed among a very large number of very small firms. To the extent that we have any information about the residual firms, we can clearly narrow the range of possible estimated H-values.

20.   If we denote this infinitesimal amount by ϵ, our new upper-bound distribution is 20, 15, 15, 10, 8, 7, 5, 5, 5, 5, 5-ϵ, ϵ. The H-index consistent with this 12-firm distribution is infinitesimally smaller than 1,188.

21.   Note that this is simply the reverse of the process done to obtain an upper bound for H. In that case, we assumed that the 20 percent share was distributed in a manner that maximized the sum of the squared shares, given our knowledge that the seventh largest firm had only a 5 percent share.

22.   Recall that for a given number of firms (in this case five), the smallest sum of the squared shares occurs when the firms are all of equal size. This is the same characteristic

that leads to equal-sized firms minimizing the H-index for a full distribution. See Section III.

23. For more discussion of H-index calculation using imperfect data see Schmalensee (17).

24. In the cases where the share shifts occur only among the top four firms, the erroneous CR_4 will be equal to the true CR_4. In a sense, the erroneous CR_4 is "right for the wrong reason."

25. Highly concentrated markets with relatively large firms are the cases where CR_4 outperforms H most clearly in terms of sensitivity to data errors. In less concentrated markets, H will be considerably less sensitive to error than it is in highly concentrated markets. For instance, assume that the true distribution of shares is 15, 15, 10, 10, 8, 7, 5, 5, 5, 5, 5, 5, where CR_4 equals 50 and H equals 938. Then assume that we observe an erroneous distribution (with an equal number of firms), such as 15, 10, 10, 10, 10, 8, 7, 5, 5, 5, 5, 5, 5, where CR_4 equals 45 and H is 888. In this example, the error in CR_4 is 10 percent, while the error in H is only 5.33 percent.

26. Examples 3, 4, and 9 are those in which variability of firm shares is decreased due to the errors.

27. This view is consistent with much of the empirical literature concerning the relationship between concentration and profitability or prices. For a review of this literature see Pautler (14). This view is also consistent with the literature that uses specific market models involving dominant firms, cartels, or tacitly collusive oligopolies to derive the theoretical relationships between market-structure measures and measures of economic performance. For examples of this literature see Dansby and Willig (3), Dickson (4), Encaona and Jacquemin (5), and Hause (6). See also Daniel Benjamin (1), this volume.

28. This view of the use of a market-structure measure is consistent with much theoretical work on oligopoly theory. See, for example, Stigler (19) and Pautler (14).

29. There may be rationales for the use of concentration measures in merger guidelines that do not flow from standard welfare economics. For instance, one commentator has argued that in passing Section 7 of the Clayton Act, Congress was more concerned with preventing transfers of wealth from consumers to sellers (due to market power) than with enhancing efficiency. See Lande (12).

30. For derivations showing that four-firm concentration can be a theoretically valid index see Saving (15), Cowling and Waterson (2), and the papers cited in note 27 *supra*. For derivations indicating that the H-index and several other market-structure measures may be theoretically valid indicia of performance see Dansby and Willig (3) and Kelly (8).

31. For the most recent work along these lines using line-of-business data see Kwoka and Ravenscraft (11). Previous papers comparing the value of alternative market-structure measures include Kwoka (10) and Miller (13).

32. The H-index consistent with the first distribution is 3,800, while the H-index for the second distribution is 1,600.

REFERENCES

1. Benjamin, Daniel. (1983) "Effect of Monopolies and Cartels on Market Prices," *Research in Law and Economics*, Vol. 5: 1–15.
2. Cowling, K., and Waterson, M. (August 1976) "Price-Cost Margins and Market Structure," *Economica*, Vol. 43: 267–274.
3. Dansby, R., and Willig, R. (June 1979) "Industry Performance Gradient Indexes," *American Economic Review*, Vol. 69: 249–260.

4. Dickson, V. (1981) "Conjectural Variations Elasticities and Concentration," *Economic Letters*, Vol. 7: 281–285.
5. Encaona, D., and Jacquemin, A. (February 1980) "Degree of Monopoly, Indices of Concentration, and Threat of Entry," *International Economic Review*, Vol. 21: 87–105.
6. Hause, J. (June 1977) "The Measurement of Concentrated Industrial Structure and the Size Distribution of Firms," *Annals of Economic and Social Measurement*, Vol. 6: 73–103.
7. Hirschman, A. O. (September 1964) "The Paternity of an Index," *American Economic Review*, Vol. 54: 761.
8. Kelly, W. Jr. (July 1981) "A Generalized Interpretation of the Herfindahl Index," *Southern Economic Journal*, Vol. 48: 50–57.
9. Kwoka, J. (July 1977) "Large-Firm Dominance and Price-Cost Margins in Manufacturing Industries," *Southern Economic Journal*, Vol. 44: 183–189.
9a. ———. (1982) "The Herfindahl Index in Theory and Practice," unpublished manuscript, George Washington University, Washington, D.C.
10. ———. (June 1981) "Does the Choice of Concentration Measure Really Matter?" *Journal of Industrial Economics*, Vol. 29: 445–453.
11. Kwoka, J., and Ravenscraft, D. (March 1982) "Alternative Measures of Concentration and the Profit-Concentration Relationship," Washington, D.C., Federal Trade Commission.
12. Lande, R. (1982) "Wealth Transfers as the Original and Primary Concern of Antitrust: The Efficiency Interpretation Challenged," *Hastings Law Journal*, Vol. 34.
13. Miller, R. A. (July 1972) "Numbers Equivalents, Relative Entropy, and Concentration Ratios: A Comparison Using Market Performance," *Southern Economic Journal*, Vol. 39: 107–112.
13a. ———. (Fall 1982) "The Herfindahl-Hirschman Index as a Market Structure Variable: An Exposition for Antitrust Practitioners," *Antitrust Bulletin*, Vol. 27: 593–618.
14. Pautler, P. A. (October 1981) "A Review of the Economic Basis for Broad-based Horizontal Merger Policy," Washington, D.C., Federal Trade Commission.
15. Saving, T. R. (February 1970) "Concentration Ratios and the Degree of Monopoly," *International Economic Review*, Vol. 11: 139–146.
16. Scherer, F. (1980) *Industrial Market Structure and Economic Performance*. Chicago, Rand McNally.
17. Schmalensee, R. (May 1977) "Using the H-Index of Concentration with Published Data," *Review of Economics and Statistics*, Vol. 59: 186–193.
18. Stigler, G. J. (1968) "The Measurement of Concentration," pp. 29–38 in *The Organization of Industry*, ed. G. Stigler. Homewood, Ill., Irwin.
19. ———. (1968) "A Theory of Oligopoly," reprinted in *The Organization of Industry*, ed. G. Stigler. Homewood, Ill., Irwin.

PART II

REGULATION AND REPRESENTATION

THE PROSPECT THEORY OF THE PATENT SYSTEM AND UNPRODUCTIVE COMPETITION

Roger L. Beck

The prospect theory, a radical new theory of the patent system, asserts that patents grant an exclusive right to develop a prospect. Patent protection of future invention clashes with the traditional view that a patent is granted after *the invention is produced and its scope is limited to what actually has been invented—a limitation which sets the stage for unproductive competition to obtain the economic rents from future inventions. The prospect theory offers an answer to the problem of unproductive competition through allocation of the property right to future invention. This paper tests the prospect theory by determining whether: (1) the present patent system authorizes creation of a monopoly on future invention, and (2) particular patents actually have monopolized future inventions. The results of these tests seriously undermine belief in the prospect theory.*

Research in Law and Economics, Volume 5, pages 193–209.
Copyright © 1983 by JAI Press Inc.
All rights of reproduction in any form reserved.
ISBN: 0-89232-419-8

I. INTRODUCTION

The purpose of this paper is to examine and test the radical new "prospect" theory of Edmund Kitch [(8); hereinafter referred to as Kitch], in which he purports to explain the actual workings of our present patent system.[1] The prospect theory denies the traditional view that patent protection is limited to what has been invented. Instead, it alleges that patents grant an exclusive right to develop a "prospect" by discovering technology which was unknown when the inventor applied for the patent. Thus the patent monopoly would extend to future invention, which may include the technology needed to commercialize the original discovery.

Insofar as the prospect theory is true, the present patent system would tend to limit unproductive competition for the economic rent from future inventions. Different forms of unproductive competition are extensively discussed in the literature. Unproductive competition may include premature invention, unproductive duplication of invention, patenting of unnecessary substitute inventions, or excessively rapid spending on research.[2] Current literature indicates unproductive competition is a serious problem.[3]

This investigation tests the prospect theory by determining whether (1) the present patent system authorizes creation of a monopoly on future invention, and (2) particular patents actually have monopolized future inventions. The results seriously undermine belief in the prospect theory. The view that "the prospect function is a significant, if not the predominate [sic], function of the American patent system as it has operated in fact" [Kitch, p. 267] appears to be without foundation.

II. IMPLICATIONS OF THE PROSPECT THEORY

If the prospect theory is true, the following implications [see Kitch, pp. 265–266, 269–270, 276] should prove valid:

Giving the patent owner an exclusive right to develop a prospect would reduce the incentive to compete unproductively for the future invention. A competitor could not take the right to the future invention by introducing it prematurely. Furthermore, there would be no incentive to duplicate research leading to the future invention. Production of the future invention would be entirely the business of the patent owner.[4]

The patent owner would, however, enlist the aid of any independent researchers thought to enjoy a relative cost advantage. The patent owner would coordinate and control the search for the new technology to ensure that independent researchers avoided accidental duplication of research and took full advantage of each others' discoveries.

Another implication is that patenting future inventions requires granting patents earlier, *ceteris paribus,* than does patenting completed inventions. Earlier patenting would lengthen the lag between patenting and commercialization. If the prospect theory is valid, the present patent system should encourage early patenting (see "Time-Bar Rule" and "Workability" in Section III and "Alleged Support for the Prospect Theory" in Section IV).

III. LEGAL AUTHORITY FOR PATENTING UNDISCOVERED TECHNOLOGY

What a patent legally may protect is determined by statutory authority and judicial interpretation. It will be shown that a patent legally may protect only what the inventor actually invented *prior* to applying for the patent, which fails to support the assertion of the prospect theory that a patent monopolizes future invention.

Protection Is Limited to What the Patent Owner Has Invented

The statutory requirements make the legal limits of patent protection clear:

> The specification shall contain a written description of the invention, and of the manner and process of making and using it, in such full, clear, concise , and exact terms as to enable any person skilled in the art to which it pertains, or with which it is most nearly connected, to make and use the same, and shall set forth the best mode contemplated by the inventor of carrying out his invention.
> The specification shall conclude with one or more claims particularly pointing out and distinctly claiming the subject matter which the applicant regards as his invention. [35 U.S.C. 112]

There is no basis here for the belief that the patent owner has exclusive control of new technology which comes after *further* development. Instead, the patent owner must particularly point out and distinctly claim his invention. Obviously, what has not yet been invented cannot be particularly pointed out and distinctly claimed, nor would it be possible to describe "the manner and process of making and using" a future invention. The patent protection the public trades for production of new technology is limited to the inventor's actual discovery [see *Kendall Co. v. Tetley Tea Co.,* 89 F.Supp. 897, DC Mass. (1950)] and the statute requires that it be described in "full, clear, concise, and exact terms." The duty to so describe the invention is the basis for the rule that ambiguous language will be construed against the patent owner [see *Hookless Fastener Co. v. G. E. Prentice Mfg. Co.,* 68 F.2d 848, Cal. 2 (1934)]. The purpose of imposing this duty on the patent owner is to ensure that the public is protected from extension of the scope of the patent [see *Universal Oil Products Co. v. Globe Oil & Refining Co.,* 332 U.S. 471 (1944)]. This decision supports the traditionally popular belief that it would be unfair to allow the patent owner to monopolize more than was invented—and it also would discourage others from seeking the undiscovered technology. Of course, prevention of unproductive competition from others is exactly what is wanted, under the prospect theory. However, the necessary legal authority is wanting.

Certain established patent practices further the objective of confining patent protection to what the patent owner has invented. For example, principles cannot be patented. A principle can be put into operation by particular mechanical structures, and structures can be patented. A principle can be put into operation by particular processes, and the steps of processes can be patented. The patenting of principles might bring future mechanical structure or process inventions within the scope of the patent.

Similarly, claims which define a result (called functional claims) are not permitted. Claims must define the means of achieving some result [see *General Electric Co. v. Wabash Appliance Corp. et al.,* 304 U.S. 364, 368–69 (1938)]. Functional claims might bring future inventions of means to achieve a result within the scope of the patent.

Inventors have been denied patents when it appeared that the invention was "speculative," that is, not yet actually invented. An application concerning atomic decomposition of uranium filed in 1944 was denied because the invention was not consistent with then-known physical laws and scientific principles. The reactor disclosed in the application had not been built. At a much later time, sufficient scientific evidence had accumulated and the patent was granted [108 USPO 231 (1956)].

"Broad" Claims

The statutory requirement is merely that the specification "shall set forth the best mode contemplated by the inventor of carrying out his invention," and that the claims should define the invention. The claims would be broader than the "best mode" when more than one method of carrying out the invention was discovered.

Broad claims increase the value of the patent because they encompass more new technology, and it may seem that the free play of the inventor's imagination could bring future inventions within the patent's scope. However, the breadth of the claim is legally limited to what has been invented. The Patent Office and the courts reject excessively broad claims.

In *Georgia Pacific Corp. v. United States Plywood Corp.* [258 F.2d 124, Cal. 2 (1958)], the claim that the patent covered the cutting of deep grooves in all plywood was rejected because this process only relieved stress and prevented edge separation in certain types of plywood. In *Corona Cord Tire Co. v. Dovan Chemical Corporation* [276 U.S. 358 (1928)], the claim that the patent covered curing rubber with all chemicals known as disubstituted guanadines was rejected because only some of the members of that chemical family actually cured rubber. The inventor *might* have brought future inventions within the patent if it had turned out that all disubstituted guanadines did cure rubber. Some inventors may make lucky guesses when drafting claims.

It is not enough, however, to guess correctly about what will work. In addition, the lucky guess must appear not to have been a lucky guess but an actual discovery of the patent owner. The court would restrict the coverage of broad claims if a later invention, although clearly covered by the claims, appeared to be an entirely "different animal" [see *Westinghouse v. Boyden Power-Brake Co.,* 170 U.S. 537 (1898)]. The court may reach this verdict on equitable grounds if coverage of the later invention was accidental.

The assertion of the prospect theory that patents systematically protect unproduced technology is based on the possibilities that an inventor might guess correctly what will work, and might make that lucky guess appear to be an actual invention—neither of which constitutes adequate support. Guessing is not a costless claim-drafting technique. An incorrect guess about what will work forfeits some of the benefit of the discovery the inventor actually did produce to the extent that its definition is part of the same claim which the court finds to be excessively broad (and therefore invalid).

A claim properly limited to what was invented *may* nevertheless cover a subsequent improvement—even an independently patented subsequent improvement. That is to say that the later invention may be *generically* covered by the earlier patent, even though the first inventor did not draft *specific* claims to the later invention because that method of carrying out the invention was not yet known. The later inventor could prevent use of the patented improvement by others (including the first inventor), but could not use it himself unless licensed to use the first invention. Thus, each patent fails to give either inventor exclusive control of the improvement. The inventors have complementary monopolies.

Even when the first inventor does have limited rights in a later improvement, this must not be confused with the prospect theory's assertion that a patent conveys an exclusive right to develop a prospect. These limited rights do not assure uninhibited flows of information between the first inventor and improvement researchers, prevention of premature improvement, or elimination of unproductive duplication in improvement research. The empirical evidence presented in Sections IV and V contradicts the notion that limited rights in a later improvement allow a patent owner to control and coordinate the search for unproduced technology.

Infringement

The patent gives the inventor the right to stop others from infringing the patent. Infringement is unauthorized use of the technology protected by a patent. Since the patent is legally limited to protection of the inventor's discovery, the patent owner cannot stop others from using later discoveries. In general, the patent owner also cannot stop others from using *part* of the discovery described in a single claim. The patent is infringed only by use of *all* of the elements recited in a particular claim. If a process is claimed, all the steps of the process must be used before that claim is infringed. However, substitution of equivalent elements or steps to achieve the same result does not avoid infringement [see *University of Illinois Foundation v. Block Drug Co. et al.,* 112 U.S.P. 204, 241 F.2d, Cal. 7 (1957)].

Amending Applications

It might be thought that the inventor's original application for a patent could be amended to include later discoveries as long as the patent had not yet been granted. However, that is prohibited by statute: "No amendment shall introduce new matter into the disclosure of the invention" (35 U.S.C. 132). Only new claims which are supported by the original application can be accepted as amendments.

Time-bar Rule

The time-bar rule is a statutory requirement alleged to support the prospect theory [Kitch, p. 270] because it appears to encourage early patenting, perhaps even before the invention has been brought through the experimental stage. The time-bar rule prohibits granting the patent if the inventor's application was filed more than one year after exploitation of the invention began. The traditional explanation of the time bar is that it prevents obtaining more than a seventeen-year monopoly (by waiting to file an application until just before competitors learn to use the invention). The traditional explanation is preferable because periods of use of the new invention which are primarily experimental rather than exploitive do not activate the time bar. See *Elizabeth v. American Nicholson Pavement Co.* [97 U.S. 126; 24 L.Ed. 1000 (1878)], in which the period of experimental use lasted six years. The time-bar rule is not designed to encourage early patenting of incomplete inventions and therefore it does not support the prospect theory.

Workability

There is no statutory requirement that the invention be a commercial success before a patent can be granted, and the absence of such a requirement is alleged to support the prospect theory [Kitch, p. 270]. This is weak support because it does not encourage early patenting, it merely allows early patenting. There are incentives not to patent early. An invention is not patentable unless it is useful [*ibid.*], and the more commercially valuable the invention the smaller the risk that it will appear frivolous or insignificant and therefore unpatentable. Another reason to delay patenting is to make the invention's operation more reliable. Patents have been denied on mechanical devices which occasionally made errors [see *McKenzie v. Cummings,* C.D. 683 (1904); *Carlin v. Crumpton,* 45 App. D.C. 166, C.D. 211 (1916)]. Reliability is particularly crucial to patentability when malfunction endangers life or limb.

IV. EMPIRICAL EVIDENCE: FIFTY INVENTIONS

Does evidence about particular inventions show that statutory authority and judicial interpretation succeed in limiting a patent's scope to what the inventor actually has invented? The fifty important inventions listed in the table were identified and thoroughly researched by Jewkes, Sawers, and Stillerman [(7), pp. 263–401]. A review (*infra*) of the evidence about some of these "inventions" makes it very clear that Jewkes *et al.* assigned an uncommonly broad meaning to the term "invention" by including the totality of major technological progress in some broad product or process area. In their view, the scope of an invention is enormous relative to the scope of a single patent. This broad definition of an invention corresponds to the prospect theory's definition of a prospect.

Alleged Support for the Prospect Theory

The first three columns of the table appear in Kitch (p. 272). The dates in the second and third columns are the year it first became possible to apply for a patent and the year of first commercial use, as determined either by Jewkes *et al.* (7) or by Kitch's interpretation of their evidence. Kitch argues that this evidence supports the prospect theory because it shows that the *lag* to commercialization is *lengthy.* However, these lags only appear "long" relative to a purely subjective notion of "short." This evidence fails to test the assertion that the lag has been *lengthened, ceteris*

Table 1. Fifty Important Inventions
—Lag to Commercialization

Invention	Patentability	Commercialized	Lag
Automatic transmissions	1904	1937	33
Bakelite	1907	1910	3
Ball-point pen	1938	1945	7
Catalytic cracking	1915	1930's	15
Cellophane	1910	1925	15
Cinerama	1937	1953	16
Continuous casting of steel	1890's	1950	50
Continuous hot strip rolling	1892	1923	31
Cotton picker	1850	1942	92
Crease-resisting fabrics	1926	1932	8
Cyclotron	1929	?	—
DDT	1874	1942	68
Diesel-electric rwy traction	1890's	1934	34
Electric precipitation	1884	1909	25
Fluorescent lighting	1859	1933	74
Freon refrigerants	1931	1933?	2
Gyro-compass	1852	1908	56
Hardening of liquid fats	1900	1909	9
Helicopter	1912	1941	29
Insulin	1920	1924?	4
Jet engine	1791	1944	153
Kodachrome	1910	1935	25
Long-playing record	1944	1948	4
Magnetic recording	1898	1939	41
Methyl methacrylate polymers	1877	1935	58
Neoprene	1921	1930?	9
Nylon and Perlon	1930	1939	9
Penicillin	1928	1944	16
Polyethylene	1935	1939?	4
Power steering	1925	1931	6
Radar	1904	1935	31
Radio	1900	1915	15
Space rockets	1920's	1944	14
Safety razor	1895	1905	10
Self-winding wristwatch	1922	1928	6
Shell moulding	1941	1944	3
Silicones	1904	1944	40
Stainless steels	1904	1915	11
Streptomycin	1921	1944	23
Sulzer loom	1928	1945	17
Synthetic detergents	1900	1930's	30
Synthetic light polarizer	1828	1935	107
Television	1905	1940	35
Terylene polyester fiber	1941	1953	12
Tetraethyl lead	1924	1935?	11
Titanium	1880's	1950?	60
Transistor	1948	1955	7
Tungsten carbide	1916	1926	10
Xerography	1937	1950	13
Zip fastener	1891	1923	32

paribus, due to patenting of unproduced technology, and therefore it does not test the prospect theory.[5]

The subjective appearance of a lengthy lag is not only meaningless, but it also owes much to the adoption by Jewkes *et al.* (7) of an uncommonly broad definition of invention. If the scope of an invention is reduced to the scope of a patent, commercialization occurs quickly. A study [Sanders (10), pp. 90, 96–97] of 245 commercially useful patented inventions patented in 1938, 1948, and 1952 showed that 88.2 percent achieved first commercial use *before* the patent was granted (39.2 percent of these 245 inventions achieved first commercial use before the inventor even *applied* for a patent). More than half of the remaining 11.8 percent were used commercially before the patent was one year old. Less than 2 percent of the inventions waited three or more years after patenting to achieve commercial use.

New Tests of the Prospect Theory

The prospect theory implies that patents conveyed an exclusive right to develop these fifty "inventions" (prospects). It follows that these patents should have monopolized the new technology developed during the seventeen years after they were granted. However, this was not the case. There was competition for most new technology, not exclusive control. Although Jewkes *et al.* (7) were primarily interested in the independent inventor's contribution to important inventions, the vigorous competition in the development of these inventions did not escape their notice (pp. 214–219).[6] They also observed that competition may have been more important and pervasive than previously thought. Inventors thought to have had exclusive control (for example, Dupont/nylon) may actually have faced competition (such as German work on synthetic fibers) or potential competition. The existence of competition in such cases may not be generally recognized if competitors never complete their research or do so only long after the first inventor has achieved commercial exploitation [*id.,* pp. 215–216].

To illustrate the reasons for concluding that evidence about these fifty inventions generally conflicts with the prospect theory, the theory will be subjected to testing using detailed evidence [taken from *id.,* pp. 263–274] in regard to the first five inventions in the table.

Automatic Transmission. The invention of a separate torque converter and hydraulic coupling by H. Fottinger in 1904 eventually led to the development of automatic transmissions. Fottinger did not control the development of automatic transmissions. He was not granted a patent which conveyed an exclusive right to develop the prospect of an automatic transmission. In fact, large numbers of *independent* individuals and companies competed to develop this prospect without the benefit of coordination through centralized control. Those who later succeeded in making contributions as important as Fottinger's also lacked patent powers permitting them to control further development.

The list of individuals and companies involved in development suggests that coordination and control were needed. They included Harold Sinclair, an American engineer working with the London General Omnibus Company in the 1920s; W. G. Wilson, a British consulting engineer; Earl A. Thompson, who began consulting with the Cadillac company in 1926; A. W. Hallpike and A. A. Miller, British independent inventors in the 1930s; Rieseler, an independent inventor in Germany in the 1920s; Alf Lysholm, a Swedish employee of the Ljungstrom Steam Turbine Company; Allan Coats, a Scottish individual inventor in the 1920s; P. M. Salerni, an individual inventor working in England in the 1930s; A. and H. Schneider and E. W. Spannhake, individual inventors who began work in the United States in 1935; various motor manufacturing companies; and H. F. Hobbs, a British individual inventor.

It cannot be determined with certainty from the evidence at hand which inventive efforts represented unproductive competition. However, there are episodes in the development of automatic transmissions which appear to have provided fertile grounds for unproductive competition due to a lack of coordination and centralized control. For example, Sinclair's work led to use of a hydraulic coupling with an epicyclic gear box in Daimler cars in 1930, while Thompson invented a *similar* mechanism, but with the important addition of an automatic control (the combination became the Hydra-Matic). An automatic control system also was invented by Hallpike and Miller. Thus, these developments may represent the duplication of inventions—the combination of a hydraulic coupling with an epicyclic gear box (Sinclair *v.* Thompson) and an automatic control (Thompson *v.* Hallpike and Miller). Whether duplication of invention is unproductive depends upon the circumstances.[7]

Two other examples also illustrate how competition provides fertile grounds for duplication in the absence of coordination. First, research aimed at adapting the 1904 torque converter to automobiles was separately carried out by three different inventors: Fottinger, Rieseler, and Lysholm. Second, there was a large number of independent research programs which successfully produced converter-couplings. These research programs were carried out by Coats, Salerni, the Trilok research society, the Schneiders and Spannhake, and various motor manufacturers.

These four examples are suggestive of duplication at the subassembly or component level. There also may have been duplication of research at the level of a complete automatic transmission by Hobbs, whose automatic transmission was "invented and developed as a solo effort" [Jewkes *et al.*, p. 265].

Bakelite. Bakelite was the first thermosetting plastic, patented by Leo Baekeland in 1909. Bakelite overcame the disadvantages of earlier plastics, which "hardened only upon cooling, softened when heated and were too soluble" [*id.,* p. 266]. Patents had been obtained on earlier plastics, but these earlier patents did not convey an exclusive right to develop a prospect. Baekeland was not subject to coordination and control by an owner of an earlier patent, despite the fact that the research of competing inventors—Smith, Luft, Kleeberg, and Story—might profitably have been coordinated. The inference that owners of earlier patents did not have exclusive rights to develop a prospect also is supported by the fact that bakelite was separately patentable. The bakelite patents themselves do not appear to have given Baekeland an exclusive right to further development: Baekeland made many subsequent improvements which probably were separately patented after their discovery, and there is no evidence that Baekeland's patents allowed him to coordinate and control later research done by others.

Ball-point Pen. Georg and Ladislao Biro applied for patents on the ball-point pen in 1938. In the 1940s they formed a company which marketed this pen in Argentina. Milton Reynolds, an American, visited South America, bought a number of Biro pens, and quite deliberately invented a ball-point pen which was not covered by the Biro patents. The Reynolds pen was introduced in 1945 and was an immediate success. The Biro patents did not convey an exclusive right to develop a prospect because a subsequently developed substitute—the Reynolds pen—was not covered by the Biro patents. In fact, the Biro patents did not even convey limited rights to the Reynolds pen (see "Broad Claims," *supra*). The patenting of substitutes for other patented inventions is a common occurrence which is well documented [Beck (2)], well understood, and clearly does not support the prospect theory. If a patent actually did convey an exclusive right to substitutes for the invention, competing inventors would have no incentive to make socially unproductive investments in the discovery of substitutes.[8]

The ball-point pen invention contradicts the prospect theory for another reason: despite earlier patent protection of the ball-point pen the evidence does not suggest that the Biro brothers' (or Reynolds') research was coordinated by an earlier inventor who had an exclusive right to the development of the prospect.

Catalytic Cracking. Catalytic cracking was a new method of refining crude oil which raised yields of the more valuable refined products. A. M. McAfee invented a catalytic cracking process in 1915, but catalytic cracking was not a commercial success until the 1930s. McAfee's invention did not bring him the exclusive right to develop the prospect of catalytic cracking. The many important developments leading to commercialization were not controlled by McAfee or any other inventor. A great deal of research in catalytic cracking was done in Germany between 1920 and 1930. Another independent research effort led by Eugene Houdry produced a catalytic cracking process which eventually was commercially successful. Houdry's patents did not give him an exclusive right to develop his own process, however. The Sun Oil Company put the finishing touches on Houdry's invention and received patents protecting its development of the Houdry process.

Independent development of other catalytic cracking plants was carried out by a number of oil companies, such as Phillips Petroleum Company and Standard Oil Company of New Jersey. Standard was a member of a group of eight oil companies which launched a cooperative research program to develop catalytic cracking. Cooperation and coordination would have involved all the firms doing catalytic cracking research—not just eight companies—if there had been an exclusive right to develop catalytic cracking.

Cellophane. Uncertainty over who actually invented cellophane is indicative of competition among inventors. There is no evidence that competition was effectively controlled and coordinated. The extent of unproductive competition, if any, cannot be determined from the available evidence. Jacques Brandenberger's European and American cellophane patents were transferred to a new French company, La Cellophane, the first company to manufacture cellophane commercially.

Dupont later became interested in cellophane and acquired Brandenberger's American patents. These patents did not protect subsequent development of the invention because new patents were granted when waterproof cellophane was developed, which contradicts the prospect theory.

V. OTHER EVIDENCE ALLEGED TO SUPPORT THE PROSPECT THEORY

In addition to claiming a "long" lag between patentability and commercialization, Kitch supported the prospect theory by: (1) listing five specific inventions alleged to have conveyed exclusive control of a prospect, and (2) describing the mineral claim system as an analogue of the patent system's alleged performance of a prospect function.

Five Specific Inventions

A re-examination of these five inventions will show why they might have appeared—mistakenly—to have conveyed exclusive control of a prospect: earlier patents may *generically* cover later independently discovered improvements which are *specifically* covered by a later patent (see "Broad Claims," *supra*). However, the first inventor does not have *exclusive* control of the later invention because the improved method of carrying out the original invention was unknown to and therefore unclaimed by the first inventor. The original inventor and improvement inventor *each* may have the right to prevent use of the improvement by the other. This differs sharply from the claim of the prospect theory that the first inventor has exclusive control of the right to develop a prospect.

Process Inventions. The five inventions include two process inventions—a chemical process and xerography. The chemical process is "a process of separating fats into glycerine and stearic, margaric and oleic acids" [Kitch, p. 268]. However, the patent did not convey an exclusive right to develop the prospect. What it did convey was the right to prevent another from using improved machinery designed to carry out the process [see *Tilghman v. Proctor*, 102 U.S. 707, 728 (1880)]. The Court speculated that the defendants' improvement might be separately patentable, but concluded that use of the improved machinery to separate fats was an infringement of the plaintiff's process patent.

The xerography example is similar: "Anyone else who makes a machine embodying that process, even though much superior due to its improvements, will infringe" [Kitch, p. 269]. However, this is merely the right to prevent the infringing use of a separately patentable improvement. The right to prevent infringement is not a patent monopoly on the improvement and it is not attributable to exclusive control of a prospect.

Nonprocess Inventions. "An inventor of a substance useful as a lubricant has a patent on that substance, and if it is later discovered to be invaluable as a fuel additive, any such use of the substance infringes his patent even though he never suspected that it had those properties" [*id.,* p. 269]. This statement is correct but incomplete. The inventor of the new use also can get a patent [Eggert (5), pp. 778–780], so the first inventor and the second inventor each would have the right to prevent the other from taking advantage of the new use. The inventor of the lubricant does not have an exclusive right to develop the prospect.

The two remaining examples—Selden's automobile patent and the diode vacuum tube patent—do not support the prospect theory for the same reason: a generic patent does not convey exclusive control of a subsequent improvement which is separately patentable. It is correct but incomplete to say that "subsequent inventors of superior automobiles will infringe that claim" [*id.,* p. 268], and that the inventor of the triode could not use his invention without infringing the diode vacuum tube patent [p.

269]. These two inventions are even less effective support for the prospect theory (compared to the first three) because their generic characteristics were stripped away by later events: the courts ruled that the automobile "patent was limited to the particular type of engine Selden had used" [*id.*, p. 268], and the diode patent was invalid [p. 269].

Mineral Claim Analogy

The prospect theory would be more believable if an analogous mechanism for the allocation of property rights could be shown to operate successfully outside of the patent system. Kitch drew an analogy to the mineral claim system developed in the American West in the last half of the nineteenth century: "The system that evolved permitted one who found mineralization on the public land to file a claim which gave him the exclusive right to develop the claim" [p. 271].

One problem with the analogy is that the mineral claim system has not operated in accordance with its statutory authority. Instead of actually finding mineralization before filing a claim, most prospectors merely said they had found mineralization, claimed the right to develop, and then looked for minerals [Senate Committee (11), p. 662].

A second problem with the analogy is that the mineral claim system's success as a property rights allocation mechanism has been seriously questioned [*id.*, pp. 657–674]. Property rights have not been unambiguously defined for a variety of reasons including vague claim location notices and multiple claims on the same property. "Such claims may be as many as seven or eight deep in the case of promising uranium properties. Much vexatious litigation as well as confusion and hard feelings result all too frequently from . . . gaps and anomalies in the law's prescriptions" [*id.*, p. 666]. Surprisingly, this property rights allocation mechanism lacks a central claim registry—claims usually are recorded at the county courthouse or office of the recorder of deeds.

A third problem with the analogy is that the mineral claim system broke down completely for many minerals (for example, oil, coal, gas) because they require a large prediscovery investment.[9] Prospectors were unwilling to make these large investments when they had not yet been assigned exclusive property rights in the minerals. (Prepatent expenditures often are large and our present patent system therefore may prevent discovery of some important new technology.) The mineral claim system was selectively revised by a 1920 statute that permitted exclusive allocation of rights to some minerals prior to the search for and discovery of those minerals [Kitch, p. 273]. This selective revision of the mineral claim system brings to mind the proposal that patents be obtainable before research gets under way through explicit competitive bidding.

VI. SUMMARY AND CONCLUSIONS

This paper has examined and tested the prospect theory. The prospect theory is a radical new theory of the patent system which asserts that a patent monopolizes future invention by granting an exclusive right to develop a prospect. This theory is important because, if it is correct, the problem of unproductive competition for patents may be solved within the present patent system. On the other hand, unproductive competition is possible if the traditional theory of the patent system is correct: the patent monopoly is only awarded after the invention is produced and the scope of the patent is limited to what actually has been invented. Under these circumstances, some new mechanism is needed to prevent unproductive competition through monopolization of future inventions. For example, the option of bidding for a patent could be added to the present patent system. Explicit competitive bidding for the patent on a future invention would transfer the expected value of the patent owner's economic rent to the Patent Office, thus removing the economic incentive for unproductive competition.[10]

Both statutory authority and judicial interpretation were examined to determine whether a patent legally can protect more new technology than the inventor actually has invented. No support was found for that belief. There is no legal basis for giving the patent owner the exclusive right to the new technology which comes from *further* development.

Evidence about particular inventions was examined and was found to be consistent with the traditional view that patent protection is limited to what the inventor actually has invented. The patents these inventors received did not grant them an exclusive right to develop a prospect. These patents did not convey a patent monopoly on future inventions. This evidence supports rejection of the prospect theory, which implies that the present patent system should be changed to curtail unproductive competition—perhaps by adding the option of explicit competitive bidding for patents.

ACKNOWLEDGMENTS

Helpful comments by C. W. Gillam, M. Percy, R. Savitt, B. Yu, and anonymous referees are gratefully acknowledged.

NOTES

1. The prospect theory has been hailed as "one of the few advances in economic theory concerning patents that has been made in several decades" [Holcombe and Meiners (6), p. 30].

2.   A large number of papers which study separate forms of unproductive competition have been integrated [Beck (3)] to show that each form can be explained by competition for the economic rent from future or present inventions. To control that competition, the option of explicit bidding for a patent could be added to the present patent system [Beck (3), pp. 103–106]. A third answer to the problem of unproductive competition (different from both the prospect theory and explicit competitive bidding) is given by Ben Yu (13), who extends Cheung (4). Yu argues that the *present* patent system controls unproductive competition through *implicit* competitive bidding—potential producers of each future invention are alleged to bid for the right to invent.

3.   This literature directly contradicts some widely accepted notions about invention. For example, the recent discovery that invention may be premature [Barzel (1)] directly contradicts the belief that it is best if the public has the benefit of new technology at the earliest possible moment.

4.   Smith and McFetridge (12) have argued that the prospect theory fails to solve the problem of unproductive competition because at most it allocates the right to commercialize without allocating the right to invent: "The prospect mechanism is a hybrid of exclusive and common property rights" (p. 198). They present an elegant theoretical analysis which clearly demonstrates that economic rent still would be eliminated by premature patenting (rather than premature commercialization), given prepatenting competition. However, the prospect theory can be defended by claiming that prepatenting competition actually does not occur. The issue is empirical, not theoretical: Is the number of firms with the special skills patenting requires small enough to permit collusive control of prepatenting competition, while the number of firms capable of developing a prospect is so large that unproductive competition would occur unless the patent system performed a prospect function? (This may be what Kitch [9] meant in his reply to McFetridge and Smith.) The prospect theory cannot be so easily refuted and deserves a more thorough examination.

5.   The observed lag is suggestive of premature invention, since the mean lag in the table is 28.2 years. Competition may bring invention so early that seventeen-year patents expire before the market for the invention develops. (However, premature invention does not *necessarily* imply a long lag to commercialization—invention may be premature even if the lag is zero [Barzel (1)].)

6.   They saw both productive and unproductive competition occurring and believed that the benefits of the former were obtainable only at the cost of enduring the latter. Recently, it has become clear that competitive bidding for patents might secure the benefits of productive competition and reduce the costs of unproductive competition [Beck (3)].

7.   If productive, duplication must come from pursuit of different research strategies (or if identical, the costs of preventing their pursuit must have exceeded the benefits) and also must meet this further requirement: Each additional research strategy carried out must have promised expected social benefits greater than expected social costs. This may not be the case, because expected private benefits can exceed expected private costs even when expected social benefits are less than expected social costs. See Beck (3), p. 100, for an analysis of the distinction between productive and unproductive duplication.

8.   Kitch does discuss patenting of substitutes [(8), pp. 278–279], but does not point out the conflict between this behavior and the prospect theory. He assumes that the substitute is, for some unexplained reason, an entirely separate prospect. He then argues that the prospect function achieves an improvement in resource allocation because the competing inventor's goal of sharing royalties on the first invention is attainable as soon as the substitute invention has been patented: no *further* development expenditures are required. However, because Section III shows that a patent cannot legally protect further development, savings from failure to commercialize the substitute cannot be attributed to the prospect function. A simpler explanation is that whenever a substitute provides no net advantage over the first

invention there is no potential gain from commercialization. It may be more correct to think of the present patent system as misallocating resources rather than saving them, however, because it encourages the invention of substitutes. Costly invention of substitutes might be avoided if there were competitive bidding for an invention and its substitutes before research begins.

9.   This would make it relatively easy to identify attempts to short circuit the statutory requirements by prospectors who first claim and then search.

10.   See Beck (3), pp. 97–106, for discussion of empirical evidence showing that unproductive competition does occur in the present patent system and an evaluation of a competitive bidding option as an addition to the present patent system.

REFERENCES

1.   Barzel, Yoram. (August 1968) "Optimal Timing of Innovations," *Review of Economics and Statistics,* Vol. 50: 348–355.
2.   Beck, Roger L. (October 1976) "Patents, Property Rights, and Social Welfare: Search for a Restricted Optimum," *Southern Economic Journal,* Vol. 43: 1045–1055.
3.   ———. (1981) "Competition for Patent Monopolies," *Research in Law and Economics,* Vol. 3: 91–110.
4.   Cheung, Steven N. S. (1977) "Property Rights and Inventions: An Economic Inquiry," unpublished manuscript, University of Washington, Seattle.
5.   Eggert, Paul H. (December 1979) "Uses, New Uses and Chemical Patents—A Proposal," *Journal of the Patent Office Society,* Vol. 51: 768–789.
6.   Holcombe, Randall, and Meiners, Roger. "The Contractual Alternative to Patents," Institute for Humane Studies Law and Liberty Working Paper 1–79, Menlo Park, Calif.
7.   Jewkes, John, Sawers, David, and Stillerman, Richard. (1958) *The Sources of Invention,* London, Macmillan.
8.   Kitch, Edmund W. (October 1977) "The Nature and Function of the Patent System," *Journal of Law and Economics,* Vol. 20: 265–290.
9.   ———. (April 1980) "Patents, Prospects, and Economic Surplus: A Reply," *Journal of Law and Economics,* Vol. 23: 205–207.
10.   Sanders, Barkev. (Spring 1962) "Speedy Entry of Patented Inventions into Commercial Use," *Patent, Trademark, and Copyright Journal,* Vol. 6: 87–116.
11.   Senate Committee on Interior and Insular Affairs. (1976) "Report to the Federal Trade Commission on Federal Energy Land Policy," Washington, D.C., Government Printing Office.
12.   Smith, Douglas A. and McFetridge, Donald. (April 1980) "Patents, Prospects, and Economic Surplus: A Comment," *Journal of Law and Economics,* Vol. 23: 197–204.
13.   Yu, Ben. (October 1981) "Potential Competition and Contracting in Innovation," *Journal of Law and Economics,* Vol. 24: 215–238.

VOTER SEARCH FOR EFFICIENT
REPRESENTATION

Roger L. Faith and Robert D. Tollison

In seeking efficient representation, voters in the United States exhibit a pronounced preference for home-grown representatives. This preference for local over outside candidates is widely known, but it has not been analyzed in terms of rational voter choice. In this paper we argue that the preference for local candidates essentially derives from the desire of voters to minimize the costs of monitoring and controlling their elected representatives, hence creating a demand for pre-election *information regarding the likelihood of inefficient representation by the voters' future political agent. The implications of the model are subjected to empirical tests using data on the House of Representatives of the Ninety-sixth Congress.*

I. INTRODUCTION

Representation of the preferences of citizens is a fundamental activity in a democracy. Candidates devote considerable resources to periodic election campaigns in which they advertise their virtues to voters, and voters

Research in Law and Economics, Volume 5, pages 211–224.
Copyright © 1983 by JAI Press Inc.
ISBN: 0-89232-419-8

search out and choose approximately one-half of these individuals as their political agents. The central task of these agents is, as Stigler [(5), p. 17] suggests, "to give efficient representation to the collection of group interests that express the desires of the citizens who compose the state."

In seeking efficient representation, voters in the United States exhibit a pronounced preference for home-grown representatives. The data in Table 1 are suggestive of this preference. In each state a large proportion of its national representatives are born in the districts that they represent. If the idea of home-grown representation is construed more loosely, an overwhelming majority of legislators in these states have longstanding ties to their districts.

This preference for local over outside candidates is widely known as a factual matter, but it has not been analyzed as an expression of rational voter choice.[1] What is the basis of this comparative advantage in representation? A major purpose of this paper is to provide an answer to this question. The investigation to follow will show that the preference for local candidates essentially derives from the desire of voters to minimize the costs of monitoring and controlling their elected representatives. These costs can be substantially reduced by judicious selection of one's representative, and thus create a demand for *pre-election* information regarding the likelihood of inefficient representation and, in the extreme, misrepresentation by the voters' future political agent.

This demand for pre-election information is not peculiar to the market for political representation. Firms also have an incentive to gather information concerning the individuals with whom they contract to provide services for the firm. But unlike firms in hiring managers, voters often do not have the opportunity to screen the prospective efficiency of politicians in alternative political employments, particularly candidates en-

Table 1. Length of Residence in District for Selected State Delegations to the U.S. House of Representatives, 1978 (in percentages)

Length of residence	All States	California	New Jersey	Ohio	Tennessee	Texas
All their lives	64.0	53.0	55.0	100.0	62.5	67.0
80% of their lives, or over 30 years	14.0	30.0	11.0	0	25.0	21.0
20–29 years	8.0	7.0	22.0	0	0	0.0
10–19 years	11.0	9.0	11.0	0	12.5	12.0
Total	97.0	99.0	99.0	100.0	100.0	100.0
Number of legislators	(434)*	(43)	(9)	(23)	(8)	(24)

* One seat vacant in 1978.
Source: Congressional Directory (1).

tering politics for the first time. Also unlike firms in hiring managers, voters find that, if they have made a poor choice in selecting a representative, recall or contract renegotiation is very costly. In such a setting, where voters are unsure about the prospective efficiency of a politician and where mistakes are costly to correct, the election of local candidates becomes a means of obtaining efficient representation. For example, local candidates will normally own specific capital in the district, and the value of this capital can be linked to their effectiveness as representatives.

Explicit entry barriers in the form of statutory residency requirements appear to play a redundant role in this analysis. If voters elect home-grown representatives because they are easier to control and their behavior is easier to predict (and thus more efficient as representatives), a natural informational barrier to entry is posed to candidates who have not lived in the district for a long period of time. Yet a variety of residency requirements for holding elective offices are observed across states. The explanation for the presence of these residency requirements will turn on the costs facing voters in finding out about the degree of home-grownness in candidates across jurisdictions.

In Section II an economic theory of voter search for efficient representation is presented. The implications of this theory are subjected to an empirical test in Section III, using data on the degree of home-grownness among members of the present U.S. House of Representatives. Some concluding remarks are offered in Section IV concerning the origin of entry barriers in politics versus markets.

II. SEARCHING FOR EFFICIENT REPRESENTATION

Consider how the market for managers of private firms operates. Potential managers will be candidates in the parent firm and in other firms, candidates in the parent firm providing the obvious analogy to home-grown labor in politics. With a given wage for managerial services, firms will follow the dictates of marginal productivity theory in selecting for employment the candidates with the highest expected marginal revenue products. An important aspect of decision-making by firms is the opportunity for observation of the performance of candidates in alternative employments, whether in parent or other firms. These observations serve as a screening device used to reduce information costs in the market for managers, and this search process enables owners to procure efficient representation of their interests. Generally, only those candidates with the highest expected marginal revenue products (net of search or detection costs) will be selected for managerial advancement.

But in this search and selection process will there be a pronounced preference for in-firm (home-grown) candidates? To a large extent the answer is yes. Candidates in the parent firm possess firm-specific human capital in the form of relatively more information about how the firm operates. By the usual definition of specific capital, this information is worth more in the training firm than in other firms, and for this reason in-firm candidates for managerial positions will possess an advantage over candidates in other firms (other things equal). Moreover, the search costs of detecting the merits of in-firm candidates will generally be lower than those associated with finding out about the potential abilities of candidates in other firms. On both counts promotion from within has a certain economic logic.[2] The degree of this tendency is clearly an empirical issue which will depend upon the importance of specific managerial training across firms and upon search costs in the market for managers. As a general rule, however, the existence of alternative signals about the potential value of managers, provided these signals are not too costly to discover and not too easy to counterfeit, should partially ameliorate the advantage that in-firm managers possess in this labor market.

Moreover, once a firm has hired a manager, market signals will continue to yield a flow of information about the manager's performance. If the firm finds that it made a poor decision and hired a manager whose actions are systematically reducing the net worth of the firm, it has recourse to contract renegotiation as a means of controlling managerial behavior. The manager can be fired or his salary can be adjusted to reflect a lower than expected level of performance. Contract renegotiation can obviously work in the opposite direction if the firm finds that it has underestimated a manager's worth to the enterprise. The details of contract renegotiations are not important; the economic substance is. The ability of firms to monitor managerial performance with market signals and to adjust managerial contracts in light of observed performance substantially lowers the costs of poor choices in the market for managers. Recall of poor managerial choices may be painful, but it is not a prohibitively costly procedure for firms to undertake. Moreover, the process of contract renegotiation will discipline potential managerial shirkers.

In the terminology of economics, voters likewise face a problem of searching for efficient representation. This process differs in two basic respects from that of firms in hiring managers. First, unlike firms, voters cannot easily screen the performance of potential representatives by observing them in alternative employments as representatives.[3] The locationally specific training and informational advantages possessed by home-grown candidates are thus likely to be substantially larger in politics than in markets. Local candidates will embody more specific training in local political conditions and will thereby have an advantage over outside candidates in winning elections. Moreover, it is relatively less costly to detect the potentiality of efficient representation in local than in outside candidates. Both of these arguments partially explain the pronounced preference for home-grown labor in politics. Second, unlike firms, the costs to voters of a poor choice for representative can be substantial. Recall procedures are costly and rarely effective, and contract termination can take place only at periodic intervals in elections. Voters will thus search for an efficient means to enforce specific performance by elected officials. In this respect local candidates with longstanding ties to the district are much more likely to have specific human or other types of capital in the district, and their net worth can thereby be more easily affected by nonperformance of political tasks.

Consider the example of the lawyer-legislator. His practice is in the district, and the extent to which he can increase the present value of his practice will depend upon his ability to combine representation efficiently with his local law practice.[4] This ability will be a function of the representation of local interests (clients or potential clients of his firm) in the legislature. If he fails to provide efficient representation for local interests, the value of his specific capital in the district will fall. Similarly, representatives whose outside occupations are closely tied to the dominant occupations in their districts (for example, farmers) may find their wealth positively correlated to their performance in representing local interests. The fact that procedures for contract adjustment are relatively costly in politics is therefore a second major reason that voters show a pronounced preference for home-grown labor in electing representatives. Local candidates can be controlled more easily through wealth effects on their future earnings (and on the value of their friendship capital) in the district.

There are, of course, exceptions to these two basic points that explain home-grown representation in politics. For example, in some cases representative performance can be observed in alternative settings. A politician seeking election to a higher office is a reasonably common example in which a legislator's performance in an alternative political office is an important input to voter choice. What should be stressed about these cases is that such additional information about potential performance reduces the advantage of home-grown candidates as long as this information is not too costly to transmit to voters. Thus, while home-grownness will be important in local elections among inexperienced candidates, it will be less important in more general elections where candidates can offer a variety of evidence about their representative abilities and trustworthiness to voters.

The argument to this point says that lacking other information about the potential reliability of politicians, voters prefer local candidates on information cost-minimizing grounds. Explicit residency requirements also reduce the costs of candidate information—a candidate must live in a district for a specified time to be eligible for elective office. Yet, if there is already a natural entry barrier posed to outside candidates in the subjective calculus of voters, what is the rationale for such entry barriers? Appeal to the motivation of local candidates to block the entry of outside candidates does not appear to offer an explanation of these requirements. Since there are usually numerous local candidates, the costs of colluding among these individuals should be high enough to deter the erection of explicit entry barriers against outsiders. Put another way, entry from within the district is so easy that any potential rents from barring outside competition would be dissipated by competition from within the district. Indeed, if voters prefer home-grown representatives, there is no point in the erection of residency requirements by local politicians. So the question is, why do we observe a variety of residency requirements across states if local voters will not vote for outside candidates in the first place? A more satisfactory answer is related to the information costs that voters face in finding out about the degree of home-grownness among candidates. The insideness of candidates is a signal. Where the identity of the insider is known by voters, no signals from candidates are necessary. Where insideness is less obvious, steps will be taken to eliminate fakers, and residency requirements will be used to ensure insideness of candidates. Thus, when normal information and monitoring devices become more costly, voters move to another signaling device—residency requirements.

This simple theory of voter choice of representatives can be stated in terms of its testable implications. Insideness of candidates is a valuable piece of information to voters with respect to obtaining good representation from their elected representatives. As with the demand for any economic good, the quantity of the inside information will be a function of its price, the prices of other information and control devices, and those factors affecting the marginal value of candidate information such as income. The prices or costs of detecting the degree of insideness in political candidates will vary, as will the availability of substitute and complementary information sources and control devices. Home-grownness will be higher where the costs of detecting this attribute in candidates are lower. Moreover, where the costs of discovering home-grownness are low, the demand for alternative signaling devices, such as residency requirements, will be low. For example, outsiders may be more easily detected in homogeneous populations, and homogeneous jurisdictions will thus exhibit more home-grownness in their political representatives and a lower demand for residency requirements.

Therefore, by observing proxies for the costs of detecting and monitoring the insideness of politicians across jurisdictions and other factors affecting the demand for information, this theory of rational voter choice of home-grown representation can be tested empirically. Home-grownness should vary predictably across jurisdictions with respect to those factors which affect the costs and benefits to voters of discovering the degree of home-grownness among candidates.

III. EMPIRICAL EVIDENCE FROM THE NINETY-SIXTH CONGRESS

The major empirical implications of the analysis concern how differences in voter information costs and benefits affect the degree of home-grownness in political candidates across jurisdictions. In this section, two sets of evidence which are consistent with the primary implications of the theory are presented.

Both empirical tests seek to explain the degree of home-grownness of elected representatives in the most recent (at the time of this writing) U.S. House of Representatives as a function of variables which proxy (1) the costs of detecting home-grownness, (2) the value of information and home-grownness, and (3) alternative sources of candidate information and control. In the first test our sample consisted of 433 congressional districts.[5]

Two dependent variables were used. The first measure of home-grownness, TENURE1, is the total time (measured in years) up to 1978 (the start of the Ninety-sixth Congress) that the current representative was a resident of the district that he represented. The second measure of home-grownness, TENURE2, is the total time that a congressman lived in the district up to the year of his first election. This latter measure of home-grownness negates the influence of incumbency on electoral decisions.

A number of independent variables were employed to proxy the effect of the various costs and benefits of voter information on a representative's home-grownness. All demographic variables are based on the 1970 Census.

DENSITY, measured as the population density (persons per square mile) in the representative's district, proxies differences in the costs of detecting the insideness of political candidates across jurisdictions. It is hypothesized that these costs are lower the greater is population density. For example, candidates will find it less expensive to advertise their insideness where population density is higher. On the other hand, if increased density lowers the costs of communicating a candidate's insideness, it most likely lowers the costs of communicating other information regarding a candidate's reliability and effectiveness, and in this case the demand for home-grownness should fall. The impact of DENSITY on home-grownness is thus ambiguous.

NONMOVER, measured as the proportion of the district's population over five years of age which resided in the same house in 1970 as in 1965, proxies the permanency of the population. This variable impacts on home-grownness in two ways. First, a more permanent population should have a higher stake in the quality of representation. Thus, there should be a higher demand for all types of candidate information and control, including home-grownness. Second, long-time residents should be expected to have lower costs of detecting insiders and thus should "purchase" more home-grownness, *ceteris paribus*. A positive sign is expected on the estimated coefficient on NONMOVER in both cases.

RENTER, measured as the percentage of occupied living units in the district that are rented, proxies the value of efficient representation to the permanent population. Economic theory tells us that a transitory population has a weak incentive to devote resources to controlling local politicians since their long-run stake in the district is small relative to more permanent residents. And when they do participate in selecting a representative, their interests as transients and as holders of nondistrict specific capital may well be in conflict with the preferences of the permanent population. Thus, in the face of an increasing transient population (proxied here by the proportion of renters), it pays the permanent population to see that their interests are represented by a candidate with like interests, for example, a long-time resident with capital tied to the district. A positive sign is expected on this variable.

INCOME, measured alternatively as per capita and median family income (both in dollars) in the representative's district, reflects the influence of income on the demand for information regarding candidate attributes. In their search for efficient representation, voters can purchase candidate information of varying sophistication. At the roughest level of information might be a candidate's party affiliation (see note 3), followed by personal attributes like sex and race. At a slightly higher level of sophistication comes the candidate's degree of home-grownness, followed by his position on various issues, previous voting record, and so on. The finer (and more expensive) classes of information are most likely the more relevant to voter choice, and so as income rises and better information is purchased, home-grownness should become a less relevant measure of a candidate's future efficiency. In economic terms information on insideness is an inferior good over some range of income. The sign of INCOME is therefore theoretically indeterminate.

BUSINESS is a dummy variable equal to 1 if the representative has a business interest in the district and equal to 0 otherwise. Among the set of occupations of the members of the Ninety-sixth Congress, the variable BUSINESS was assigned a value of 1 if the representative was a lawyer, farmer, private professional or businessman, and/or the like, and assigned a value of 0 if the representative was a housewife, clergyman, educator, and so forth. As argued in Section II, one way of increasing the expectation of efficient representation is to select a representative with business ties to the district. Since this implicit information and control device is a substitute for information on home-grownness, a negative sign is expected on this variable.

BLACK, measured as the percentage of the district's population that is black, is included to see if some measure of social homogeneity impacts on the decision to select inside candidates.[6] Greater homogeneity of the population may be expected to reduce the costs of detecting insiders. Since the proportion of blacks exceeded 50 percent in less than 3 percent of all districts, an increase in BLACK measures an increase in heterogeneity. A positive sign is expected on BLACK.

Finally, INCUMBENT, measured as the numbers of years of prior service in the House, is included when the dependent variable is TENURE1, time in the district up to 1978. This variable is entered to control for the obvious positive relationship between time in district and time in service.

The two equations run using microdata on individual representatives are:

$$\text{TENURE1} = \text{CONSTANT} + \alpha_1 \text{ DENSITY} + \alpha_2 \text{ NONMOVER} + \alpha_3 \text{ RENTER} + \alpha_4 \text{ INCOME} + \alpha_5 \text{ BUSINESS} + \alpha_6 \text{ BLACK} + \alpha_7 \text{ INCUMBENT} + \mu_1; \text{ and}$$

$$\text{TENURE2} = \text{CONSTANT} + \beta_1 \text{ DENSITY} + \beta_2 \text{ NONMOVER} + \beta_3 \text{ RENTER} + \beta_4 \text{ INCOME} + \beta_5 \text{ BUSINESS} + \beta_6 \text{ BLACK} + \mu_2.$$

The ordinary least squares estimates of the α and β coefficients are reported in Table 2.

The results of both specifications support the expectations of our model. In both equations all of the independent variables, with the exception of BLACK, assume the predicted signs. In Eqs. (1) and (2), where the dependent variable is time lived in the district up to 1978, NONMOVER and BUSINESS are both strongly significant (at better than the 5 percent level), while RENTER is significant at the 10 percent level. DENSITY carries a negative sign, indicating perhaps that the costs of communicating candidate information other than home-grownness fall more with population density than do the costs of communicating or detecting insideness. This interpretation is tempered by the relatively high insignificance of the estimated coefficient. INCOME (both per capita and median family) has a negative and significant effect on home-grownness, indicating that home-grownness is indeed an inferior good in practice.[7] The proportion of blacks in the district has the opposite effect of that predicted in the model, but the estimated coefficient is likewise insignificant. Finally, as

Table 2. Estimated Regression Coefficients for Congressional Districts

Independent Variables	*(1)* TENURE 1	*(2)* TENURE 1	*(3)* TENURE 2	*(4)* TENURE 2
	Dependent Variable			
INTERCEPT	22.95	24.19	23.20	24.46
	(2.94)**	(3.02)**	(2.96)**	(3.04)**
DENSITY	−.00008	−.00009	−.00006	−.00007
	(.67)	(.80)	(.51)	(.63)
NONMOVER	32.10	32.96	31.29	32.14
	(2.91)**	(3.00)**	(2.83)**	(2.92)**
RENTER	17.17	15.52	15.58	13.96
	(1.89)*	(1.72)*	(1.72)*	(1.55)
BLACK	−.057	−.056	−.06	−.06
	(.95)	(.94)	(1.01)	(1.01)
INCOME (per capita)	−.0018		−.0018	
	(1.81)*		(1.78)*	
INCOME (median family)		−.0007		−.0006
		(1.93)*		(1.91)*
INCUMBENT	.849	.850		
	(9.98)**	(10.00)**		
BUSINESS	−5.23	−5.32	−5.99	−6.07
	(4.54)**	(4.61)**	(5.59)**	(5.67)*
R^2	.220	.220	.093	.094
F-statistic	17.08	17.16	7.28	7.36

* t-value significant at the 10% level or better.
** t-value significant at the 5% level or better.
Note: t-values in parentheses.
Sources: Congressional District Data Book (2); *Congressional Directory* (1).

one would expect, INCUMBENT has a strong positive effect on the dependent variable. Both overall regressions are significant at the 5 percent level (the F-statistics).

Our second sample consists of aggregating the data on each congressional district and representative to the state level. In this sample the independent variables are the mean values for each state of the explanatory variables used in the first sample. For example, DENSITY is measured as the average district population density in a state. The dependent variables are the average time that members of a state's House *delegation* lived in the districts that they represent up to 1978 and prior to their first election to Congress.

We test our theory on aggregated data for several reasons. First, we want to see if home-grownness transcends district boundaries. That is, it is conceivable that a candidate may be considered to be a native son of district A although he actually may reside in a neighboring district B. In addition, aggregating from our microdata we believe removes the effect of district-specific influences on the election habits of individual districts. Finally, district boundaries are redefined with every decennial census, and thus for many current House members the district they now serve is not the same geographic or demographic district they represented upon first election to office.

The specification of the model for the aggregate sample of fifty states is the same as given in Eqs. (1) and (2) with two exceptions. First, BUSI-NESS is removed from the regression equation. Second, residency requirements for gubernatorial candidates (RESIDENCY) are entered to proxy the level of artificial barriers to entry in a state's political system. Gubernatorial requirements are used since residency requirements for national office are not subject to state discretion. Implicitly, we are assuming that information costs regarding candidates for state office and national office are highly correlated. The theoretical expectation, as discussed in Section II, is that artificial barriers will be higher where natural informational barriers are low. A negative sign is expected on this variable.

The results of ordinary least squares estimations on the aggregated data are reported in Table 3.

All of the independent variables retain the same signs as they had using the microdata. NONMOVER and RENTER are significant at the 5 percent level, but INCOME and INCUMBENT drop and DENSITY rises in significance. It is worth noting here that RENTER becomes substantially more significant in the aggregate specification. This seems plausible since in a *given* district, particularly large cities, many renters are part of the permanent population. Yet when considered as part of an entire state's population, renters as a group reflect a transient population, and this should show up in a more highly significant RENTER variable. The new variable, RESIDENCY, enters with the expected negative sign and is significant at about the 20 percent level. The overall regressions are both significant at the 5 percent level, but less significant than when microdata is used, suggesting that the notion of insideness does not significantly transcend current district boundaries.

In sum, all eight equations shown in Tables 2 and 3 seem to confirm that the more important determinants of the demand for home-grownness lie along economic rather than social lines. This can be best seen with respect to the NONMOVER and RENTER variables. Nonmovers represent the permanent portion of a district's population, and it is plausible that such individuals have a significant fraction of their wealth (house and property) tied to the district in which they reside. On the other hand, renters or the transitory portion of the population do not have such ties in the district. An increase in the transitory population increases the incentive of long-time residents to protect their interests by searching out candidates who will efficiently represent them at the national level.

Table 3.   Estimated Regression Coefficients
for State Averages

	Dependent Variable			
Independent Variables	(1) TENURE 1	(2) TENURE 1	(3) TENURE 2	(4) TENURE 2
INTERCEPT	−8.28	−9.56	−11.58	−13.20
	(.46)	(.56)	(.60)	(.72)
DENSITY	−.00058	−.0006	−.0006	−.0007
	(1.19)	(1.35)	(1.21)	(1.37)
NONMOVER	77.36	79.44	73.31	75.33
	(3.75)**	(3.94)**	(3.30)**	(3.46)**
RENTER	64.72	67.50	65.37	67.44
	(2.75)**	(2.81)**	(2.57)**	(2.59)**
BLACK	−.103	−.112	−.17	−.17
	(.84)	(.91)	(1.32)	(1.35)
INCOME (per capita)	−.0032		−.0029	
	(1.08)		(.90)	
INCOME (median family)		−.001		−.0009
		(1.19)		(.94)
INCUMBENT	.319	.311		
	(1.33)	(1.30)		
RESIDENCY	−.523	−.541	−.599	−.611
	(1.27)	(1.31)	(1.35)	(1.37)
R^2	.360	.364	.288	.290
F-statistic	3.38	3.43	2.91	2.93

* t-value significant at the 10% level or better.
** t-value significant at the 5% level or better.
Note: t-values in parentheses.
Sources: Congressional District Data Book (2); *Congressional Directory* (1); Council of State Governments (3).

The evidence presented in this section thus offers some reasonable support for the theory of voter search for efficient representation presented in Section II. Voters opt for home-grown candidates where the costs of doing so are low; natural informational barriers to the entry of outside competition in politics tend to be high when explicit barriers such as residency requirements are low; and home-grownness among politicians tends to be related to their holdings of specific capital in the districts that they represent. Some of the major points in the theoretical discussion therefore carry over into practice.

IV. CONCLUDING REMARKS

The role of explicit entry barriers in politics is similar to the role played by apprenticeships in market occupations. Both institutions serve to restrict the supply of labor into various endeavors by imposing time costs on the prospective employee or representative. The difference in the two institutions is that in politics entry barriers seem to be more often demand-side motivated while in the private market entry barriers are more often supply-side motivated. That is, residency requirements are an expression of a supplementary screening device for voters in their search for efficient representation rather than an attempt by legislators to protect their incumbency status. Although private firms also have similar incentives to use apprenticeships as a screening device, most occupational entry barriers derive from the desire of current members of an occupation to restrict competition for their jobs.

Finally, in more recent times technological improvements in communications have diminished the economic advantage of explicit barriers to entry in politics. It is not surprising therefore to find that residency requirements for state offices have generally been falling. However, as the empirical results put forth in this paper show, implicit entry barriers in the guise of home-grownness are still a fact of contemporary political life.

NOTES

1. See Wahlke *et al.* [(6), p. 488], who present comparable evidence on the home-grownness of state legislators, but who are at a loss to explain the phenomenon.

2. For a more general discussion of the internal organization of firms, particularly the employment relation, see Williamson, Wachter, and Harris (7).

3. One might plausibly argue that the political party serves as a screening function for voters when it supports a particular candidate for election. But, ultimately, the candidate qualities sought by a party must coincide to a large degree with the qualities sought by the voters.

4. That lawyers, for example, can successfully combine outside earnings with legislative service has been shown by McCormick and Tollison (4).

5. Two districts were deleted from the sample due to missing values for some of the variables.

6. The proportion of foreign-born in the population and the fraction of the workforce holding blue-collar jobs were also tried. Neither of these variables did better than BLACK nor significantly affected the estimates of the other variables in the model.

7. Since voter search is the underlying process in our model, the results on the INCOME variable may be proxying the effect of education (the ability to interpret information?) among voters. The simple correlation coefficient between INCOME and the proportion of the population with at least a high school education in the data is .698 (significant at the 1 percent level).

REFERENCES

1. *Congressional Directory*. (1978) Washington, U.S. Government Printing Office.
2. *Congressional District Data Book*. (1978) Washington, U.S. Government Printing Office.

3. Council of State Governments. (1976) *Book of the States 1976–1977*, Lexington, Kentucky, Iron Works Pike.
4. McCormick, Robert E., and Tollison, Robert D. (1981) *Politicians, Legislation, and the Economy: An Inquiry into the Interest-Group Theory of Government*, Boston, Martinus Nijhoff.
5. Stigler, George J. (January 1976) "The Sizes of Legislatures," *Journal of Legal Studies*, Vol. 5: 17–34.
6. Wahlke, J. C., *et al.* (1962) *The Legislative System*, New York, John Wiley and Sons.
7. Williamson, O. E., Wachter, M. L., and Harris, J. E. (Spring 1975) "Understanding the Employment Relation: The Analysis of Idiosyncratic Exchange," *Bell Journal of Economics*, Vol. 6: 250–278.

LIABILITY RULES, PROPERTY RIGHTS, AND TAXES

Robert J. Staaf

A considerable literature exists on the internalization of externalities by way of the infamous Coase Theorem. This note examines the tax consequences, under the current Internal Revenue Code, of alternative entitlements available to the Court to enforce a right to be free of certain externalities (that is, the right to bring a nuisance action). Despite the fact that there are significant tax consequences depending on which entitlement the court chooses, the familiar distributional results of the Coase Theorem apply under conditions of risk. Under conditions of Knightian uncertainty, however, significant distributional effects do occur through the tax system and the chosen entitlement may have implications for economic growth and progress.

INTRODUCTION

The purpose of this note is to incorporate basic tax considerations into the analysis of externality-creating activities. Coase (4) in his seminal

Research in Law and Economics, Volume 5, pages 225-233.
Copyright © 1983 by JAI Press Inc.
All rights of reproduction in any form reserved.
ISBN: 0-89232-419-8

paper on social cost showed that Pareto-relevant externalities will be "internalized," thereby guaranteeing an efficient outcome.[1] In Coase's classic rancher-farmer example, ranching creates a negative externality when cattle stray onto the farmer's land and damage his crop. Following Coase's analysis, the right to use the farmer's land eventually will be assigned to its highest valued use through court decisions or private contracts. The implicit entitlement used by Coase was the property rule. Calabresi and Melamed (3) extended the analysis by examining the transactions costs resulting from the assignment of different entitlements, such as liability and property rules. Buchanan and Faith (1) then examined the consequences of a property rule versus a liability rule in creating incentives for entrepreneurial activity and economic growth.[2] This note goes one step further by examining the tax consequences to the rancher and farmer of alternative entitlements. This institutional consideration is important in certain instances because of the size of the tax wedge, and leads to a modified Coase Theorem result. Moreover, it can lead to a much different interpretation of the internalization of the externality.

ENTITLEMENT ALTERNATIVES AND TAX CONSEQUENCES

Consider the case of *Boomer v. Atlantic Cement Co.*,[3] in which neighboring landowners brought a nuisance action alleging injury to their property from dirt, smoke, and vibrations emanating from the defendant's cement plant. The court held these to be a nuisance[4] and proceeded to choose among several possible remedies to enforce the landowners' entitlement.

First, the court could classify the action as a continuing nuisance and award periodic damages. Second, it could grant an injunction compelling the plant to abate the nuisance as a condition of operation. Third, it could award permanent damages, thereby permitting the plant to continue operations.[5] To illustrate the tax consequences of these alternatives, assume the present value of the damages to the landowners is $100,000, or $10,000 each year at a 10 percent discount rate.

The first remedy is a damage rule. The cement company can treat the periodic damage award as a necessary business expense, tax deductible under §162 of the Internal Revenue Code of 1954. To the extent that the nuisance lowers the land value, in this case by $100,000, the landowners also receive a tax break on a future sale or exchange because they have reduced their capital gains tax.[6] However, the periodic damage award would normally run with the property and thereby the property value before and after the award will remain the same, all other things equal.

The second remedy is a property rule enforced by injunction. If the plant owners desired to continue operations, they would have to purchase a servitude or easement from the landowners awarded the injunction. Assuming the plant pays $100,000 or more for the property interest, the expenditure would no longer be tax deductible. Rather, it would be considered a nondeductible capital expenditure under §263 of the code.[7] Because only an interest in land is acquired, depreciation of the $100,000 capital expenditure is not permissible. The landowners may be subject to capital gains on the sale of their property interests or to a reduction in their tax basis.

The tax consequences of whichever of these two remedies is awarded can be dramatic. Compared to the property rule, in this example, the liability rule will result in $46,000 in tax savings to the firm if it is in the 46 percent marginal tax bracket. Moreover, the decision as to which rule is imposed may also have allocative effects, such as whether the plant will maintain operations and purchase an easement or shut down. This aspect will be explored in more detail in the following section.

The third remedy is a borderline case. The courts discuss these cases in terms of "private inverse condemnation." One interpretation of permanent damages is that they are not damages at all, but an involuntary sale of a property interest such as a servitude on the land. Therefore, the firm would not receive favorable tax treatment. On the other hand, if permanent damages are interpreted as damages, the plant would receive tax benefits similar to the periodic damage rule.

A case in point is *Clark Oil and Refining Corp. v. United States.*[8] The action was for a refund of $185,431.24 in federal income taxes, based on a theory of improper disallowance of a business expense deduction. The facts are that Clark owned property adjacent to that of the Richards, who operated a paint business. Clark eventually purchased all the property surrounding the Richards' land, except for an access highway. The existence of a paint factory in the middle of an oil refinery created potential threats of explosion. In order to eliminate this dangerous situation, Clark attempted to purchase Richards' land in 1953, prior to litigation, but negotiations broke down because of a disagreement over the price. The *actual*, as opposed to the *expected*, nuisance damages over the years was minimal, and Richards' out-of-pocket losses never exceeded $5,000. In 1958 Richards filed suit against Clark requesting an injunction against nuisances and trespasses committed by Clark and sought $1 million in damages. The district court judge informally indicated that he was inclined to grant an injunction that would have cost Clark at least $25,000 a day. At this point, the parties settled the dispute and Clark eventually paid $287,500 for Richards' property. On stipulation the action was then dismissed. Clark treated $25,000 of the settlement as the purchase price for

Richards' property and treated the balance as a payment for liquidating damages for which he took a deduction pursuant to §162 of the Internal Revenue Code [*Clark* at 1219].

The circuit court disallowed the deduction and treated the expense as a nondeductible capital expense. The court based its decision, *inter alia*, on the fact that the "origin and character" of Clark's claim was an attempt to establish a price for Richards' property even though the lawsuit took the form of a nuisance action for damages [*id.* at 1220].[9]

The fact that Clark took actions to acquire the property appeared to influence the court. If Clark would have waited and let Richards bring the nuisance action, the outcome might have been different. Or if the potential hazard were not so great, such as in the *Boomer* case, the court might have awarded damages that might have been deductible.[10] The entitlement outcome of the *Clark* case is a property rule. The disallowance of a $297,500 business expense less the true fair market value of Richards' property will increase the expected price of entrepreneurial activity that creates externalities. Under a damage rule the entrepreneur will be encouraged to undertake activities, even though he may underestimate the damages from externalities, because he is permitted to claim these as necessary business expenses.

IMPLICATIONS AND CONCLUSION

The property rule, relative to a damage rule, imposes a significant tax cost on entrepreneurial activity. In the *Clark* example, assume that the nuisance in fact lowered the value of Richards' property from $287,500 to $25,000, as Clark claimed on its tax return. The difference, $262,500, represents the expected cost (damages) of the externality. If Clark was in the 46 percent marginal tax bracket and the deductions were allowed, the after-tax cost of Clark's activity would be only $141,750 as compared to the full $262,500 under the property rule. Such a tax wedge would significantly affect allocative decisions. Under the actual ruling, it is likely that the owners of Clark suffered an unanticipated wealth loss of $120,750 (that is, $262,400 minus $141,750).

The allocative effect arises only under special circumstances of *uncertainty* as opposed to *risk* [Knight (6)].[11] The *Boomer* case represents a situation in which there is uncertainty regarding the entitlement that the court will award. The *Clark* case carries this result one step further by creating uncertainty regarding the tax consequences of the decision. Under uncertainty, a property rule represents a wealth loss to the owners of the firm. On the other hand, a damage rule results in a situation in which the government in effect is a silent partner with the firm because general taxpayers bear a portion of the loss in the form of foregone tax revenues.

If a damage rule *or* a property rule were firmly established as precedent, the externality would simply be internalized within the firm and be passed on to consumers as an ordinary cost of doing business. Under conditions of risk, with a known probability distribution, it would make no difference whether entitlements were enforced by a property or a damage rule.[12]

In the *Clark* case, the purchase price of buying out the owner affected by the externality was assumed equal to the amount recovered under a damage rule less the fair market value of the externally affected land. The liability for the externality under either rule is simply a cost and, like any other cost, it will be passed on to consumers regardless of the tax consequences. Thus, the Coase Theorem is operative in the sense that the externality will be internalized as a cost of production.

In any economy characterized by growth, however, not all externalities may be represented by a known probability distribution of events. Uncertainty, in the Knightian sense, is more likely for new inventions, new techniques, and new discoveries. The Coase Theorem, by definition, is not applicable to a case of Knightian uncertainty. However, the combined effects of what rule is used to enforce entitlements and the tax code treatment of these rules is applicable. Under current I.R.C. provisions, a liability rule creates a greater incentive ex ante to undertake entrepreneurial activities in the face of uncertainty. The social costs generated by such activity is, in part, distributed beyond the particular market to society as a whole in the form of tax consequences. Whether this is a desirable consequence is a normative question beyond the scope of this note.

ACKNOWLEDGMENT

The author is indebted to the editor of this journal, an anonymous referee, and Louis De Alessi for useful criticisms and comments. I, of course, assume all liability for errors.

NOTES

1. For a definition of Pareto-relevant externality, see Buchanan and Stubblebine (2).
2. Their thesis is that entrepreneurs who create externalities estimate the anticipated damages from their activities at a lower value than the individuals who are potentially affected by the externalities. From this basis they argue:

> The case for a liability rule arises only when the dynamic properties of the economic process are recognized. Whereas the value of existing resources will tend to be higher under a generalized regime of property rules, the rate of increase in this value through

time will tend to be larger under a regime that offers only liability rule protection of established entitlements against new and untried intrusions that may be minimal requisites for any development at all.

The economy could scarcely be characterized by growth and development while nominal entitlements are all protected by strict property rules. Such legal arrangements would tend to insure that little change from an existing *status quo* is possible. The potential for the profitability-productivity of new resource combinations can first be imagined only in the minds of entrepreneurs. Others in the economy cannot share such visions.

Briefly, Buchanan and Faith's argument is that because the liability rule has characteristics of a "private" right of eminent domain, the optimistic entrepreneur—who anticipates low damages to others—will anticipate lower costs than if he were subject to a property rule requiring him to bargain with the persons who would be affected by externality and who anticipate higher damages. Therefore, the liability rule lowers the ex-ante, anticipated price of entrepreneurial activity.

3.   *Boomer v. Atlantic Cement Co.*, 26 N.Y. 2d 219, 257 N.E. 2d 870, 40 A.L.R., 3d 590 (N.Y. Ct. of App., 1970).

4.   It is interesting to note that the law does not classify *all* externalities as nuisances. It follows a methodology similar to Buchanan and Stubblebine's (2) definition of a Pareto-relevant externality (*id.* at 873).

5.   The court granted an injunction which would be vacated upon payment by the defendant of permanent damages.

6.   The landowners *may* be able to treat the damage award as a tortious recovery that *may* not be taxable income.

7.   Alternatively, the landowners may be in a better bargaining position with the injunction than with an easement or equitable servitude because they are in a position to force a sale of the whole property.

8.   *Clark Oil and Refining Corp. v. United States*, 473 F.2d 1217 (7th Cir. 1973).

9.   The test used by the court comes from a Supreme Court decision described as follows:

Accordingly, we hold that the origin and character of the claim with respect to which a settlement is made, rather than its potential consequences on the business operations of a taxpayer is the controlling test of whether a settlement payment constitutes a deductible expense or a nondeductible capital outlay. *Woodward v. Commissioner*, 397 U.S. 572 (1970).

10.   Damages paid pursuant to a judgment or in settlement of a suit or claim are generally treated as losses under §165 of the Internal Revenue Code of 1954. However, a general rule is that an expenditure should be treated as a nondeductible capital expense if it brings about the acquisition of an asset having a useful life in excess of one year or if the expenditure secures a like advantage to the taxpayer which has a life of more than one year. *American Dispenser Co., Inc. v. Commissioner*, 359 F.2d 191 (2d Cir. 1966). Therefore, periodic damages would be more likely to be treated as deductible than permanent damages. But the law seems unsettled.

11.   For a different interpretation of entrepreneurship but similar in view to Knight, see Kirzner (8).

12.   Liability is like any other tax-deductible expense such that when it is fully anticipated it will be passed on to the consumer like any other cost.

REFERENCES

1. Buchanan, J., and Faith, R. (1981) "Entrepreneurship and the Internalization of Externalities," *Journal of Law and Economics*, Vol. 24: 95.
2. Buchanan, J. M., and Stubblebine, W. C. (1972) "Externality," *Economica*, Vol. 29: 371.
3. Calabresi, G., and Melamed, A. D. (1972) "Property Rules, Liability Rules, and Inalienability: One View of the Cathedral," *Harvard Law Review*, Vol. 85: 1089.
4. Coase, R. H. (1960) "The Problem of Social Costs," *Journal of Law and Economics*, Vol. 3: 1.
5. Kirzner, I. (1973) *Competition and Entrepreneurship*, Chicago, University of Chicago Press.
6. Knight, F. (1921) *Risk, Uncertainty and Profit*, Boston, Houghton Mifflin.

AUTOMOBILE SAFETY REGULATION:

A REVIEW OF THE EVIDENCE

Richard J. Arnould and Henry Grabowski

Only 10 to 20 percent of automobile occupants choose to wear seat belts despite findings that their use is highly effective in the prevention of deaths and injuries. This low utilization rate has prompted an examination of several sources of market failure, more specifically, information imperfections and market externalities. On the premise that consumers purchase suboptimal amounts of safety, policy makers have been considering passive restraint systems, that is, requiring either automatic seat belts or air cushions. Other policy approaches, some of which have been adopted in various countries, include mandatory belt-use laws, information campaigns professing the efficacy of seat belts, tort law reform, and insurance reform. This paper provides an extensive review of the Peltzman effect and the arguments for market failure that could call for occupant restraint regulation. Empirical evidence is evaluated that pertains to both arguments. New evidence is provided that reveals that the benefit/cost ratio is very high for use of the L/S belt and passive belt systems but that the results for air cushions are mixed. Various policy options available to the government are assessed in

Research in Law and Economics, Volume 5, pages 233–267.
Copyright © 1983 by JAI Press Inc.
All rights of reproduction in any form reserved.
ISBN: 0-89232-419-8

relation to the empirical findings. It is concluded that government intervention in the market may be necessary to provide for the optimal social welfare with respect to the purchase of safety equipment in the United States.

I. INTRODUCTION

The safety of automobiles has received much attention in the United States over the past two decades; a period of growing and often controversial government regulation of automobiles. Over 27,000 front-seat occupants die each year as a direct result of being involved in motor vehicle accidents, 70,000 are severely injured, and over 2.5 million suffer injuries requiring hospitalization or attention by a physician [National Safety Council (30)]. Technologies exist that are capable of drastically reducing the death and injury rates resulting from motor vehicle accidents. These technologies include various types of occupant restraint systems. However, the technologies are not utilized voluntarily at significant levels [Robertson (43), Nordhaus (10)]. Thus, we have those who argue that safety standards should be required. Others purport that if left to their own devices, consumers would purchase optimal amounts of safety based on calculated decisions about individual benefits and costs from the devices [Peltzman (35, 36)].

The problem of high automobile death and injury rates is not unique to the United States. Neither is the problem of the efficiency of various forms of regulation. However, many foreign jurisdictions have gone beyond U.S. regulations, requiring all cars to be equipped with seat belts and have taken the added measure of passing mandatory seat-belt use laws. In jurisdictions where penalties are imposed for noncompliance, seat-belt use is as high as 60 to 70 percent [Robertson (43)]. This can be compared to findings of field studies which estimate that voluntary seat-belt usage in the United States is between only 10 and 20 percent for front-seat occupants [Opinion Research (34), Robertson (42)] and lower than 9 percent for those involved in tow-away accidents [Hedlund (22), p. 2].

Two interrelated issues emerge from these situations. First, can the low voluntary utilization rates of occupant restraint systems be explained by costs systematically exceeding benefits? Second, if the first question is answered negatively then we must ask what is the appropriate form of governmental intervention? In what follows, we analyze the possible sources of market failure and evidence that supports or refutes those possibilities. We then analyze various forms of governmental intervention. The issues are of important policy concern due to the changing policies toward automobile regulation by the Reagan administration. A brief history of occupant restraint regulation in the United States and foreign jurisdictions will set the stage for the issues being reviewed.

Formal regulation by the federal government began in 1966 when Congress passed the National Highway and Traffic Safety Act [Subcommittee (50), GAO (58)]. That act created the National Highway and Traffic Safety Administration (NHTSA) and empowered it with broad rule-making authority. NHTSA has established safety standards across a broad range from the construction of highways to the provision of safety devices such as lap belts, padded instrument panels, energy-absorbing steering columns, shoulder belts for left and right front-seat occupants, penetration-resistant windshields, and dual braking systems on automobiles.

Regulations pertaining to seat belts have been the most controversial. Seat belts and lap/shoulder belts (L/S) differ from other mandated equipment in that they require the active participation of the occupant. Although numerous studies have verified the success of seat belts in reducing serious injury in car accidents, as noted above, and some engineering studies indicate they are, by far, the most effective means for saving lives, consumer usage has been discouragingly low. A benefit/cost analysis conducted by the authors of this paper and reported elsewhere [Arnould and Grabowski (4)] does provide evidence of benefits from a higher utilization rate even when subjected to various forms of sensitivity analysis. But other evidence indicates that utilization rates are declining [Hedlund (22), p. 2].

One policy approach for increasing protection is the requirement of passive restraints. An amendment to the lap/shoulder belt requirement, known as Federal Motor Vehicle Safety Standard 208 (FMVSS 208), was initiated in 1977 by former U.S. Transportation Secretary Brock Adams [Federal Register (17), p. 3529]. This was rescinded, however, by the Reagan administration in 1981 shortly before it was to be implemented. The amendment would have required that new automobiles sold in the United States be equipped with a passive restraint system that protects front-seat occupants in head-on collisions, and crashes up to 30° off center, at speeds up to 30 mph into a rigid barrier. Two technologies would satisfy this type of safety standard. The passive belt (PB) is a relatively low-cost alteration of the existing active belt system. It is designed so that a belt system automatically restrains the occupant when the door is closed. The air cushion (AC) is a much more costly device in which air cushions activate, protecting the occupant from the dashboard of the automobile upon an impact to the front of the car.

Another policy approach for increasing utilization includes the mandatory belt-use laws that have become common in many industrialized nations [Pulley and Scanlon (38), Robertson (43)]. Such a law has two benefits in addition to its potential effectiveness reported earlier. It requires no additional equipment purchases and it applies immediately to the full population of automobile owners. However, belt laws may be viewed as placing unacceptable restrictions on individual behavior and hence may be ignored and resisted by many. Evidence suggests that this would be a more serious problem in the United States than in Europe.[1]

Intermediate government policies which stop short of direct regulation can be promulgated. For example, a policy to provide the consumer with crucial information about the value of wearing seat belts would maximize freedom of choice. This is the approach currently favored by the Reagan administration. However, past saturation campaigns aimed at the public have had little influence on seat-belt use [Robertson (43, 44), Teknekron (51)].

Another possibility is to use tort law to provide economic incentives for using restraint devices. For example, courts could hold defendants liable for injury damages only to the extent of injuries that would have occurred if the restraint device had been in use at the time of the accident. This has been referred to as the mitigation theory.

Another example of tort law reform is the adoption of universal no-fault insurance. This would facilitate the use of insurance premium discounts for the voluntary consumption of effective safety protection. Under a fault or no-fault system, insurance rates will decline if occupant restraint-system use increases and this leads to insurance claim reductions that are passed on to the insured in the form of lower rates. However, in fault states liability premium rates are based on the collective experience of a particular insurance class and use of a restraint device by a particular individual does not directly affect his premium rate (except personal medical expense coverage). On the other hand, premium discounts can be used as an up-front incentive for restraint protection in no-fault states since coverage is first person in character.

In the remainder of this paper we discuss various rationales for types of market failure that could result in the need for a policy toward occupant restraint systems. We then examine the empirical evidence that supports and contradicts the need for governmental intervention. Section IV of the paper is devoted to a review of benefit/cost analysis of passive restraints. Finally, we relate those results to the policy options available to the government.

II. MARKET FAILURE AND REGULATORY RESPONSE:
A Review of Relevant Theoretical Analyses

Suppose that the market for safety equipment functions in a socially optimal fashion. Then an option to the policies discussed above would be total deregulation. Proceeding from this point, Walter Oi (32) has developed a model in which the socially optimal level of safety equipment is consumed when the sum of injury and injury avoidance costs are minimized. This outcome requires not only a competitive market and rational behavior but also perfect and symmetric information about the probability distribution of product defects and personal injuries on the part of individuals and producers and the absence of any externalities. Such stringent preconditions limit the model.

Peltzman (35, 36) takes the Oi approach one step further. He argues that even if the market does not lead to a social optimum, government regulations may be unable to produce any welfare gains. In Peltzman's model, a policy mandating safety devices on automobiles changes relative "prices" that drivers place on accident probabilities and other driving outputs referred to as driving intensity. If driving intensity is a normal good, a reduction in ". . . risk price of driving intensity, that is, [a reduction in] the probability of death given an accident . . ." will result in drivers substituting more driving intensity for reduced probability of death [Peltzman (35), p. 681]. If that occurs, deaths will not be reduced by mandatory safety devices to the levels predicted by the status quo estimates. Thus, his model predicts that more safety regulation will lead to a ". . . (1) reduced severity of accidents [to drivers] for each level of intensity, (2) increased driving intensity, and so increased probability of accident, the net result being that (3) an equilibrium increase in the expected cost (e.g., death) from accidents cannot be ruled out . . ."[2] [*ibid.*, p. 683]. This Peltzman effect is, thus, a "moral hazard" type of phenomenon where government reduction of the "price" of accidents causes disincentive effects to occur that may defeat the original intention of the policy. The evidence concerning such offset behavior, frequently referred to as the "danger compensation" principle, will be discussed below.

In contrast to the Oi and Peltzman analyses, two basic market failures are usually stressed as factors possibly justifying government intervention—imperfect market information, and externalities.

Decisions concerning the benefits and costs of seat-belt protection are subject to uncertainty. The individual is faced with a very low probability of an adverse outcome such as loss of life or serious injury. However, that probability is a complex function of endogenous and exogenous forces that make a well-informed decision difficult. To further complicate matters, costs and benefits are asymmetric in the sense that costs are incurred in the present with relative certainty; whereas benefits, which depend on a complex set of probabilities, occur in the future.

Kunreuther (26) and others [Thaler (52), Tversky (54), Tversky and Kahneman (55)] suggest that individuals subjected to similar situations tend to err on the side of purchasing too little safety. Kunreuther (26) conducted an extensive analysis of decisions regarding the purchase of flood insurance. He found that most eligible individuals failed to purchase highly subsidized flood insurance. His analysis led to the rejection of the possibility that the insurance was not being purchased because of expectations that the government ultimately would bail out those subjected to a flood disaster. Kunreuther concluded that the behavior of those studied was more accurately predicted by the theories of Tversky and Kahneman (54, 55), that is, when subjected to a low probability of an extreme outcome, individuals' behavior is driven more by the low probability of the event's occurrence and less by the potential losses. This insensitivity to the potential cost of the low probability outcome has been used by some to explain the low utilization of L/S belts [Arnould and Grabowski (4)]. Others argue that the low utilization is the result of benefits being less than the costs of L/S belt use. In the next section, we provide some empirical evidence in support of the conclusion that individuals err on the side of too little L/S belt use.

Externalities provide the other potential source of market failure. The cost imposed on others from injuries or deaths as a result of automobile accidents includes losses of utility to family and friends, medical cost subsidized with funds generated by government programs, productivity losses due to team-oriented tasks, and group-rated insurance programs.

In addition, as another type of externality, insurance programs may provide a disincentive for individuals to purchase safety equipment because group rating systems do not impose on the individual the full cost of restoring health or well-being after accidents occur. Individual rating systems that would reduce the extent of this moral hazard are limited by transaction costs and other legal arrangements. However, the extent of these disincentives to invest in safety is limited by the fact that we are dealing here with "irreplaceable" assets (in the limit, one's life) which are not in a real sense fully insurable [Cook and Graham (13)]. Nevertheless, moral hazard may lead to underutilization of safety equipment.

We are therefore faced with the following questions: If either information problems or externalities exist to any significant degree, this could lead to suboptimal utilization of safety equipment. At the same time, the benefits of any particular type of government policy remedy must be weighed against its costs. In this regard, the effectiveness of government regulation may be corrected by Peltzman-type offset behavior as well as other factors. These are empirical questions, the evidence for which will be examined in detail below.

III. HISTORICAL STUDIES OF AUTOMOBILE SAFETY

A. The Effects of Regulation

Sam Peltzman (35, 36) was the first economist to do a major empirical analysis of the effects of government regulation on the death and injury rates from automobiles. Peltzman constructed a model of the factors influencing accident death and injury rates for the period 1947–65, prior to the introduction of any major safety regulation (namely, the lap seat-belt). He estimated the effectiveness of automobile safety regulation in the post-regulation period 1965–72 by projecting the death and injury rate which would have occurred without regulation, using the preregulation model estimates. He then compared these projected values to actual death and injury rates during the postregulation period. The difference was attributed to regulation. Similar cross-section rates were estimated to determine if differences exist between short-run and long-run influences.

Two rather surprising conclusions were drawn from these estimates by Peltzman (35). First, the reduction in fatalities for motor vehicle occupants attributed to regulation was quite small (approximately 7 percent). Second, and more surprising, Peltzman found a much larger than projected increase in expected deaths to pedestrians from motor vehicle accidents in the postregulatory period. Peltzman interpreted these findings as consistent with the danger compensation effect of drivers responding to increased safety equipment regulation by taking increased risks in their driving behavior. Combining the above two findings, Peltzman concluded there was a 100 percent offset to the desired regulatory objective of reducing automobile fatalities and injuries—that is, the small gains in auto fatality reductions for vehicle occupants were completely offset by a higher death rate for pedestrians as the result of the increased risk-taking induced by regulation.

Much of the controversy stirred by these results centers on the relationship between the theory and the empirical analysis. MacAvoy (28) has pointed out that the increase in pedestrian deaths is counter to the predictions of the theory. Specifically, some types of safety devices, such as dual braking systems, may reduce the risk of death by reducing the frequency of accidents. Other devices, such as padded dashboards, collapsible steering columns, and seat belts do not reduce the incidence of accidents but do reduce the risk of death or injury should an accident occur. These latter safety devices, which make up a major part of those considered by Peltzman, do not reduce the liability costs of accidents or the costs to those in other cars. Most importantly, they do not change the cost to the driver of injuries or death inflicted on pedestrians if accidents involving an automobile and a pedestrian have virtually no probability of injury to the driver, a seemingly safe assumption to make. Therefore, we should not expect a significant change in pedestrian deaths as a direct result of these types of safety regulation.

Empirically, the model links an increase in accident rates to an increase in teenage drivers and drunken driving. However, the model does not really explain how increases in teenage driving or drunken driving are related to automobile safety regulation. In fact, the increase in the number of teenage drivers involved in accidents more likely has to do with demographics and teenage driving habits than with safety equipment [Nelson (31)]. Another statistical problem with the results generated by this model may arise because a general time trend variable used to generate the differences between actual and predicted death rates explains most of the decline in the pre-1965 accident death rate. Again, many factors that may or may not be related to safety regulation could explain that trend [Nelson (31), Pitovsky (37)]. In general, the reduced form model developed by Peltzman does not exclude other theories that might explain Peltzman's results.

Since Peltzman's analysis was first published, some attempts have been made to directly test the danger compensation or risk offset phenomena. In this regard, Evans, Wasielewski, and von Buseck (15), three researchers at General Motors, analyzed the time duration of following headway maintained by seat-belt users and nonusers in high-flow freeway traffic in mandatory belt use (Ontario) and nonmandatory belt use (Michigan) jurisdictions. They hypothesize that the Peltzman effect should result in belt users maintaining less headway regardless of jurisdiction and a lower average headway in Ontario, where mandatory belt laws have drastically increased belt usage. In both jurisdictions ". . . a smaller percentage of users than nonusers drove at close, risky headways . . . In the Ontario study, mandatory usage, rather than producing increased risk taking as suggested by the danger compensation principle, was also associated with the avoidance of risk" [ibid.]. This is contrary to the Peltzman hypothesis. In another study, Rumer, Berggrund, Jernberg and Ytterbom (45) found the margin of safety greater for those using studded tires in Sweden than those using conventional snow tires, even though those using studded tires drive at greater average speeds. Their findings were also not generally supportive of Peltzman's analysis.

In sum, while risk offset is a theoretically possible response, there is a real question concerning its empirical significance. This is a question on which further research should be forthcoming. For the present, the idea of a *100 percent* offset to automobile regulation suggested by Peltzman's work has been met with considerable doubt and skepticism by social scientists.

It also should be observed that while most of the attention to Peltzman's work has focused on his findings of risk shifting to pedestrians, his first result cited above of a very small effect of auto safety regulation in reducing motor vehicle occupant fatalities can be explained on other grounds than risk offset behavior. In particular, the most important device from a safety standpoint mandated by regulation was the seat belt. (Other devices like padded dash or penetration-resistant windshields have much lower potential effectiveness.) However, we know that the vast majority of individuals do not use their seat belts. Surveys indicate a usage rate for the general population in the range of 10 to 20 percent [Robertson (41)]. Furthermore, the usage of seat belts by drivers in tow-away accidents was observed to be less than 10 percent in one major study [Hedlund (22)].

The implications of this low utilization rate for automobile injury and fatality reduction in the postregulatory period can be evaluated quantitatively. Engineering estimates on the effectiveness of seat belts in saving lives and preventing injury showed that these devices would prevent 30 to 60 percent of the deaths and serious injuries that will occur without such devices in operation. However, if these devices are actually utilized by only about 10 percent of motor vehicle occupants involved in accidents, the expected reduction in fatalities and serious injuries, even if all cars are equipped with these devices, is only 3 to 6 percent—well within the estimated range of safety benefits observed by Peltzman, especially given all the empirical and measurement problems associated with a model of this kind.

Hence, the low observed benefits for motor vehicle occupants from mandatory safety equipment can be explained to a large degree by the lack of seat-belt utilization rather than risk offset behavior or other more complicated phenomena. Of course, this raises the more fundamental question of why the majority of people do not utilize their seat belts. Is this a "market failure" phenomenon that should be addressed by further regulation? Alternatively, does it reflect "rational behavior" on the part of consumers? The empirical evidence regarding these questions is considered in the next section.

B. Why Don't People Wear Seat Belts?

In two recent papers, Bloomquist (7) and Bloomquist and Peltzman (8) argue that the current low level of belt use is the result of rational calculations of the benefits from reduced probabilities of death or injury. Further, they argue that the time and discomfort costs are sufficient to discourage use and would outweigh the benefits for many individuals. However, the time and discomfort costs are very sensitive to the estimation procedures used with other important explanatory variables, and are subject to similar criticism applied to the earlier Peltzman (35) work.

On the basis of this kind of analysis, Bloomquist (7) predicted that improvements in L/S belt design and comfort would increase belt usage to 51 percent. Contrary to that prediction, large-scale reports show that belt usage actually is declining [Opinion Research (34), p. 5]. This conclusion is drawn from the results of periodic large-scale field studies conducted by Opinion Research Corporation for the Department of Transportation. In its 1978 study involving 69,000 field observations the mean safety belt usage was found to be 14.1 percent. That updated usage rate reflects a decline from the results of this group's research conducted the previous year.

Thaler and Rosen (53) also argue that low voluntary utilization may be explained by low benefits relative to the time and inconvenience of buckling up. Using values on what individuals would be willing to pay to avoid risk based on labor market analysis, they estimate that individuals would be willing to forego $200 to reduce the probability of death by 1 chance in 1,000. Multiplying that estimate by the estimate of the National Safety Council that lap belts reduce risk of death by 1 chance in 20,000, Thaler and Rosen conclude that the expected annual benefits from lap-belt use are approximately $10. This, obviously, could be less than the time and inconvenience of buckling up for most individuals, thus explaining the low utilization of government-mandated seat belts.

In another paper [Arnould and Grabowski (4), p. 32], however, we point out that Thaler and Rosen's benefit estimates are subject to significant downward bias because they ignore the value of injury reduction from buckling up and consider only the lap-belt case. Most cars are now equipped with the more effective lap/shoulder belts. Adjusting for these problems and expressing the benefits in 1981 dollars, we find the estimated annual individual benefits from buckling up in our analysis to range from $63 to $130 (depending on the weighting scheme used for valuing injury reductions).[3] Thus even the low end of our sensitivity analysis provides for benefits substantially greater than those found by Thaler-Rosen and the estimates of time and discomfort costs used by Bloomquist. Our estimates further do not include any value for reduced insurance premiums. Even though insurance companies may be unwilling to individually rate on the basis of L/S belt use, a substantial increase in L/S belt utilization would reduce accidental deaths and, therefore should bring about substantial premium reductions over the long run [GAO (58)].[4]

An alternative hypothesis for the low observed levels of seat-belt use that we discussed above is that individuals are generally insensitive to low probabilities. Several strands of evidence in the literature are consistent with this hypothesis. A survey of 1,500 licensed drivers by Teknekron Research Corporation [(51), p. A3], for example, found that only 23 percent expected the probabilities of their being in an accident would be equal to or greater than the national average. Over 80 percent believed that they had "a lot of control" or "almost total control" to prevent an accident. Clearly, both perceptions are inconsistent with the actual probabilities of being in a serious automobile accident.

The behavior toward low probability events may also be viewed as a manifestation of "bounded rationality" [Simon (46)]. Slovic, Fischoff, and Lichtenstein (51) found that a substantially higher percentage of those surveyed responded affirmatively to the use of seat belts when confronted with the probability of being involved in a serious accident over a fifty-year period (one chance in three) than when probabilities were stated on an annual basis (where the odds are very small). Similarly, when the sizable benefits found by Arnould and Grabowski (4) are calculated on a per-ride basis, they amount to less than 10 to 20 cents per ride in 1975 dollars. Clearly, this could be below the threshold value necessary for individuals to invest time in the decision. The implications of learning-by-doing are also quite different for rare events of a hazardous nature compared to more probable outcomes. In the present case, the choice not to buckle up is repeatedly reinforced by the lack of any negative consequences. At the same time, one serious accident may "truncate" the individual from the sample and preclude the opportunity for a change in behavior. Learning-by-doing is thus not a viable option here and learn-ing-by-study may fail to influence individual behavior because of the abstract character of low probability odds.

In summary, the "insensibility to low probabilities" appears to us to warrant serious attention by social scientists. At the same time, considerably more analysis is needed of the decision process of individuals before policy can singularly rest on such evidence.

C. Government Policy Efforts To Increase Seat-belt Utilization Here and Abroad

Public information campaigns by government agencies and private organizations have been generally unsuccessful in efforts to increase L/S belt use in this country. The Motor Vehicle Manufacturers Association commissioned Yankelovich, Shelly, and White to conduct a study to determine if advertising campaigns would affect attitudes toward seat-belt usage [Subcommittee (50), pp. 22–23]. Grand Rapids, Michigan, was chosen as the test city with Milwaukee, Wisconsin, as the comparison city. Advertising messages geared to emotional appeal were broadcast over radio and television during prime time. The follow-up survey results indicate that the level of belt use increased from 29 to 41 percent and that those approving of mandatory belt-use laws increased from 48 to 62 percent [Subcommittee (50)].

The Insurance Institute for Highway Safety (IIHS) conducted its own survey of seat-belt use in Grand Rapids shortly after the earlier survey was completed. Through direct observation of vehicle occupants, IIHS found that 87 percent of the drivers observed were not wearing seat belts in Grand Rapids while in Milwaukee 88 percent were not [Robertson (42), Subcommittee (50), p. 23].

A second study [Robertson (44), Subcommittee (50), pp. 23–24] with equally disheartening results used cable TV to control messages going to individuals. Residents on one side of a street received messages; those on the other side did not. Automobile vehicle registrations were used to identify the inhabitant of a street. Actual observation revealed that the commercials had no influence on seat-belt use, leading IIHS [Robertson (43)] and GAO (58) officials to conclude that increased information dissemination has no perceptible impact on seat-belt use.

Utilization rates of L/S belts achieved in jurisdictions with mandatory use laws provide an interesting contrast to the U.S. experience as well as a basis for analyzing policy options. Data on areas for which mandatory use laws were in effect in 1977 are shown in Table 1. Information about usage rates before enactment of mandatory use laws is provided where available [Opinion Research Corporation (34), Thaler (52)]. Those rates range from a low of 1 to 3 percent in Japan to an average of 43 percent in Switzerland. Overall average use rates in these jurisdictions were comparable to or slightly higher than the United States. After the enactment of the laws, use rates (Table 1, col. 6) increased dramatically to more than 70 percent, on average. Moreover, the increases were not temporary. Australia, where mandatory use laws were first enacted, reported increases to above 70 percent in the late 1970s. But in Ontario, Canada, belt use dropped off slightly, to around 50 percent.

These results from mandatory belt-use laws are significant when compared to utilization rates in the United States. The one notable exception is the case of Japan where the law requires that belts be used on expressways but provides no enforcement or penalty for noncompliance. Pulley and Scanlon (38) report belt use in Japan to be 8 percent, as shown in Table 1. But Robertson (43) observed cars entering expressways in two Japanese cities and discovered fewer than 1 percent of the front-seat occupants were wearing seat belts.

Another important issue is whether increased utilization levels in these countries have resulted in the expected declines in automobile fatalities and injuries. The last two columns provide some preliminary estimates in this regard. The information at this stage is very limited and subject to qualification. For some jurisdictions, inadequate control was maintained over other factors that were changing, such as design, other safety features, and, most importantly, changes in speed limits.

Foldvary and Lane (19) found, after careful controlling for other factors, that deaths were reduced in Victoria, Australia, by 20 percent in urban areas and 10 percent in rural areas. That is somewhat below the forecasted reduction of 20 to 30 percent from 70 percent L/S belt utilization assuming

Table 1. Effect of Safety-belt Usage around the World, 1977

Country	Effective Date of Law	Penalty for Non-compliance	Enforcement	Public Information Program	Belt Usage before Law Effective	Belt Usage after Law Effective	Occupant Fatality Reduction	Occupant Injury Reduction
Czechoslovakia	1–1–69	Max $10						
Japan	2–1–71	None	0	None		Aug. 1975 8%		
Australia (all states)	1–1–72	Max $20	1	Yes	1971 25%	1972–1974 68–85%	1972–1974 25%	1972–1974 20%
New Zealand	6–1–72	Max $200	1		May 1972 30%	1972–1975 62–83%		
France	7–1–73 (1)	$10–20	1	Yes	March 1973	March 1974 64% 1975: 85% (outside cities) In city: Daytime 15% Nighttime 30%	1975 22%	1975 32%
Puerto Rico	1–1–74	$10	0–1	Yes	July 1973 26%	July 1976 25%		
Sweden	1–1–75	Max $100 Usual $10	1	Yes	36%	March 1976 79%		
Spain	10–3–74 (2)	$15						

Table 1. (Continued)

Country	Effective Date of Law	Penalty for Non-compliance	Enforcement	Public Information Program	Belt Usage before Law Effective	Belt Usage after Law Effective	Occupant Fatality Reduction	Occupant Injury Reduction
Belgium	6-1-75	$1.50–$15.00				July 1975 92%	June–Sept. 1975–39%	June–Sept. 1975–24%
Luxembourg	6-1-75	$5–12.50						
Netherlands	6-1-75	20¢–$120			Oct. 1974 Rural: 28% Urban: 15%	June 1975 Rural: 72% Urban: 58%		
Finland	7-1-75	None	3	Yes	June 1975 9–40%	Dec. 1975 53–71%		
Norway	9-1-75	None	0	Yes	Sept. 1973–75 Rural: 37% Urban: 15%	June 1975 Rural: 61% Urban: 15%		
Israel	7-1-75	Max $110	3	Yes	June 1975 8%	Aug. 1975 80% July 1976 80%		
Switzerland	1-1-76	$8	1–2	Yes	May 1975 35–40%	May 1976 87–95%		
West Germany	1-1-76	None	1	Yes		Jan. 1976 70–77%		
Canada Ontario	1-1-76	$20–100	1	Yes	Oct. 1975 17%	Mar. 1976 77% June 1976 64%	Jan.–July '76 17%	Jan.–July 15%

246

USSR	1-1-76	$1.50	1	None
Canada Quebec	8-15-76	$10-$20	0-1	None
Austria	7-1-75			
Denmark	1-1-76			
Yugoslavia	1-1-77			

0 – Essentially none
1 – When motorist stopped for another purpose
2 – Strict (when observed not wearing belt)
3 – Only requested to "buckle up" by officer
Note: Blanks indicate no information available.
Source: Pulley and Scanlon (38), GAO (58).

(1) On roads outside city limits 1–1–75 usage required on city roads between 10 p.m. and 6 a.m.
(2) Usage not required in cities

an effectiveness rate of 50 percent. Estimates from other studies summarized in columns 7 and 8 of Table 1 range from 17 to 39 percent for reduction in deaths and from 15 to 32 percent for reductions in injuries. Robertson (43) contends that the lower end of the range, that is, 10 to 20 percent, probably provides the "best" current estimate.

It might be argued that these results are consistent with the danger compensation principle—or Peltzman's "moral hazard" effect [O'Neill (33)]. If so, deaths are not reduced as much as expected because drivers are willing to increase driving intensity due to the increased safety afforded by the use of L/S belts. Also consistent with the Peltzman effect, Conybeare (12) found that automobile-related nonoccupant deaths increased by more than predicted values while occupant deaths decreased after the introduction of belt-use laws in Australia.

At the same time, another explanation for lower than expected reductions in injuries is that those who obey usage laws tend to be the safer drivers whereas those who disobey the laws tend to be willing to take more risk in driving situations. Williams and O'Neill (60) advance this kind of hypothesis. It is also consistent with evidence from NHTSA that shows that those likely to be involved in accidents in the United States are the least likely to be users of L/S belts [DOT (14)]. It is plausible that this group would be the most likely to violate mandatory belt-use laws.

In any event, while observed safety benefits from mandatory belt regulation have been less than those projected based on engineering studies, it is worth emphasizing they have been sizable in countries like Australia which have implemented these programs in a serious manner. Indeed, if comparable gains of 10 to 20 percent fatality reduction could be accomplished in the United States, it would mean an annual savings of several thousand lives and many times that in serious injury reductions.

While mandatory seat-belt laws have been adopted by many foreign countries and have had apparent success in significantly reducing automobile fatalities and injuries, compulsory legislative proposals have not fared well in this country. NHTSA tried to encourage individual states to pass mandatory belt laws during the 1970s by offering to provide federal grant funds. Only Puerto Rico enacted such a law. In addition, this policy option has consistently ranked last in several public opinion polls conducted regarding possible regulatory approaches for increased protection. This suggests that consumer disutility costs from belt laws would be much higher in this country than abroad and implementation and administrative costs would also be correspondingly higher.

As noted in the introduction, policy attention in this country has focused instead on passive restraints rather than mandatory belt usage laws. The benefit/cost case for passive restraint regulation is considered in the section which follows.

IV. BENEFIT/COST ANALYSES OF PASSIVE RESTRAINT REGULATIONS

A. Effectiveness of Different Occupation Restraint Systems

Clearly the private and social benefits that result from occupant restraint systems depend upon the technical effectiveness of the devices, their expected levels of utilization, and their costs. Controversy surrounds each factor. In this section, we examine the reported effectiveness of lap/shoulder belts (L/S), passive belts (PB), and air cushions (AC) in the prevention of deaths and injuries, assuming complete utilization. Effectiveness rates are defined as the ratio of lives saved or injuries prevented to the number that would have occurred without the use of a restraint system. These are determined from actual road experience for the L/S and PB. For the AC rates, simulated crash tests were used.

Table 2 indicates that lap/shoulder belts, passive restraints, and air cushions have comparable effectiveness. There is actually much more variance in the estimated effectiveness for each device arising from alternative methods of testing and data collection than there is across devices using any particular methodology and data. The reason for this high variance across studies is that there is a considerable degree of judgment inherent in the determination of potential prevention of deaths or injuries if a restraint system had been in use. Also, these results reflect different sampling conditions in terms of driver and driving conditions. For example, the Huelke-O'Day (25) sample of tow-away crashes was heavily weighted toward rural accidents which, on average, are more severe than urban accidents, and where restraint systems are less effective. In addition, engineering test data are also sensitive to test conditions.

The effectiveness rates in Table 2 are divided into levels of injury ac-

Table 2. Estimates of Effectiveness Rates of Restraint Systems

	Lap/Shoulder			Passive Belt			Air Cushion			Air Cushion and Lap Belts		
	AIS	AIS	AIS	AIS	AIS	AIS	AIS	AIS	AIS	AIS	AIS	AIS
NHTSA	60	60	59	50	50	45	40	40	30	66	66	46
GM(a)	31	—	—	—	—	—	18	—	—	29	—	—
GM(b)	50	—	—	—	—	—	18	—	—	30	—	—
Ford	65	—	—	—	—	—	37	—	—	63	—	—
Huelke-O'Day	32	64	64	28	58	58	25	58	58	34	58	58

Effectiveness rate = $\dfrac{\text{Fatalities or injuries without restraint} - \text{Fatalities or injuries with restraint}}{\text{Fatalities or injuries without restraint}}$

Source: Huelke and O'Day (25), Subcommittee (50).

cording to the Abbreviated Injury Scale,[5] with ranges of severity from AIS-6, an injury that will result in death, to AIS-1, a minor non-life-threatening injury.

NHTSA estimates of effectiveness for each type of system exceed the estimates of others except in the prevention of serious injuries. They indicate that L/S belt use will reduce the probability of death in an automobile accident by 60 percent for the average driver. Benefits from PBs are estimated to be 50 percent [Federal Register (17), p. 3529]. Unlike the L/S and PB data, the AC data comes from experimental tests. Therefore, it is subject to greater variability. However, NHTSA estimates the AC to be 66 percent effective when used with a lap belt. The rates for the AC system are very sensitive to the use of the lap belt because the AC is designed primarily to provide protection in frontal crashes and provides little or no protection against lateral, roll-over, or secondary accident impacts unless the lap belt is worn.

Compared to NHTSA estimates, those of GM are consistently low. GM's initial estimates were 31 percent, 18 percent, and 29 percent for L/S, AC, and AC with lap belt, respectively. Later estimates of L/S effectiveness increased dramatically to 50 percent. However, no change occurred in the AC estimate, and the AC with lap belt increased only one percentage point.

A more interesting contrast to the NHTSA estimates is provided by the Huelke-O'Day (25) study. These estimates, from on-scene field investigations of a sample of accidents by a team of medical and other experts, are considerably lower than those of NHTSA. However, their estimates of serious injuries prevented are greater. These contrasting estimates of restraint system effectiveness indicate that a meaningful benefit/cost analysis must be subjected to sensitivity analysis. The NHTSA and Huelke-O'Day estimates can be thought to encompass the high and low estimates of restraint system effectiveness [Arnould and Grabowski (4)].

B. Utilization Rates

Potential societal benefits of passive restraint systems rest primarily on the extent to which they result in a much higher level of utilization than the currently mandated manual belt systems. In the case of passive belts, there is some basis for this expected increase in utilization provided by the historical experience with VW Rabbits and other cars equipped with these devices. At the same time, the representativeness of this experience for a universal regulation requiring passive restraints clearly is open to question.

VW first introduced a PB and knee bolster system as an option on its 1975 Rabbit models. Over 180,000 models equipped with PBs were sold between 1975 and 1979, a large enough sample to make valid comparisons with similar VWs not equipped with PB. Opinion Research (34) conducted a study of the VW experience released in 1978. They found usage of PBs to be 78 percent compared to 33 percent for similar VWs equipped with manual L/S belts or an incremental usage gain of 45 percent.

In a more recent study of VW Rabbits and GM Chevettes equipped with PBs it was found that the incremental usage of PB-equipped cars over the same model automobile equipped with manual L/S belts was 38 and 39 percent for the 1979 and 1980 Chevettes, respectively, and 41 and 43 percent for the 1979 and 1980 Rabbits, respectively [Nordhaus (10)]. If the national average usage rate of 14 percent is assumed, and these incremental gains were used to project PB utilization under government mandate, the total usage rate for automobiles equipped with PBs would be between 50 and 60 percent.

Some contend these rates are exaggerated due to poor design of the studies. First, the VW Rabbit and the 1979 Chevette were equipped with interlock systems while the 1980 Chevette was not. Yet incremental usage figures showed an increase over the 1979 model. A second problem could result from a "self-selection" bias, that is, those who knowingly purchase PBs are more likely to be users. However, as pointed out by Nordhaus [(10), p. 9], usage patterns of owners of second or previously owned cars not equipped with PBs were compared to usage of PBs. Incremental rates were 44 percent for Chevettes and 56 percent for VW Rabbits. Second, less than 12 percent of those purchasing PB-equipped Chevettes or VW Rabbits requested PBs. Finally, insurance claims for the 1975–78 model VW Rabbits reveal only minor differences in risk categories, physical claim experiences, and frequency of accident claims between drivers of passive and manual-equipped VW Rabbits [Highway Loss Data Institute (25)]. Thus there is little reason to expect that these estimates are significantly upward biased due to self-selection.

There is still, however, reason to believe that national utilization rates for PBs would not reach the current levels achieved by VW Rabbits and Chevettes. Small car owners, in general, use belts with a higher frequency than do large car owners [Opinion Research (34)]. An average of 33 percent of the owners of VW Rabbits equipped with manual belts use those belts compared to 14 percent for all U.S. automobiles. It does seem reasonable, however, to assume that PB utilization rates would be on the order of or exceed 50 percent in value if comparable incremental shifts occur in other driver populations [Nordhaus (10)].

Essentially no information exists about utilization rates for the more expensive ACs because of their newness. GM introduced the AC as an option on large automobiles in the mid-1970s. Due to lack of promotion and/or consumer acceptance, less than 15,000 AC equipped automobiles are on the road. Therefore, it is impossible to determine the extent to which owners will attempt to bypass the system. Nevertheless, there is the problem that many consumers may fail to expend funds for the costly replacement process after the system has been activated in minor accidents. However, it is reasonable to assume that utilization will be very high for those purchasing ACs.

C. Passive Restraints—the Potential for
Saving Lives and Reducing Injuries

It is instructive to examine the aggregate implications of the above estimates on utilization and effectiveness rates. Our own sensitivity analysis estimates of the potential benefits to society in terms of the deaths and injuries prevented from a passive restraint rule are substantial. Total lives saved and serious injuries prevented from ACs and PBs under alternative assumptions are shown in Table 3.

The estimates of total lives saved and injuries prevented are derived by multiplying the effectiveness rate for the safety device times the number of lives that would have been lost and severe injuries that would have occurred (AIS 3-5) if no restraint system had been used times the percent of front-seat occupants that utilize the restraint device [Arnold and Grabowski (4), p. 32]. The columns labeled NHTSA reflect the higher effectiveness rates estimated by NHTSA (17) and those labeled H-O'D reflect

Table 3. Steady State Estimates of Annual Benefits to Society from Occupant Restraint Devices

Restraint Device	Estimated Lives Saved*		Estimated Severe Injuries (AIS 3–5) Prevented*	
	NHTSA	H-O'D	NHTSA	H-O'D
Passive Belts				
I. 50% usage rate	6,800	3,808	16,315	20,503
II. 60% usage rate	8,160	4,570	19,578	24,601
III. 70% usage rate	9,520	5,331	22,841	28,704
Air Cushions with				
I. 0% lap belt use	10,880	6,800	22,840	41,006
II. 20% lap belt use	12,294	7,290	24,667	42,420
Manual lap shoulder belts				
I. 20% usage rate	3,264	1,741	8,375	9,050
II. 10% usage rate	1,620	864	4,188	4,525

* These estimated steady state values are computed using NHTSA's distribution of injuries (without protection) for 1975 [Arnould and Grabowski (4), p. 32] according to the formula:

Estimated Lives Saved = Effectiveness Rate ×
　　No. of Lives Lost without Restraint Device × Utilization Rate

Source: NHTSA (17), Table 1; 22.

the less optimistic effectiveness rates estimated by Huelke-O'Day (25) shown in Table 2. The rows provide estimates for the various restraint devices assuming various levels of utilization by front-seat occupants. A steady state situation is assumed in which the safety devices do not change the distribution of accident severity, number of accidents, and population and mix of automobiles. Also, we assume an equilibrium situation in which all automobiles are equipped with passive restraints. The range of utilization rates assumed for PBs are somewhat less than current experience with the VW Rabbit. Zero and 20 percent lap-belt use with the ACs are two common reference points used in safety studies.

Estimates indicate that from over 3,800 to over 12,000 lives could be saved and from over 16,000 to over 42,000 serious injuries prevented by the use of passive restraints. Lives saved and injuries prevented from 10 and 20 percent manual L/S belt use are presented as reference points. Marginal benefits from passive restraints can be determined by deducting those values from the respective values shown for PBs and ACs.

D. Costs of Passive Restraints

It is clear that air cushions involve a more elaborate and expensive technology than passive belts. However, both devices have been subject to considerable variance in terms of projected costs under large-scale production conditions. At the time of its introduction, the passive belt system has an incremental cost allocation by VW of approximately $25 (that is, relative to manual belt systems). As a consequence of inflation and various development refinements (including in some cases electronic switching devices), passive belt devices on the market today range from $50 to well over $100 per car. In testimony before NHTSA, GM maintained that even basic passive belts would cost over $114 per car under large-scale production conditions. However, Nordhaus (10) demonstrated that these cost estimates were subject to considerable self-serving exaggeration and were inconsistent with prior capital budgeting estimates at GM.

In this case of air cushions, there has also been considerable debate and uncertainty over costs. In 1976, the DOT estimated the initial equipment cost of the AC would be $97 plus $32 for lifetime operating costs. GM and Ford estimated initial cost plus *annual* operating costs of $193 plus $14 and $235 plus $26.80, respectively [Subcommittee (50)]. Of these original estimates, the GAO (58) contends that those of the automobile manufacturers were more reasonable. Over time, however, the auto manufacturers estimated original equipment cost for air cushions have also escalated substantially. Original equipment costs for air cushions are now quoted at over $500 per car.[6] Part of this reflects general cost inflation since 1976. In addition, it reflects low projected production volumes. Air cushion production is subject to considerable scale economies so that exact costs would depend on how many cars are equipped with the device each year.

While the estimated costs of passive restraints have been apparently subject to self-serving biases by both government and automobile officials, there remains a considerable zone of uncertainty concerning levels of those costs under a universal passive restraint requirement. This also must be incorporated into any benefit/cost sensitivity analysis.

E. The Valuation of Safety Benefits

Before examining specific benefit/cost estimates on passive restraints, it is useful to discuss the analytical approach in some detail. The major benefits from this type of safety regulation accrue in the form of lives saved and injuries prevented. Placing monetary values on these benefits has been a controversial process in policy circles. We therefore discuss here the alternative concepts for valuing lives that have been employed in benefit/cost analysis.

Three methods of placing monetary values on life have been used [Acton (1)]; the livelihood method [Rice and Cooper (39)]; the value of insurance [Acton (1)]; and the willingness-to-pay method [Thaler and Rosen (53)]. The livelihood method most closely relates to the individuals' discounted future-earnings stream and bears only a remote relationship to the value individuals place on risk reduction [Conley (11)]. Also, it places no value on the lives of fatally ill children for whom parents may be willing to spend large amounts to avoid further risks or to the retired who may be very risk conscious.

Similarly, the amount of life insurance held by an individual is more closely related to that individual's desired bequest to survivors than to attitudes toward risk.

The willingness-to-pay approach of valuing life, which is based upon the revealed preferences of individuals, most closely responds to the theoretical condition of benefit/cost analysis by providing a measure of the marginal social benefits from enhanced life as opposed to increased production benefit. Recent studies have used the concept of wage-risk premium or survey methods to derive estimates of the amount individuals are willing to forego in wages to accept a job that has a marginally lower risk than other jobs. One criticism is that the wage-risk premiums may measure ability-to-pay and not willingness-to-pay. As such, those measures may place a discriminatorily low value on health and safety if poorer, less skilled workers are forced into riskier jobs. However, the livelihood method is more closely tied to income than is willingness-to-pay. Also, estimation techniques may be used to adjust for potential areas of discrimination such as sex, race, and age.

More troubling is the assumption made in the use of willingness-to-pay estimates that the risk premiums are transferable across different risky situations and differing groups of people [Smith (48)]. For example, a person may have the same risk of death from a heart attack, intestinal cancer, or an airplane crash, yet not be willing to place the same value on the opportunity to reduce the probability of death in each case. Similarly, Thaler (52) has found that peoples' attitudes are not necessarily symmetrical across risk reductions and risk increases.

The willingness-to-pay method, despite measurement difficulties and other frailties, provides the soundest theoretically based method for placing monetary values on loss of life for use in social policy analysis.

F. Benefit/Cost Analysis of FMVSS 208

A number of formal benefit/cost analyses have been conducted on FMVSS 208 (the passive restraint rule). The U.S. Department of Transportation (57) published the benefit/cost ratios for passive restraints shown in Table 4 in 1976. The relevant values are the ratios of incremental benefits to incremental costs. To determine these incremental values, nominal values for each system (AC and PBs) are compared to nominal values for manual L/S belts. Similarly, optimistic values are compared to optimistic values. The nominal projections assume 15 percent L/S belt usage and 5 percent lap-belt usage while the optimistic projections assume 35 percent L/S belt usage and 5 percent lap-belt usage. Similarly, the nominal and optimistic projections for lap-belt use with ACs is assumed to be 20 and 40 percent, and PB use is assumed to be 60 and 70 percent, respectively. Then benefits and costs of those currently using L/S and lap belts are deducted from total benefits and costs for AC and PB use

Table 4. DOT Benefit Cost Ratios for Various Restraint Systems

	Total Benefits/Total Cost	*Incremental Benefits* *Incremental Cost*
Active Belt System		
15% L/S and 5% lap use	1.5	NA
35% L/S and 5% lap use	3.1	NA
Full Front Air Cushion		
Nominal projection	2.1	2.6
(20% lap-belt use)	2.4	1.9
Optimistic projection		
(40% lap-belt use)	3.5	8.7
Passive Belts	3.8	5.8
Nominal projection (60%)		
Optimistic projection (70%)		

Source: GAO (58).

to get the incremental benefit/cost ratio. In all cases, the benefit/cost ratios pass the crucial test of being greater than one. However, the ratios for the lower cost PBs substantially exceed those for the AC system.

These estimates are subject to criticism for numerous reasons.[7] In particular, they employ NHTSA's estimates for effectiveness and utilization which were on the high end of the plausible range presented above in Tables 2 and 3. They also employ cost estimates which were much lower than that of the automobile manufacturers. Hence, NHTSA employed "optimistic" assumptions for all the critical parameters in their benefit/cost calculations.

We reported a benefit/cost analysis elsewhere using the same steady state assumptions as DOT but incorporating sensitivity analysis on these parameters [Arnould and Grabowski (4)]. These results are summarized in Table 5. Specifically, we use a willingness-to-pay estimate of value of life of $300,000 which is the 1975 equivalent of the Thaler-Rosen estimate adjusted according to Bailey (6) for injuries and Arnould and Nichols (5) for insurance. We employ two weighting schemes to assign values to out of pocket cost, disability, and disutility from injuries, as suggested by Lave and Weber (27). For both schemes, deaths (AIS-6) and critical injuries (AIS-5) are given weights of one, and severe and life threatening injuries (AIS-4) a weight of .67. However, the scheme referred to in columns headed I of Table 6 assigns a weight of .05 to severe injuries (AIS-3), .01 to moderate injuries (AIS-2), and .001 to minor injuries (AIS-1).

Table 5. Incremental Benefit Cost Ratios for Alternative Cost and Effectiveness Rates

	Passive Belts											
Case	*VW Costs (25)*						*$50 Purchase Price*					
Effectiveness	*Utilization Rates*						*Utilization Rates*					
	50%		60%		70%		50%		60%		70%	
	I	II	I	II	I	II	I	II	I	II	I	II
(1) NHTSA	3.56	6.31	4.98	8.99	6.39	11.66	1.90	3.37	2.66	4.80	3.41	6.22
(2) Huelke-O'Day	3.00	6.11	4.12	8.58	5.25	11.05	1.60	3.26	2.20	4.58	2.80	5.90

	Air Cushions							
	NHTSA Cost				*Ford Cost*			
	Associated Lap-Belt Usage				*Associated Lap-Belt Usage*			
	0%		20%		0%		20%	
	I	II	I	II	I	II	I	II
(1) NHTSA	1.37	1.87	1.65	2.28	.54	.73	.64	.89
(2) Huelke-O'Day	1.44	2.25	1.56	2.55	.56	.88	.61	.99

Note: I and II refer to the weighting systems for assigning values to life and injury.
Source: Arnould and Grabowski (4), p. 42.

The scheme referred to in columns II of Table 6 assigns weights of .25, .1, and .01 to AIS-3, AIS-2, and AIS-1 injuries, respectively. Two measures of externalities were included in our incremental benefits. The Social Security Administration (56) reports that 40 percent of total expenditures on health care are paid from public funds. Therefore, we included 40 percent of expected savings in medical cost from reduced automobile deaths and injuries. Also, we included savings in court and legal expenses [Fagin (16), p. 2]. Other externalities were not included due to difficulty of measurement. Therefore, our estimates of annual societal benefits should be conservative. Our conservative estimate must be qualified because we do not account for Peltzman-type negative externalities. Evidence reviewed earlier in this paper reveals doubts concerning the existence of those negative externalities. For example, it is doubtful that insurers would be willing to grant discounts for ACs if actuarial experience was expected to support the Peltzman effects. Also, the VW Rabbit experience in which claims experiences in terms of physical damage awards and overall frequency of accidents claims were virtually identical for PB and manual L/S belt-equipped automobiles strongly refutes the existence of Peltzman's "moral hazard" effect [Highway Loss Data Institute (23)].

Utilization rates were assumed to be 20 percent for L/S belts. However, we use utilization rates of 50, 60, and 70 percent for PBs for the columns shown in Table 6, implying incremental changes in usage of 30 to 50 percent. Mendeloff (29) argues that these values may be very optimistic due to the generally higher than average manual L/S belt-utilization rates of VW Rabbit owners and the existence of an ignition interlock system on the PB equipment of VW Rabbits. However, his position is somewhat diluted by the recent experience with the PB-equipped Chevettes (discussed earlier) and comparisons of occupant experiences for owner-operated manual and passive belt cars.

Finally, we examine the sensitivity of the benefit/cost ratios to effectiveness rates of the passive restraint systems. That is accomplished by using the rates estimated by NHTSA (57) and Huelke-O'Day (25). These values distinguish rows 1 and 2 in Table 5.

The results of these adjustments to the benefit/cost computations are shown in Table 5. Benefit/cost ratios for the PB range from 1.6 to 11.7. Thus, the system remains cost beneficial when subjected to sensitivity analysis that takes the form of changing the assumptions about the relevant parameters. Although not shown in Table 6 the results remain robust to sizable increases in the disconnect rate and increases in the assumed value of life.

Similar results were not obtained for the AC system. That system was cost beneficial only for the cases when NHTSA's low-cost estimates were used. This is so unless a much higher value of life than the $300,000 figure

Table 6. Net Annual Benefits for Alternative Cost and Effectiveness Ratios

| | Benefit/Costs, Passive Belts | | | | | |
| | 50% | | 60% | | 70% | |
	I	II	I	II	I	II
VW Costs ($25):						
NHTSA	1,275,027,700	2,644,686,300	1,982,269,600	3,979,480,900	2,684,530,900	5,309,294,400
Huelke-O'Day	998,115,400	2,545,074,800	1,553,940,000	3,775,277,200	2,116,745,200	5,005,479,700
GM Costs ($50):						
NHTSA	839,553,800	2,210,825,000	1,548,510,300	3,544,782,600	2,248,138,500	4,869,411,900
Huelke-O'Day	559,702,500	2,108,212,800	1,119,405,000	3,339,558,400	1,679,107,600	4,570,903,900

Air Cushions

| | 0% | | 20% | |
	I	II	I	II
NHTSA:				
NHTSA	4,386,377,600	6,907,284,300	5,798,085,400	8,974,428,000
Huelke-O'Day	4,739,304,500	8,823,174,000	5,344,322,200	10,335,718,000
Ford:				
NHTSA	−2,967,117,400	−1,741,569,000	−2,322,091,900	−709,528,100
Huelke-O'Day	−2,838,112,300	−774,030,700	−2,515,599,600	−645,020,000

258

employed in our analysis is used (with correspondingly higher values on injury avoidance using the weighting schemes in Table 5).

The total annual net incremental benefits (costs) society would receive from passive restraints are shown in Table 6. Total net annual incremental benefits derived from PBs range from $0.5 billion to $5.3 billion while total annual incremental benefits for ACs ranged from a high of $10.3 billion to a low of negative $3.0 billion. The large upper bound for ACs reflects the fact that they result in the elimination of substantially more fatalities and injuries than PBs (given their assumed 100 percent utilization rate). At the same time, they are much more expensive and their estimated net benefits are subject to much higher variance. Specifically, the absolute net benefits for ACs in Table 6 are large and positive when the relatively low costs of NHTSA are assumed, but they become negative in value when the higher cost figures of the automobile makers are used. In contrast, PBs exhibit positive benefit estimates under all conditions considered.

Certain qualifications must be placed on the results in Tables 5 and 6. First, although PBs appear to be more cost beneficial under most assumed conditions, neither DOT nor our cost estimates included discomfort cost. Thus, those individuals who place a higher disutility on belt use may purchase the more costly ACs (especially if they are affluent). One study suggested that at the price differential expected to exist between PBs and ACs, about one-third of the population of automobile buyers would purchase ACs [Hart (21), p. 6]. GM predicted that 10 percent of new car buyers would purchase ACs [GAO (58), pp. 54, 114]. However, all manufacturers have indicated they would initially satisfy a passive restraint requirement with passive belts. This makes passive belts the more relevant case for public policy analysis.

Second, the steady state equilibrium values used to derive the benefit/cost ratios will not be realized upon the enactment of a passive restraint rule. Approximately 10 percent of the automobile population is replaced annually. Thus, it would take at least ten years to achieve these equilibrium levels.

Third, the distributional effects of a passive restraint law are not necessarily the same across all individuals. Those who already use L/S belts would be made worse off (except for possible collective reductions in insurance). Those in groups having a greater probability of being involved in an accident, for example, young drivers, or those who drive while intoxicated, will have greater than average gains. Although, as pointed out by Mendeloff [(29), pp. 8–9], saving the lives of the high-risk drivers may have a countervailing effect by increasing the pool of higher risk drivers. However, this effect probably will be very small.

Finally, benefits may be overstated because, even though the high-risk drivers could gain the most from restraint system use, evidence suggests they may be the least likely to wear belts. Unpublished data provided to us by the University of North Carolina Highway Safety Research Institute at Chapel Hill reveal a substantially lower voluntary usage of L/S belts among very young and old drivers and those who drive while intoxicated [see Waller and Barry (59)]. Similarly, evidence from other countries (to be discussed later) is consistent with this. In those countries where mandatory use laws have results in substantial increases in L/S belt use, reductions in fatalities and injuries have been somewhat less than would be predicted using current estimates of effectiveness rates [Robertson (43)]. Thus, behavioral factors may result in a reduction in effectiveness rates not taken into account in the estimates used in any of the benefit/cost studies of restraint systems in the United States.

Two recent benefit/cost analyses confirm that substantial positive net benefits would result from the passive restraint rule. Nordhaus [10] developed benefit/cost ratios for four policies: Amended Rule 208 (requiring a phase-in of passive restraints beginning with large 1982 model-year cars); Reversal (phasing small cars in first); Simultaneous Introduction of all 1983 model year cars; and Rescission. Using cost and effectiveness data developed by NHTSA, Nordhaus concluded that rescission of the passive restraint rule would result in a net annual loss of $2.4 billion. Assuming a mix of air bags and passive belts consistent with a projection of large, intermediate, and small car sales, a 41 percent incremental usage of passive belts, 1981 prices, and based on the life of new automobiles equipped with passive restraints on all model years from 1983 on, the total net discounted benefits from the passive restraint rule were estimated to be $32.9 billion. Under the same assumptions, the estimated benefits from reversal are $33.3 billion and for simultaneous introduction, $33.1 billion. This ranking of positive benefits remained intact when subjected to sensitivity analysis of cost, usage, and the mix of passive belts and air bags.

In a more recent unpublished study, Graham, Herrion, and Morgan (20) have performed a benefit/cost sensitivity analysis of Amended Rule 208, as well as other policy alternatives, using the "Delphi" method for obtaining probabilistic distributions on key parameters. In particular, they interviewed occupant crash protection specialists and other professional experts from academia, government, and industry to obtain parameter estimates with respect to effectiveness, utilization rates, costs, and the value of lifesaving. Their findings are similar to our own regarding Amended Rule 208 in that they find positive net benefits and benefit/cost ratios for most plausible scenarios. In addition, they find that the net benefits estimated for Amended Rule 208 tend to significantly exceed those for the alternative policy approach of a large-scale educational campaign to increase belt usage.

Two other interesting findings emerge from the Graham, Herrion, and Morgan analysis. First, they suggest that the net benefits of Amended Rule 208 could be increased by a design modification that would require installation of passive belts that were more difficult to disconnect than the belts which most automobile makers were planning to install under Amended Rule 208. Second, they found that the benefit/cost performance of air bags relative to passive belts is quite sensitive to the value of lifesaving. At sufficiently high values of lifesaving, they find that the greater lifesaving benefits of air cushions more than compensate for their higher costs.[8] Their finding in this regard suggests a nonnegligible portion of the population would probably elect to purchase air bags if given the opportunity to do so under Amended Rule 208 or some other basis.

In sum, the evidence from several separate benefit/cost analyses, although subject to the various qualifications discussed above, support the position that positive benefits would accrue from a passive restraint rule. Hence, the rescission by NHTSA, in 1981, of the passive restraint rule, in favor of an information program (which has proved ineffective in the past) is at variance with prevailing benefit/cost analyses. Recent changes in that policy decision and possible future repercussions are discussed in the next section of the paper.

IV. SUMMARY AND CURRENT POLICY DEVELOPMENTS

Experience with seat belt and other occupant restraint systems has provided one of the most interesting case studies of health and safety regulation. The history of occupant restraint systems has been traced from the voluntary introduction of lap belts as a purchase option on automobiles in the late 1950s to the formation of NHTSA in 1966 to the issuance of FMVSS 208 in 1967 requiring that all cars be equipped with seat belts. Seat belts were one of the earliest safety requirements for which clear engineering evidence existed of their effectiveness. Yet as early as 1969 the U.S. Department of Transportation had concluded that the level of seat-belt use was too low to reduce traffic injuries to an acceptable level.

The low levels of utilization promoted government efforts to increase the utilization of occupant restraint systems. Early efforts mainly were directed toward the provision of better information and educational campaigns that stressed the benefits from seat-belt utilization (or, in many cases, the cost of nonuse). As reported earlier in this paper, these efforts were singularly unsuccessful at providing long-term increases in seat-belt utilization. The reasons for lack of success are consistent with our analysis of decision-making under low probabilities—namely, when faced with a low probability of an extremely adverse outcome, people tend to err on the side of purchasing too little safety.

The failure of information and education campaigns led to more direct means of regulation. NHTSA required that all cars built between August 1973 and August 1975 be equipped with passive restraints or L/S belts and an ignition interlock system [State Farm (49), p. 8]. Automobile manufacturers choose to supply ignition interlocks and not passive restraints. The ignition interlock system met with such public outcry that Congress, in 1974, rejected the part of the standard relating to ignition interlocks and continuous buzzers and also required that any further changes in FMVSS 208 be submitted to Congress.

In subsequent periods, policy attention has focused on two alternatives—passive restraint equipment regulations, and compulsory belt-use laws. Several foreign countries have adopted the latter policy approach. Compulsory belt-use laws have proved to be a successful policy tool in a number of countries and provinces where they were adopted. Specifically in those countries where compulsory use laws have been enacted with penalties for noncompliance, use has increased to the 50 to 70 percent level and fatalities have declined by approximately 20 percent. However, in the United States, compulsory use laws have not met with similar acceptance. NHTSA tried to induce states to pass these laws through Federal Highway Program incentives, but not one state elected to pass them.

The U.S. federal government's efforts have been concentrated instead on the development of a passive restraint regulation. After many years of delay and court challenges (spanning several administrations), the former Secretary of the Department of Transportation, Brock Adams, finally issued a passive restraint regulation in 1977. That requirement, the subject of much of our earlier discussion, required the phasing in of passive restraints beginning with large cars in model year 1982. Several analyses of this regulation, reviewed earlier in this paper, confirm that passive restraints are highly cost beneficial and remain so when subjected to sensitivity analysis. In fact, only when it was assumed that FMVSS 208 would be satisfied with ACs and no passive belts, and when the high range of cost of ACs was assumed did passive restraints fail the benefit/cost test.

This brief history leads to the current position of "limbo" in which policy related to passive restraints rests. Secretary of Transportation Lewis reopened the rule-making in February 1981, based on "changed economic circumstances" and the "difficulties of the automobile industry" [*State Farm* (49), p. 14]. In October 1981, NHTSA formally rescinded the passive restraint rule [Federal Register (18), p. 53.419].

In the rescission order [Federal Register (19)], NHTSA argued that the passive restraint requirement could be justified only if seat-belt usage rose by 13 percentage points. Furthermore, FMVSS 208 could be satisfied by ACs or "detachable" or "continuous" passive belts. NHTSA found that most new cars would be equipped with the detachable belts, and further concluded that when detached, the passive belt requires the same active participation on the part of the occupant as manual belts. Hence, they argued ". . . one cannot reliably predict even a 5 percentage point increase as the minimum level of expected usage" [Federal Register (19)]. Furthermore, NHTSA argued that elimination of detachable PBs as a means of meeting FMVSS 208 would meet with public reactions similar to those brought on by the ignition interlock system.

A group consisting of State Farm Mutual Automobile Insurance Co., National Association of Independent Insurers, Automobile Owners Action Council, and numerous individuals filed petitions for review of the NHTSA order to rescind the passive restraint requirement. On June 1, 1982, the U.S. Court of Appeals for the District of Columbia Circuit handed down a decision in which the rescission of the passive restraint standard was described as "arbitrary, capricious, an abuse of discretion, and a violation of law . . ." [*State Farm* (49), p. 4].

The court concluded that most of the rescission decision by NHTSA officials was based on undocumented notions about public attitudes toward governmental safety regulation. In particular: "The agency has offered no evidence that seat belt usage will fail to increase as was expected when the standard was first promulgated . . ." and ". . . has failed to consider or analyze obvious alternatives to rescission . . ." [*State Farm* (49), p. 50]. The court declined, however, to reinstate the passive restraint rule, but instead referred the matter back to NHTSA. It concluded ". . . that rescission of the standard must be subject to 'thorough' probing, in-depth review . . ." [*State Farm* (49), p. 47].

Most recently, it was reported in the *Wall Street Journal* (August 5, 1982) that, after interchange with NHTSA, the court ruled that Amended Rule 208 be reinstated. However, the court left NHTSA with a number of alternatives. First, NHTSA must determine by October 1, 1982, if the 1983 deadline for provision of passive restraints is feasible. Already, the automobile manufacturers have resisted that date. Further, the court left it open for NHTSA to conduct further impact analysis of the regulation, issue new rules subject to court review, or get congressional action to rescind the amended rule.

Predictions concerning where automobile safety regulation policy will now lead must be highly speculative. The most likely immediate prospect is for delaying action on the current court ruling followed by more efforts directed to studies of alternative policies and possibly to halfway solutions that go beyond information and education campaigns. These include demonstration projects and, possibly, specific requirements aimed at high-risk populations of drivers such as teenagers. From a research perspective, studies of insurance incentive schemes, tort law changes, and other more market-oriented approaches to increasing safety protection might yield high dividends [Allen (2), Comment, *Chicago Law Review* (9), Huelke (26)]. These have been given little attention in this case, but have proved useful in other regulatory situations [Arnould and Grabowski (4)].

In any case, the current situation does not appear to us to be an equilibrium one. The present level of fatalities and serious injuries from automobile accidents remains very high, given that relatively low cost technologies exist to significantly reduce these occurrences. In addition, U.S. policy now diverges sharply from the stringent compulsory belt-use policies that prevail in many foreign countries. The benefit/cost studies reviewed in this paper emphasize the high potential societal benefits achievable from greater utilization of occupant restraint systems. We expect that government regulation will again play a major role in attempting to change this situation, although the exact form of this regulation remains uncertain at the current time.

NOTES

1. A Gallup Poll [Hart (21)] found that over 70 percent of the people sampled strongly opposed mandatory belt-use laws. In other surveys, mandatory belt-use laws have been ranked very low by respondents. Similarly, numerous states have rescinded or their supreme courts have declared unconstitutional laws requiring motorcyclists to use safety helmets.

2. The model produces the same results when increased income induces an increased demand for safety.

3. Our calculations [Arnould and Grabowski (4), p. 32] are based on 1975 dollars and use a value of life of $300 for reduction in the risk of death by one chance in 1,000. Our calculations here are presented in 1981 dollars using a straightforward inflation adjustment procedure.

4. The General Accounting Office [(58), p. 62] indicated that five insurers have proposed discounts of from 1 to $3\frac{1}{2}$ percent for automobiles equipped with ACs in fault states and considerably greater discounts in no-fault states. Greater discounts are possible in no-fault states due to the first party's insurance carrier not being liable for damages or injuries to the second party.

5. The Abbreviated Injury Scale (AIS) is a six-point scale for classifying injury levels where 1 and 2 are minor to moderate, 3 is severe but not life-threatening, 4 is severe and life-threatening but full recovery is probable, 5 is critical, survival is uncertain and paralysis or other permanent impairment of bodily function is likely, and 6 is maximum severity, currently untreatable resulting in immediate or short-term death [AMA (3)].

6. In a 1979 report, the GAO indicated that GM and Ford planned to charge in excess

of $500 (in current 1979 dollars) for air cushions introduced in 1982 and 1983. More recently, a GM official indicated that their current estimates of AC costs were between $900 and $1,000. The latest cost increases are alleged to be caused by inflationary pressures and reduced volume brought about by the shift to smaller automobiles.

7. Although the livelihood method was used by DOT to determine value of life, the resulting values were very close to those derived using the willingness-to-pay criteria and used in our study (4). Monetary benefits from reduced injuries may be understated by DOT due to their placing no value on pain and suffering but, likewise, may be overstated because of their inclusion of all medical costs (many of which are a transfer) and other costs that either would not be eliminated or would be only partially eliminated if injuries were prevented but the distribution of accidents was not changed.

8. This latter finding results from the fact that at high values of lifesaving, the higher costs of air cushions are more than compensated by their greater lifesaving potential (as shown in Table 6 above). The Graham, Herrion, and Morgan [(20), p. 79] analysis suggests a value of lifesaving of $350,000 is sufficient to make air cushions the preferred device. However, their analysis appears to ignore the substantial costs associated with reinstallation of deployed air cushions that will occur for many motorists over the lifetime usage of their automobile. Incorporation of this cost could cause the break-even value to increase substantially. Nevertheless, their point in this regard appears generally valid.

REFERENCES

1. Acton J. (Autumn 1976) "Measuring the Monetary Value of Lifesaving Programs," *Law and Contemporary Problems,* Vol. 60(4): 46–72.
2. Allen, C. C. III. (1977) "Non Use of Seat Belts as Failure to Mitigate Damages," *American Law Reports,* 3rd edition, Vol. 80: 1033–1070.
3. American Medical Association for Automotive Medicine, Joint Committee on Injury Scaling. (1976) *Abbreviated Injury Scale,* rev. ed., Chicago.
4. Arnould, R., and Grabowski, H. (1981) "Auto Safety Regulation: An Analysis of Market Failure," *Bell Journal of Economics,* Vol. 12: 27–48.
5. Arnould, R., and Nichols, L. (1983) "Wage Risk Premiums and Workmen's Compensation: A Refinement of Estimates of Compensating Wage-Differential," *Journal of Political Economy,* forthcoming.
6. Bailey, M. J. (1980) *Reducing Risks to Life: Measurement of the Benefits,* Washington, D.C., American Enterprise Institute of Public Policy Research.
7. Bloomquist, G. (1979) "Value of Life Saving: Implications of Consumption Activity," *Journal of Political Economy,* Vol. 87: 540–558.
8. Bloomquist, G., and Peltzman, S. (1979) "Mandatory Passive Restraint Systems and Social Welfare," unpublished manuscript, Illinois State University.
9. Comment. (1973) "Self-Protection Safety Devices: An Economic Analysis," *Chicago Law Review,* Vol. 40: 418–424.
10. Comments. (May 26, 1981) William Nordhaus on Notice of Proposed Rulemaking on Federal Motor Vehicle Safety Standard Occupant Crash Protection, Docket No. 74–14, Notice 22.
11. Conley, B. (1976) "The Value of Human Life in the Demand for Safety," *American Economic Review,* Vol. 66(1): 45.
12. Conybeare, J. A. C. (1980) "Evaluation of Automobile Safety Regulations: The Case for Compulsory Seat Belt Legislation in Australia," *Policy Sciences,* Vol. 12: 27–39.
13. Cook, P., and Graham, D. (February 1977) "Demand for Insurance and Protection: The Case of Irreplaceable Commodities," *Quarterly Journal of Economics,* Vol. 91: 143–157.

14. Department of Transportation. (1977) "Supplementary Analysis to DOT FMVSS 208,"
     Washington, D.C.
15. Evans, L., Wasielewski, P., and Von Buseck, C. (Sept. 24, 1980) "Compulsory Seat
     Belt Usage and Driver Risk-Training Behavior," GMR-3413, GM Research Labora-
     tories, Warren, Mich.
16. Fagin, B. M. (1915) *Societal Costs of Motor Vehicle Accidents, 1975,* Washington,
     D.C., NHTSA.
17. *Federal Register.* (July 5, 1977), Vol. 42: 3529.
18. *Federal Register.* (Oct. 29, 1981) (Notice 25), Vol. 46: 53, 419.
19. Foldvary, L. A., and Lane, J. C. (1974) "The Effectiveness of Compulsory Wearing
     of Seat Belts in Casualty Reduction," *Accident Analysis and Prevention,* Vol. 6: 59–
     81.
20. Graham, John, Herrion, Max, and Morgan, M. Granger. (November 1981) "An Anal-
     ysis of Federal Policy toward Automobile Safety Belts and Air Bags," unpublished
     manuscript, Carnegie Mellon University, Pittsburgh, Pa.
21. Peter D. Hart Associates. (August 1978) "Public Attitudes toward Passive Restraints,"
     DOT Report, p. 6.
22. Hedlund, J. (April 1979) "Preliminary Findings from the National Crash Severity
     Study," Washington, D.C., NHTSA.
23. Highway Loss Data Institute. (June 1979) "Comparisons of Claim Frequencies of Volks-
     wagen Rabbits with Automatic and Manual Seat Belts," Research Project HLDL A-
     10, Washington, D.C.
24. Huelke, D. (1970) "Practical Defence Problems—The Expert's View," *Marquette Law
     Review,* Vol. 53: 200–209.
25. Huelke, D., and O'Day, J. (November 1979) "The National Highway Traffic Safety
     Administration Passive Restraint Systems—A Scientist's Viewpoint," paper prepared
     for the Conference on the Scientific Basis of Health and Safety Regulations, Wash-
     ington, D.C., The Brookings Institution.
26. Kunreuther, H. (Spring 1976) "Limited Knowledge and Insurance Protection," *Public
     Policy,* Vol. 24(2): 229–261.
27. Lave, L., and Weber, W. (1970) "A Benefit-Cost Analysis of Auto Safety Features,"
     Applied Economics, Vol. 2: 265–275.
28. MacAvoy, P. W. (1976) "The Regulations of Accidents," pp. 83–89 in H. Manne and
     R. L. Miller, eds., *Auto Safety Regulation: The Cure or the Problem,* Glen Ridge,
     N.J., Horton.
29. Mendeloff, J. (February 1981) "Passive Restraints and Auto Safety: Another Look,"
     unpublished manuscript, University of California, San Diego.
30. National Safety Council. (various years) *Accident Facts,* Chicago, NSC.
31. Nelson, R. (1976) "Comments on Peltzman's Paper on Automobile Safety Regulation,"
     pp. 63–70 in Manne and Miller, *Auto Safety Regulation, supra* (28).
32. Oi, W. Y. (Spring 1973) "The Economics of Product Safety," *Bell Journal of Eco-
     nomics and Management Science,* Vol. 4(1): 3–29.
33. O'Neill, B. (1977) "A Decision-Theory Model of Danger Compensation," *Accident
     Analysis and Prevention,* Vol. 9: 157–165.
34. Opinion Research Corporation. (December 1978) "Safety Belt Usage: Survey of Cars
     in the Traffic Population," Princeton, N.J.
35. Peltzman, S. (August 1975) "The Effects of Automobile Safety Regulations," *Journal
     of Political Economy,* Vol. 83(4): 677–725.
36. ———. (1975) "The Regulation of Automobile Safety," pp. 1–52 in Manne and Miller,
     Auto Safety Regulation, supra (28).
37. Pitovsky, R. (1976) "Regulation Reform: Techniques for Evaluating Challenges to the
     Wisdom of Existing Programs," pp. 73–81 in Manne and Miller, *Auto Safety Regu-
     lation, supra* (28).

38. Pulley, C., and Scanlon, M. (October 1977) "Seat Belt Use Laws in Europe," paper presented at National Conference of Governors' Highway Safety Representatives, Portland, Oregon.

39. Rice, D., and Cooper, B. (1967) "The Economic Value of Human Life," *American Journal of Public Health*, Vol. 57: 1954–1966.

40. Robertson, L. S. (1974) "A Controlled Study of the Effect of Television Messages on Safety Belt Use," *American Journal of Public Health*, Vol. 64: 1071–1080.

41. ———. (September 1976) "Estimates of Motor Vehicle Seat Belt Effectiveness and Use," *American Journal of Public Health*, Vol. 66(99): 76–82.

42. ———. (1977) "Auto Industry Belt Use Campaign Fails," Washington, D.C., Insurance Institute for Highway Safety.

43. ———. (April 1977) "Automobile Seat Belt Use in Selected Countries, States, and Provinces with and without Laws Requiring Belt Use," Washington, D.C., Insurance Institute for Highway Safety.

44. ———. (1977) "Car Crashes: Perceived Vulnerability and Willingness to Pay for Cash Protection," *Journal of Community Health*, Vol. 3: 136–141.

45. Rumer, K., Berggrund, U., Jernberg, P., and Ytterbom, U. (1976) "Driver Reaction to a Technical Safety Measure—Studded Tires," *Human Factors*, Vol. 18: 443–454.

46. Simon, H. A. (1957) *Models of Man*, New York, John Wiley.

47. Slovic, P., Fischoff, B., and Lichtenstein, S. (December 1977) "Accident Probabilities and Seat Belt Usage: A Psychological Perspective," Eugene, Oregon, Decision Research.

48. Smith, R. (April 1979) "Compensating Wage Differentials and Public Policy: A Review," Institute of Labor and Industrial Relations, Ithaca, N.Y., Cornell University.

49. *State Farm Mutual Automobile Insurance Co., et al. v. Department of Transportation, et. al.,* Slip Decision (D.C. Cir., June 1, 1982).

50. Subcommittee on Consumer Protection and Finance. (September 1977) "Report on the Department of Transportation Automobile Occupant Passive Restraint Rule," Washington, D.C., U.S. Senate.

51. Teknekron Research Incorporated. (July 1979) "1979 Survey of Public Perceptions on Highway Safety," prepared for U.S. Department of Transportation, Washington, D.C.

52. Thaler, R. (1978) "Toward a Positive Theory of Consumer Behavior," unpublished manuscript, Stanford, Calif., NBER.

53. Thaler, R., and Rosen, S. (1975) "The Value of Saving a Life: Evidence from the Labor Market," in N. E. Terleckyj, ed., *Household Production and Consumption Studies in Wealth and Income*, No. 40, New York, NBER, Columbia University Press.

54. Tversky, A. (1974) "Judgment under Uncertainty, Heuristics and Biases," *Science*, Vol. 185: 1124–1131.

55. Tversky, A., and Kahneman, D. (1973) "Availability: A Heuristic for Judging Frequency and Probability," *Cognitive Psychology*, Vol. 5: 207–232.

56. U.S. Department of Health, Education, and Welfare. (April 1977) *Social Security Bulletin*, Washington, D.C.

57. U.S. Department of Transportation. (Dec. 6, 1976) "The Secretary's Decision Concerning Occupant Crash Protection," Washington, D.C.

58. U.S. General Accounting Office. (July 27, 1979) *Passive Restraints for Automobile Occupants—A Closer Look*, Report to the Congress CED-79-93.

59. Waller, P. F., and Barry, P. Z. (1969) "Seat Belts: A Comparison of Observed and Reported Use," University of North Carolina Safety Research Center, Chapel Hill.

60. Williams, A. I., and O'Neill, B. (June 1979) "Seat Belt Laws: Implications for Occupant Protection," SAE paper No. 790683, presented at SAE Passenger Car Meeting, Dearborn, Mich.

TABLE OF CASES

Case and page where cited:

American Dispenser Co., Inc. v. Commissioner (1966); p. 230 n.10.

Berkey Photo, Inc. v. Eastman Kodak (1978, 1979, 1980); p. 151 n.1; p. 153 n.14; and p. 131ff.

Boomer v. Atlantic Cement Co. (1970); p. 231 n.3.; and see pp. 226, 228.

Brass v. North Dakota ex rel. Stoesser (1894); p. 54 n.49; and see p. 47.

Budd v. New York (1892); p. 47.

Carlin v. Crumpton (1916); p. 199.

Cement Manufacturers Association v. U.S. (1925); p. 2.

Central Elevator v. People (1898); p. 51 n.12.

Chicago Board of Trade v. United States (1918); p. 49 n.1; and see 17ff.

Clark Oil and Refining Corp. v. United States (1973); p. 230 n.8; also see pp. 227, 228, 229.

Corona Cord Tire Co. v. Dovan Chemical Corporation (1928); p. 197.

John Dickinson v. Board of Trade (1904); p. 52 n.22.

Elizabeth v. American Nicholson Pavement Co. (1878); p. 198.

FTC v. Kellogg Company et al.; p. 186 n.2.

FTC v. Litton Industries, Inc. (1973); p. 186 n.2.

General Electric Co. v. Wabash Appliance Corp. et al. (1938); p. 196.

Georgia Pacific Corp. v. United States Plywood Corp. (1958); p. 197.

Gordon v. New York Stock Exchange (1975); p. 53 n.42; also see pp. 45, 48.

Hookless Fastener Co. v. G. E. Prentice Mfg. Co. (1934), p. 196.

Kendall Co. v. Tetley Tea Co. (1950), p. 195.

McKenzie v. Cummings (1904); p. 199.

Marathon v. Mobil etc., et al. (1981); p. 186 n.2.

Mogul Steamship Co. v. McGregor (1892); p. 127 n.83.

Munn v. Illinois (1876); p. 50 n.5; and see pp. 19, 46, 47.

Munn et al. v. People (1874), p. 47.

National Assoc. of Window Glass Manufacturers et al. v. U.S. (1923); p. 49 n.2; and see p. 50 n.2.

Payne v. Kansas (1918); p. 54 n.51.

Silver v. New York Stock Exchange (1963); pp. 49–50 n.2; and see pp. 45, 46.

State Farm Mutual Automobile Insurance Co. et al. v. Department of Transportation et al. (1982); p. 267 n.49; and see p. 263.

Tilghman v. Proctor (1880); p. 205.

U.S. v. Board of Trade of City of Chicago (1974); p. 53 n.39.

U.S. v. Christie (1905); p. 49 n.1; and see p. 25.

U.S. v. Trenton Potteries (1927); p. 50 n.4; and see pp. 45, 48.

United States v. Addyston Pipe and Steel Co. (1898, 1899); p. 14 n.1; p. 122 n.1; p. 125 nn.41,42; see also pp. 2 and 57ff.

United States v. Black and Decker Manufacturing Co. and McCulloch Corp. (1976); p. 186 n.2.

United States v. Eastman Kodak Co. et al. (1915, 1921) (1957, 1961); p. 152 nn.5,11.

United States v. Grinell Corp. (1969); p. 157 n.59.

United States v. E. C. Knight (1895), p. 122 n.2; and see p. 82.

United States v. Joint Traffic Ass'n. (1898), p. 122 n.2; and see p. 125 n.55.

United Stated v. Trans-Missouri Freight Ass'n. (1897), p. 122 n.2; and see p. 125 n.55.

Universal Oil Products Co. v. Globe Oil & Refining Co. (1944); p. 196.

University of Illinois Foundation v. Block Drug Co. et al. (1957); p. 198.

Valentine v. Berien (1900); p. 54 n.51.

Westinghouse v. Boyden Power-Brake Co. (1898); p. 197.

White Motor Co. v. U.S. (1963); p. 49 n.2.

Woodward v. Commissioner (1970); p. 230 n.9.

INDEX

Advertising:
  brand loyalty, 143–144, 146
  political, 211
Antitrust laws:
  limits of, 60
  market price, 2ff.
  regulation of, 18, 60–61

Benefit/cost:
  automobile restraints ratio,
    235–237, 241–242, 249–261

Call Rule:
  effects of, 19
  price differences, 23–24
  testimony in, 21–23, 27
  to-arrive rule, 18
Cartelization:
  bonus system, 75–80, 97
  conspiracy assumptions, 60,
    75–84, 121
  efficiency, 111
  failure, 73
  geographic factors, 68–86
  limit-pricing, 75–76, 87, 113
  reserved city system, 75–84
Coarse theorem:
  modified, 226, 229

Competition:
  behavior in, 60–61
  control of, 195–196, 201–204
  coordination in, 202–204
  duplication in, 194, 202–204
  excessive, 63, 73, 103
  failure in, 61
  nature of plant costs, 70–72
  in technology, 201
  unrestricted in question, 72–73,
    114
Competitive market:
  failure in, 141–142
  product improvements, 146–149
Competitive price:
  elasticity, 6–8
  fringe firms, 2, 11
Consumer:
  attitudes toward auto safety,
    234, 237–238, 241–243,
    251–252
Control:
  exclusive, 195–196, 197, 201–
    206
  political, 212
Costs. *See* Marginal cost-pricing;
    Transportation

Cost (Cont.)
  affecting competitive behavior,
    61
  automobile accidents, 237
  automobile safety restraints,
    253–254
  entitlement rulings, 226–228
  fixed, 117–118
  location, 65–67
  market coordination, 58
  nature of plant, 63–67, 102–107,
    114
  political, 212, 215–217
  product differentiation, 121
  short-run, 64–68
  transportation, 62, 75
  to voters, 215

Demand. *See* Elasticity
  effect of uncertain, 60, 73–75
  factors in, 5, 6–7, 10, 13
  and market friction, 108–109
  stock price, 93–96
Dominant firm:
  exclusionary practices, 132–133
  first-mover advantages, 132–
    133, 141–146, 149
  managerial superiority, 141–
    143, 149
  persistence of, 141–149
  superior product, 132–133

Economies of scale:
  and plant size, 63–64
Efficiency:
  anticompetitive behavior, 133
  Call Rule, 22–28
  of cartel, 111
  of dominant firm, 149–150
  in market, 18, 19, 22–28
  political vs. managerial
    compared, 213–215
  of regulation, 234
  of sealed bid auction, 97–98

Elasticity:
  of market demand, 2, 7–9
  fringe supply, 2–13
  marginal costs, 7, 12–13
  measure of, 41–42
Entitlements:
  damage rule, 226–227
  private inverse condemnation,
    227–228
  property rule, 226, 227

Government:
  automobile safety intervention,
    233, 235–236, 238–239,
    255–256
  mandatory automobile safety,
    235–236, 237, 244–248,
    262–264
  passive restraints, 243, 249–
    254, 255–261, 262–264

Herfindahl Numbers Equivalent:
  uses of, 170–173
Horizontal Merger Guidelines:
  as reference point, 174–176

Information. *See* Market power;
    Consumer
  effect in automobile safety,
    243–244, 261–262
  entry barrier, 213
  for H-index, 176–180
  incentive in automobile safety,
    233, 236, 243–248
  political cf. private firm, 214–
    215
  voter, 212–213
Insurance:
  consumer attitudes, 237–238
  no-fault automobile, 236
  underutilization, 240, 241–248,
    261–262
  willingness-to-pay, 254–255, 256

Inventions. *See* Control; Property
rights; Technology
coordination in, 202
definitions, 199
early patenting, 198–199
examples of, 201–206
lag to commercialization, 195,
199–204
protection, 195, 197–199
speculative, 196–197

Legislation:
automobile safety, 235–236,
261–264

Management:
superior, 14
Marginal cost-pricing:
bonus system, 97–102
feasibility, 60–61, 107, 114,
118–119
prices, 92–93, 101–107
production costs, 62ff., 103, 107
short-run consequences, 59
Market. *See* Price; Regulation
decline in Chicago grain, 43
equilibrium, 57
information, 21, 22, 25–26
measuring performance, 167ff.,
180–181
monopoly power in, 33–34
plant location, 68–72
under Securities Exchange Act,
45–46
to-arrive price, 22
transportation costs, 27–38
Market failure:
in automobile safety, 236–238,
241
sources of, 234, 236
Market power:
bases for, 108–109
entry barriers, 138–139

information a tool, 110, 135,
144, 146
noncompetitive solutions, 109–
114
Market shares:
in antitrust analysis, 167–168
effect on prices, 2–3, 7–8
Merger. *See* Cartelization
to consolidate prices, 84–88
efficiency in, 111–113
failure in, 75
and firm size, 111
four-firm concentration
measures, 168, 172–173,
176, 180–181
guidelines for, 168ff.
H-index a tool, 173–174
measures compared, 180–181
regional factors in, 68–87
of related industries, 87
Models:
competitive equilibrium, 58
dominant firm, 3
Monopoly:
efficiency in, 109
on future inventions, 193, 196–
197
by horizontal acquisition, 132,
136
natural, 57
and stock prices, 93–96

Passive restraints. *See*
Government; Regulation
effectiveness of, 235, 249–
250ff., 261–264
social benefits, 235, 237, 242–
243, 248, 249–255, 260–261
government rule rescinded,
261–264
Political choice:
variables in, 217–222
Price. *See* Competitive price;
Market

Price (Cont.)
    after-hours market, 21–24, 27–
        28
    artificial, 2–3
    cartelizing, 17ff.
    in destructive competition, 90–
        93
    distortion, 23
    effect of market shares, 3
    and marginal cost, 92–93
    premium, 5–6
    short-run, 58–59, 103
    slack capacity, 119–120
Price-fixing:
    buyers, 113–114
    evidence of conspiracy, 83–84,
        104–107
    policing device, 17, 19–21, 30–
        32
    Supreme Court, 18
Product:
    brand loyalty, 143–146
    control, 146–149
    superiority, 132
Property rights:
    court cases, 226–229
    exclusive, 196–206
    future invention, 197, 198, 201
    mineral claim system, 206

Rates:
    fixed commision, 17, 19, 24ff.,
        29–43
Regulation:
    antitrust law, 18, 60–61
    case law in grain trade, 19, 45–
        49

National Highway and Traffic
        Safety Act, 235
    private firms, 57
    railroads, 20
    warehouses, 20
Restraint of trade:
    Addyston Pipe case, 2
    in Chicago Board of Trade
        case, 18
    price effects, 3
Risk:
    danger compensation principle,
        239–240, 241, 248
    reducing, 27
Rule of reason:
    in Chicago Board of Trade
        case, 17, 18
    in merger considerations, 114

Supply:
    geographical location, 68–72, 86
Systems selling:
    exclusionary practices, 133–137
    efficiency motives, 137–141
    as strategic tool, 135, 138

Technology:
    automobile safety, 234ff.
    control over, 195–199, 201–206
    undiscovered, 196
Transportation:
    market costs, 27–38
    nature of, 70–72
    not a cost, 121
    plant costs, 62, 65